M000234568

JOHN R. BISAGNO

Letters to Timothy

JOHN R. BISAGNO
Letters to Timothy

A HANDBOOK
FOR PASTORS

BROADMAN
&HOLMAN
PUBLISHERS

Nashville, Tennesseee

0–8054–2387–7

Published by Broadman & Holman Publishers, Nashville, Tennessee

Dewey Decimal Classification: 253
Subject Heading: CHRISTIAN MINISTRY

Scripture quotations, unless otherwise noted, are from the King James Version. Biblical citations marked NKJV are from the NKJV, New King James Version, copyright © 1979, 1980, 1982, Thomas Nelson, Inc., Publishers. Those marked TLB are from The Living Bible, copyright © Tyndale House Publishers, Wheaton, Ill., 1971, used by permission.

New International Version, © copyright 1973, 1978, 1984. Many authors have made their own translations.

Library of Congress Cataloging-in-Publication Data

Bisagno, John R
    Letters to Timothy : a handbook for pastors / John R. Bisagno
      p. cm.
    Includes bibliographical references.
    ISBN 0–8054–2387–7
Pastoral theology—Handbooks, manuals, etc. I. Title.
BV4016 .B57 2001
253—dc21
2001025125

1 2 3 4 5 6 7 8 9 10 05 04 03 02 01

Contents

Part 3   The Pastor as Spiritual Leader

Part 4   The Pastor as Organizational Leader

Contents

Part 8   The Church Staff

Part 9   The Church Finances

Part 10   Facilities and Operations

Part 11   Other Important Matters

FOREWORD

I was 17 years old when I first read John Bisagno's classic book *How to Build an Evangelistic Church*. My life was permanently impacted. As a young man just beginning a life of ministry, I devoured John's wise and practical advice about pastoring and leading a local congregation. Over the years I reread the book many times, gleaning new insight each time I read it. Bisagno was a long-distance mentor to me. He modeled pastoring with a big vision and loving with a big heart.

Of course, I am only one of thousands of pastors who have been marked by the ministry of this wonderful, creative man. John has been, and continues to be, a pastor's pastor. He has loved those of us in ministry, so we couldn't help but love him back.

Now John has finally put in print all the insights, all the lessons, and all the wisdom he's gathered from a lifetime of faithful service to Jesus Christ. This book is a goldmine! It represents a virtual seminary education in a single volume. And it is classic Bisagno—clear and simple, convicting yet loving, practical and profound, humorous, and, above all, biblical. If you've never read Bisagno, you are in for a treat.

John was innovative before innovation became "cool." He has never been afraid to shake up the status quo. He was always more interested in being effective than in holding to the party line. As a result, he grew one of the greatest churches in the world.

There are some great pastors who excel in one particular area. But John has excelled at it all—preaching, leading, evangelism, discipleship, planting churches, transitioning churches, leading worship, raising money, doing world missions, resolving conflict, motivating members, and loving everyone. Thank God he took the time to write it all down in this book.

My prayer is that an entire new generation of pastors and church planters will use this book to develop the necessary perspective, convictions, character, and skills needed for ministry in the twenty-first century from this giant of the twentieth century.

Rick Warren, author
The Purpose Driven Church

Introduction

For nearly half a century, it has been my joy to serve the Lord. I began as a traveling evangelistic singer directing the music for the popular weekend youth revivals of the 1950s that produced men like Jackie Robinson, Jess Moody, Freddie Gage, Homer Martinez, and others who are legends in my denomination.

Then I had the privilege of traveling with Dr. Hyman Appelman, the most prominent evangelist on the scene between the ministries of Billy Sunday and Billy Graham. I served as crusade planner, public relations man, program director, platform manager, and music director for three years. It was one of the most important training periods of my life. I have had the opportunity to organize and lead numbers of citywide evangelistic crusades as well as preach in hundreds of them.

Just out of college, I served as associate pastor in charge of music, education, and youth at First Baptist Church of Sallisaw, Oklahoma. Since that time, I have pastored five years in First Southern Baptist Church, Del City, Oklahoma, and thirty years in First Baptist Church, Houston. I received only a bachelor of fine arts degree with a major in music from Oklahoma Baptist University, never dreaming I was not preparing for what I would ultimately do in life. In many ways, I have only stumbled by trial and error into the things I'm going to share with you. With the help of the Holy Spirit and the good counsel of pastor friends of many denominations, it has been my joy to successfully pastor two wonderful churches.

Through the years, however, I have longed to see something in writing that would spell out the ABCs, the practical "what-to-do's" and "what-not-to-do's" of the ministry, which could have made it so much easier. These truths have been produced in the fiery crucible of trial and error and refined at both the cost of failure and the surprise of success. In this book I have, therefore, attempted to anticipate most of the areas and issues that will confront a pastor in his ministry. More than one hundred topics are contained in this book, and none of them have been exhaustively treated. To do so would require a large set of books—probably an unrealistic pursuit. These pages provide an encapsulation, an overview, and answer many of the most obvious and difficult questions under each title. The chapters are short and succinct. They are tried and proven. I'm sure they will be helpful to you.

I shall never forget my first experience in serving the Lord. I became a Christian August 1, 1952, being called into vocational ministry simultaneously with my conversion. Within three weeks I was invited to Pryor, Oklahoma, to lead the music in a weekend youth crusade with evangelist Paul McCray, who would later be the best man in my wedding. As the bus arrived at the station in Pryor, I picked up my trumpet, Bible, and suitcase and stepped out into the aisle to leave the bus. Then it hit me, "Oh, my goodness! I wonder what they do in revivals."

It has been a long time since that bus station in Oklahoma, and I often feel I still have more questions than answers. However, here is hard information—practical, tested, and written from a heart of conviction and love for the Lord, his people, and my fellow pastors.

I call these pages "Letters to Timothy." Like the apostle, I have a beloved son in the ministry named Timothy, whose tender ministry to young people "on the edge" is the most effective I know. Unlike the apostle, he is my own flesh and blood. To my son Timothy and all the Timothys out there who will follow in the footsteps of the Master for years to come, I dedicate this book with a prayer and with a heart of love.

"But continue thou in the things which thou hast learned and hast been assured of, knowing of whom thou hast learned them; and that from a child thou hast known the holy scriptures, which are able to make thee wise unto salvation through faith which is in Christ Jesus."

2 Timothy 3:14–15

Part 1

The Church

Chapter 1

God's Glorious Church

Someone said it well, "Only one life, 'twill soon be past, only what's done for Christ will last." Let me say it a bit differently: "Only one ministry, 'twill soon be past, only what's done through Christ's church will last." Before the world was formed, God planned the church to be his instrument of redemption in the world. The word *church* is the Greek word *ecclesia,* meaning "the called out ones." The idea is a town hall meeting where persons are called-out for discussion and leadership. Jesus referenced himself when he said in Matthew 16:18, "Upon this rock I will build my church." Jesus is saying the church is "My called out-ones; My town hall meeting," and it is the only thing he ever established on this earth.

The word *church* in the New Testament is used two different ways. The first is the universal or invisible church. When you become a Christian, the Holy Spirit baptizes you into oneness not only with Jesus but also with all other believers everywhere. It is a church that exists beyond buildings, denominational lines, and international borders. It is the body of Christ, the family of God on earth. Ninety percent of the time, however, the New Testament use of the word *church* means a visible, locally assembled body of baptized believers worshiping together, ministering to one another, honoring him, and winning the lost.

The church is less than perfect. There have always been the charlatans and the naysayers—those who like Simon the sorcerer would buy the power of the Holy Spirit and those who today use the church for their own selfish ends and financial purposes. Let them be accursed. But perhaps it is a just commentary on the failure of some of us within the church that so many extracurricular and "parachurch" organizations have developed in the world. Most call themselves extensions of the church or arms of the church, and I am grateful for each. But the fact is that far too often, parachurch organizations give only lip service to their commitment to the local church.

When Christ came, he died for the church. He established the church. He loved the church. Today, he continues to indwell the church, and one day he will come to receive his church. She is his bride, and he is her groom. The old spiritual says:

> There's a woman in the church,
>   and she talks too much.
> Tell me, what we gonna do?
>   *Let the church roll on.*
>
> There's a singer in the church,
>   and he won't sing right.
> Tell me, what we gonna do?
>   *Let the church roll on.*
>
> There's a deacon in the church,
>   and he won't "deac" right.
> Tell me, what we gonna do?
>   *Let the church roll on.*

God's church has endured and will do so until Jesus comes to take her to heaven. *Let the church roll on.*

Throughout your ministry you will be confronted with many opportunities of service. Some of them might indeed be God's perfect purpose for your life. You will seek his heart, hear his voice, and do his will. But consider this: That which is not truly birthed of the church, emanates therein, extends therefrom, and culminates therein is doomed to make little lasting impression for God and good in this world. Well over a century ago, the YMCA was born as a soul-winning organization to bring young boys to Jesus and train them in the Word of God. Is that the purpose of the YMCA today?

Devote yourself to the church. Christ loved the church and gave himself for her. She is flawed, imperfect, wrinkled, and blemished, but the end is not here yet. He is her unfailing strength, and you will do well to commit your life to her service.

Chapter 2

Five Ingredients
of Growing Churches

I n the early 1970s Adrian Rogers, pastor of Bellevue Baptist
Church, Memphis, Tennessee, and Edwin Young, pastor of Second
Baptist Church, Houston, Texas, independently of each other and
unknown to each other, conducted a study of the twenty-five fastest-
growing churches in America to determine whether there were common ingredients in each. Some churches were in the north; some were
in the south. Some were African-American, some were Anglo. Some
were charismatic; most were not. Some had marvelous new facilities;
many were very old. But each had these five factors in common.

1. *They were strongly pastorally led.* Boards, presbyters, deacons,
elders, and committees abounded. There was a large variance in eccle-
siastical structure. But in each case, they reported, "It didn't take long,
analyzing the inside workings of the church, until it became obvious
where the power was."

But it is imperative that you understand: *Leadership is not
demanded; it is deserved.* Pastoral leadership is taught in Scripture,
granted by the people, and must be earned by the pastor. When you
have to start telling them "I'm the pastor," you no longer are. God's
people are better led than driven. Remember, a wise man will seek
counsel and work with his leaders while humbly assuming the position of leadership with which God has entrusted him.

2. *They were strong Bible churches.* Each pastor believed the Bible
to be inerrant and infallible, the unflawed, perfect Word of God—not

just a record of God's Word, but God's Word itself. These men were not attempting to be apologists. They were not defending the Bible, debating it, or trying to prove it. They were *preaching* it, explaining it, applying it, and illustrating it. Once, asked why he didn't spend more time defending the Bible, Billy Graham responded: "The Bible is like a lion. When you have a lion, you don't have to defend him. Just turn him loose; he'll defend himself."

3. *They were good-time churches.* This is not to say the Sunday service was a hootenanny or the atmosphere carnivalistic. They were happy churches with bright, warm, friendly atmospheres. The people felt the freedom to laugh, to cry, and to respond. Remember, you can't hatch eggs in a refrigerator. A warm, fluid service that allows for the freedom and spontaneity of the Spirit is conducive to the tender response of the Spirit to God. Often such services are considered to be only emotional, and decisions made therein naturally shallow.

Consider this: emotion is fully one-third of human personhood. Jesus said we are to love the Lord our God with all our mind, heart, and soul. The mind is the seat of the intellect, the place where we know. The heart is the seat of the emotions, the place where we feel. The soul is the seat of the will, the place where we resolve and commit. The person who is stimulated in his mind and stirred in his heart will commit in his soul. We thwart the work of the Lord among us when we stifle the freedom of the Spirit with stilted, overly formal services.

"Where the Spirit of the Lord is there is liberty." This is not, of course, to suggest an inherent fallacy in planning. An order of service can be directed by the Holy Spirit and still be printed in advance, but the freedom, warmth, and ease with which it should be carried out can and must be allowed.

4. *They were churches in unity.* The people gave a high priority to their oneness in Christ. Social and socioeconomic diversity are a great plus in the church. Ideally, your church will be a cross section of your city, and its leaders will be committed to preserving its unity. When a church is in harmony with itself, it becomes the beautiful body of Christ on earth through which the Lord Jesus in heaven recreates his presence every time the people of God gather. Song writer Bill Gaither

said it well: "I love the thrill that I feel when I get together with—God's wonderful people."

5. *Each church had an indomitable spirit of conquest.* There was a "holy drivenness" about the congregation. They would never be satisfied. Each church pulsated with an atmosphere of more, more, more. They must cross the next river, climb the next mountain, give the next dollar, build the next building, and win the next soul. They would not be deterred. The Nissan Motor Company, formerly the Datsun Motor Company, once had a marvelous slogan: "We Are Driven." Pastor friend, we, too, are driven. God's children are a driven people. We are driven to the ends of the earth by the Great Commission. We are driven to the end of ourselves by the love of Christ. We are driven to the end of time by the imminent return of Jesus.

The tone of each of these five ingredients is clearly set by the pastor. It all starts in the pulpit. It starts in your heart. Keep your eyes on the Lord. Keep your ears open to the Great Commission. Keep your chin up and your knees down. The best is yet to come.

Chapter 3

The Offices of the Church

E very home needs a husband; every team, a coach; every nation, a president. Every church needs a leader, and leaders cannot have two heads, let alone five or ten. Church government by committee has no place in the biblical record. The purpose of committees is to offer counsel to the pastor. God calls one person to lead the local congregation, and that person is the pastor. But always remember, leadership is never demanded. It is deserved.

God has placed deep in the heart of every woman the desire for a man she can look up to as the head of the home and spiritual leader of the marriage. In the same way, he has put in the heart of every congregation an undershepherd to lead and for them to follow. Shepherds don't follow the flock; they lead the flock. But that leadership must be deserved, earned, and won by integrity, faithful ministry, vulnerability, true humility, godliness, service, and by faithfully feeding the flock the Word of God. And this takes time. The longer you pastor a congregation, the more freedom you will be granted to lead. The pastor may be called bishop, elder, rector, or some other title, but the purpose of leadership is to lead, and the function of leadership is to get things done.

It appears from the New Testament record that churches often had several pastors. Perhaps this was a shared leadership, but I am more inclined to think there was a chief shepherd and others who served with him more in the vein of today's associate pastors and/or staff.

Whatever else is wrong about the church, the concept of an earthly shepherd as pastor/leader is right. And, remember, we are talking about a concept, a position, an office, not just a person. The person may fail and even need to be removed by the congregation, but the office itself is always to be honored.

A delicate balance exists in many churches between pastor, deacons, and congregation, but the office of pastor must be reserved as the ultimate position of leadership and authority.

A young soldier greatly disliked his superior officer and threatened not to salute. His commander said, "Son, you're saluting the office, not the man." Deep in the heart of his people is a God-given desire to salute both the man and the office. I have found when we earn leadership, God's people are more than willing to grant it.

As I read the New Testament, while there are many gifts, there are only two offices in the local church: pastor and deacon. But a wise pastor, however, will have a group around him on whom he depends for wise counsel and shared leadership. They might be called the board of trustees, the presbytery, the deacons, or the elders, but a successful pastor will solicit their help and counsel. The Book of Proverbs says, "In many counselors, there is much wisdom."

Chapter 4

God's Gift to the Church

G od gave many spiritual gifts to the church. The gift of the gifted leader, the body-edifying gifts, and the evangelistic sign gifts for unbelievers. As the gift of God to the local congregation and to the church-at-large, the gifted persons do not simply have spiritual gifts; they themselves *are* the gift. They are the pastor and/or pastor/teacher, teacher, and evangelist. Certainly pastors must be teachers, and the correct title may be pastor-teacher.

Regardless of the categories, God gave pastors as gifts to the church first and foremost to be his undershepherds. I know some churches think they won the "booby prize," but their pastor is still the gift of God to their congregation.

In the Book of Revelation, God calls pastors His "stars." Peter promises a special crown for faithful pastors: "And when the chief Shepherd shall appear, ye shall receive a crown of glory that fadeth not away" (1 Pet. 5:4).

The greatest joy you will know is to "pastor the flock of God, which is among you." Treasure each moment as a special gift and sacred trust. As God's gift to your congregation, your pastorship is also God's precious gift to you. Remember, it is at once valuable and fragile. Handle with care.

I am constantly amazed at pastors who confess how much they hate what they do and can't wait to get out of the ministry. Can you imagine how much our heavenly Father, our greater Shepherd, the Lord Jesus, loved his sheep when he laid down his life for them? Can you comprehend the honor and the privilege that has been bestowed upon you in being entrusted by our Lord Jesus to shepherd his little flock?

A cross is an "I" crossed out and is the heart of the Christian faith. And certainly at the heart of ministry stands a life of selfless service and giving. It is often said, "You can't outgive God." Neither can you outgive the people of God. Pastoring a church is like looking into a mirror; it tends to give back what it gets.

If you truly love your people, pour out your life for them and serve them with all your heart, they will love you back. Yes, there will be some Simons along the way and some Judases and Thomases, but the overwhelming majority of God's people are good, good people. They will love you, bless you, support you, follow you, primarily as they see the integrity and selflessness of your devoted service and ministry to Christ and to them.

I don't know any congregations that despise Jesus. Why do some seem to despise their pastor? Is it because they do not see Jesus in him? Unrelenting, unavailable, proud, ambitious, self-serving, unapproachable, unprepared—these are words far too often used in describing pastors.

Some of you might be reading this book as a last hope. Perhaps you're greatly discouraged, looking for a way out, and you've hoped to get enough encouragement within these pages to hang on just a little longer.

Dear pastor friend, you've got to go back, way back, all the way to the cross. Go back to where the journey started and kneel before the Lord Jesus. Let the words of "The Old Rugged Cross" well up again within your soul. Ask our Lord to form again his heart, his character, and his love within your heart.

If you cannot get there, you probably should get out of the ministry. It is not impossible that you have missed God's call altogether. Something is desperately wrong when pastors hate the body of Christ that our Lord loved and called us to serve. A fresh new touch of Jesus, a fresh look in his face, a greatly increased morning devotional time in the Word and in prayer—these are essential ingredients in rekindling the fire.

Herschel Hobbs was a patriarch of the faith. He served as president of the Southern Baptist Convention and pastored the First Baptist Church of Oklahoma City for thirty years. He died at nearly ninety years of age, still preaching every day. In his memoirs, he wrote, "If I had 10,000 lives to live over, I should want to be a pastor in each of them." And I say, "Me, too, Dr. Hobbs. Me, too."

May God grant us the faithfulness and integrity to be worthy gifts of his grace to our people.

Chapter 5

The Prayer Life
of the Church

From 1970 to 1986 the First Baptist Church of Houston, Texas, experienced strong and continual growth. In the mid to late 1980s this began to flatten out. By the early 1990s the membership had declined 5 to 10 percent. Then the church began to grow again.

The reasons for the most recent growth were threefold:

1. The people didn't panic. They stayed the course and did what they do best.
2. The people knew who they were and their unique purpose. They didn't try to be like anybody else. They tried to stay at the task God had given them and be who he had made them to be.
3. The church turned up the prayer knob by several notches.

Prayer became more important. New prayer groups were formed—some inside the walls of the church, some outside. Today there are about twenty-five weekly prayer meetings somewhere across the city in the life of this church. Ten years ago there was one. Additionally, the church began giving priority to prayer in the weekly staff meetings and evening services.

Most Protestant churches call their Wednesday night gathering "prayer meeting." Yet in most churches, prayer is the last thing we do. We take prayer requests, we write prayergrams, we sing hymns about prayer, and we talk a lot about prayer. We even have devotionals and Bible studies on prayer. In an average one-hour "prayer meeting," however, we usually spend less than five minutes actually praying.

Call the people to the front, get on your knees, call on three or four to lead, ask the people to pray one after the other, leaving no time between prayers. When you are finished, close. But, whatever you do, spend at least twenty to thirty minutes actually praying.

Rotate among the various prayer meetings of your congregation. Join them in their homes. Be seen. Be heard. Be there. Pray. Your presence lends support and approval, and your heart encourages theirs.

Many of the members of First Houston have support groups and Bible studies around town and early prayer breakfasts in various restaurants. Go to some of these groups and pray with them.

When there is a special need, call the people to prayer. Have a prayer line. Develop a prayer chain. Build a prayer room. And, by all means, remove the lock from the prayer room door and throw it away.

God is waiting for His people to pray, and prayer moves the hand of God. No prayer means no power. Little prayer means little power. Much prayer means much power. Call on the Lord. Be a person of prayer.

God loves to reveal his glory and pour out his power, and it might as well be on you.

Chapter 6

The Church Committees

C hurch committees are a vital part of the church. A wise pastor will respect and appreciate official groups in the church, commissioned to help do the work of the ministry.

Various committees to implement the many facets of a growing church will be vitally important. Varying degrees of authority/leadership are assigned to four different entities within the church: pastor, congregation, deacons, and committees.

There is an important place for each of these in the life of the church, but each must consider the other more important than itself. The pastor must be the vision-caster. This means he must have a vision to cast, which presupposes time with God to receive the vision. It is important that each committee sense this in the heart of the pastor.

The purpose of committees is to give counsel and input to church leaders in helping make decisions. The purpose of the deacon body is to refine and recommend (remember those legitimizers), and the responsibility of the congregation is to affirm and commit.

When the body of Christ feels uneasy about a decision, a wise leader will back off and reassess. Committees, deacons, and congregation are a marvelous insulation and support to the pastor in the decision-making process. Good committees will think of things you haven't thought of and view from different perspectives the various aspects of the subject. Remember not to stack the deck with committee members who agree with you. While you do not want to choose persons who are obviously not supportive of the pastor, it is still profitable to hear from all sides. Good leadership is secure enough to hear without being threatened. The other opinion just might be the one you need to hear.

The wise pastor will use the committee as a sounding board to refine and massage major decisions before taking them to the congregation. But committees are not only recommenders, they are also enactors. Often, when I was a pastor, I would take an issue to a committee and say: "I really don't care how you handle this, and I trust your wisdom completely. Make your decision and implement it. Just get it done."

Conversely, in an average week, I would make twenty-five to fifty decisions and just say, "This is the way it is." Most of the time I did not feel the need to bring a committee into the matter. It is neither feasible nor prudent to call your committees into session a dozen times a week to make every little decision that comes along.

Sometimes, however, there were decisions I felt the need to refer the deacons for approval and support. Again, very often, the decisions will stop there, but occasionally there are major things that need to go on to the congregation for final discussion and approval. *Doctrinal issues are never decided by congregation or committee.* They are defined and articulated by the pastor. If the congregation does not have confidence in the pastor to do this, they need to call a new pastor in whom they have such confidence. But doctrinal stance by committee is not an option. Sometimes it takes courage. Sometimes it will cost. Sometimes you will lose members. But the people will support you.

The obvious questions then are: "Which decisions should a pastor make? Which should he ask a committee to assist in making? Which should be referred to the deacons? Which should be made by the entire congregation?" It is not possible to predetermine categories for every decision and define the levels at which each decision is made.

That issue arose in my fifth year in Houston, and I went to our deacons with this proposal: "Give me the authority to be the one to determine at which of the four levels issues are determined as they arise. In a year, let's review and see if you are pleased. If not, we'll find another way."

They agreed, and a year later they were pleased. About fifteen years later, another sticky issue arose over who had the authority to do what. Again, I went to the deacons, reminding them of their earlier decision and asked if it was their pleasure to reaffirm the policy. They chose to do so, and the church continues to live by that policy today.

I need to say that when I am uncertain, I always err on the side of caution. I would rather have too much input and too much support than too little when I go into battle over an important matter.

Chapter 7

Appointing the Committees

A church can have many committees. First Baptist of Houston has one pastor, one staff, one deacon body, and a host of committees. Currently, this church has the following committees:

- Christian Life Center
- Committee on Committees
- Finance
- Personnel
- Properties
- Children
- Preschool
- Youth
- Benevolence
- Recovery
- Resource Center
- Social
- Baptismal
- Lord's Supper
- Missions Council
- Scholarship
- First Place Council
- First Kids Council

In my opinion, the two most important committees in the church are the finance committee and the personnel committee. Depending on each church's individual needs and priorities, other committees will run a close second, third, or fourth. This will, of course, vary with each church. In First Baptist, Houston, the missions committee and the properties committee are also important. In previous years, the media committee, handling radio and television, were also very important. Ministries come and go and priorities change, but the crucial importance of personnel and finance in the committee structure of a church remains constant.

The purpose of the finance committee is to prepare the budget annually, review the budget monthly, and monitor expenditures. Consistent overages in any line item must be dealt with. But generally it is best to raise the budget across the board on a percentage basis in good times and even lower it the same way in difficult times. But this should seldom, if ever, be done during the midst of the church fiscal year. The church budget must be prepared and administered in faith.

Unproductive ministries should be considered for termination. New money should be allocated to ministries that are enjoying the blessing of God in great measure.

Absolutely no church members should serve on the finance committee unless they are tithers *to the church.* And it goes without saying that the same is true of the staff. We must not tolerate a situation in which those who live by the tithes of the people are not tithers themselves.

The personnel committee will aid the pastor when called upon in the hiring and firing of staff, appraisal of job performance, and related pertinent matters. At First Houston I had the right to hire and fire, but I always did so, particularly at upper-level positions, in consultation with the personnel committee. Not only was their counsel and input of great value, but also they were be a tremendous buffer when the firing of a person was handled as a personnel committee matter.

The personnel committee and finance committee, as well as all church committees, should be appointed by a committee on committees, which is the other high-priority committee in your church. The question then becomes, "Who appoints the committee on committees?" Who names the persons who will name the persons who make up the committees? Therein, friends, is the sticker. Ideally, it should be the pastor. In some cases, it can be the committee on committees itself.

But when the committee on committees names the committee on committees, they obviously become a self-perpetuating body. This can work only when you have a pliable, tender-hearted, mature, wise, unselfish group of committee members who truly want to work with the pastor, have the best interest of the church at heart, and have no interest in naming their friends or themselves in perpetuity.

For nearly three decades at First Houston, we were blessed with a fine group of men and women who comprised our committee on committees. They were wise enough and gracious enough to consult with their pastor before naming any other members to the committee on committees as well as the other major committees of the church.

When you have this situation, you've got heaven on earth, and that is as it should be. Under no conditions should a pastor be saddled with a group of people on the main committees of the church with whom he cannot work. It is the responsibility of the committee on committees to honor the position of pastor by seeking his input and blessings on all potential committee members for their own committee and others.

And by all means, no person should ever be asked to serve on any committee until after the pastor and committee have agreed that he or she be asked. Don't put your pastor in the embarrassing position of saying: "Pastor, we've asked Bill Smith to serve on the building committee. Is that OK with you?" If it's not OK with you, you're a dead duck. You can't say no, or you will be at odds with a good member of the church because he's already been asked. Furthermore, the committee can't go back and say, "The pastor doesn't want you." Working together in humility and grace, in honor preferring one another, is the key to good committee work in your church.

Another possibility is that the chairman of your deacons and three or four other important committee heads can work with the pastor in naming the committee on committees. Or, they may be elected from the floor of the church. The problem with this is that some people might be nominated who are not qualified to serve, leading to unpleasant discussion, hurt feelings, and resulting problems. The gracious and respectful consideration of each other, between pastor and the committee on committees, is the best way.

Committees should rotate. Ideally, there should be one-year, two-year, and three-year terms on each committee. At any given time, some members will be going off, some will have another year or two, and some will be coming on. Stagnation and stubbornness can then be bred out and freshness and flexibility bred in. It is unthinkable that Brother "So and So" has been on the finance committee, let alone chairman of this group, for fifteen or twenty years. God bless Brother "So and So" for his faithful service, but this is not the way to do the work of the Lord.

From time to time it will be necessary to appoint "ad hoc" committees. This is normally done by the pastor for a stated purpose, for a short time, and with a stated termination date.

Our own Vision 2000 Committee at First Houston was such a committee. Its purpose was to help the pastor examine the effectiveness of every program in the church as we approached the new millennium.

Personal and public appreciation for committees is always in order. I never cease to thank God for the expertise and time that various committee members brought to the work of the Lord, as we worked together through the years in the First Baptist Church of Houston.

Chapter 8

Deacons and Their Ministry

In Acts chapter 6, we have the record of the first deacons. Simply stated, the preachers needed help. Overwhelmed with ministry, Peter and the disciples were spending too much time meeting the physical demands of the people and too little time in spiritual preparation to teach and preach the Word.

God's answer? Set aside deacons. The catalyst was the distribution of daily food to the widows. The Grecian widows complained that the Hebrew widows were getting priority, while they were being neglected. Dr. Luke says it this way: "There arose a murmuring among the Greeks against the Hebrews."

Even a cursory reading of the text shows that the most important issue was not the food but the argument over the distribution of the food. The fellowship was divided. The church was split. And we know that divided fellowships go nowhere. Luke's statement, "Look ye out among you seven men of honest report, full of the Holy Ghost and wisdom, whom we may appoint over this business," (Acts 6:3) may well be interpreted, "Find seven men whom you can appoint over this *mess.*"

Clearly, the apostles were disturbed over the division of the fellowship. The primary purpose of deacons was not to do the physical work of the church but to preserve the fellowship of the church that is often disturbed in the process of doing the physical.

Division within the church is devastating. The unity of the body of Christ is everything. The unbeliever may disbelieve God and doubt the Bible, but when he comes into the presence of Jesus as created in the life of a unified people, something mystical and wonderful happens. And in that presence, there is life. People are drawn to Christ and converted. Unity in the church must be preserved at all costs.

And to whom is the responsibility given to preserve the unity of the congregation? That responsibility is placed squarely on the shoulders of the deacons. Never forget, deacons were ordained not just to meet the physical needs of the congregation—the serving of tables—but also to preserve the fellowship that had been broken over the issue of serving tables.

Unfortunately, however, in some churches the deacons, far from maintaining the fellowship of the church, are themselves the cause of disharmony within the congregation. I speak bluntly here, perhaps even harshly, but I do so in the context of honoring deacons at the churches I served as pastor. They were masters at maintaining the fellowship. But I must say that the most consistent problem with which I have helped young pastors deal through the years is deacons who are creating a power struggle with the pastor and who are actually dividing the church rather than unifying it. Running off the pastor, administering the budget, fighting over secondary issues, and creating power struggles are not what deacons are supposed to do.

Frankly, in far too many churches, the whole issue is a mess and churches are desperately hurt, going nowhere, even declining because of it. But where deacons do what deacons are supposed to do, the church prospers and the deacons are happy. The deacons should protect the fellowship and assist the pastor in ministering to the congregation.

The very word *deacon* is the Greek word *doulos,* which means "servant." He is not one who leads; he is one who serves. Yes, admittedly, 1 Timothy 3:5 says, "If a man know not how to rule his own house, how can he take care of the church of God?" But the deacon, as well as the pastor, is in a place of *earned* leadership. He leads only because he serves. If I do not serve, I cannot lead.

But too often deacons think they can lead without serving. Deacon, seize the initiative! Find a problem and meet the need. Go to the hospital. Win the lost. Mow the yard. Empty the trash. Take food to the widows. Say to the pastor, "I'll do that . . . here, I'll handle that . . . let me . . . don't worry about it . . . we'll do it." *That is to be the attitude of the deacon.*

Deacons who don't serve but love to lead are unhappy deacons, and their churches are dying. Deacons who protect the fellowship, honor the pastor, have an humble servant's heart, and love to work are deacons who are happy and whose churches are alive and growing.

My best friends are deacons. I have worked with the best deacons in the world. They supported me, and I supported them. Sometimes they corrected me, and sometimes I corrected them. In honor, we preferred one another, we exalted one another, we supported one another. For thirty years First Baptist Church of Houston worked in harmony and went forward. And I say to the credit of deacons and the glory of my God, "Thank the Lord for deacons who understand the ministry to which God has called them and who serve and protect the fellowship of the congregation."

Chapter 9

Deacons and Divorce

Let's talk first about the oldest controversy surrounding the positions of pastor and deacon. I speak, of course, of the issue of divorce. First Timothy 3 lists qualifications for bishops and deacons, among them the controversial second verse, "The husband of one wife."

This issue regarding the ordination of church leaders has been greatly debated through the years. The general assumption has been that it simply means one may never have been divorced. Others have suggested it is a reference to bigamy—one wife at a time. We do speak, do we not, of a former wife as an "ex-wife"? Then there is the question, Must a deacon be married? Is this a prohibition against a single deacon? The answer, of course, is no.

Other problems abound. What about a man who remains married to a woman but is a practicing homosexual? Is he or is he not qualified under this apparent restriction? If one divorces his wife, does he then denounce his pastorate or his deaconhood? And what about the grace of God? Are we or are we not new creatures in Christ Jesus? Are old things passed away, or are they not? Or what if the divorce occurred before a person became a Christian, or if he is the classic innocent party? On and on goes the controversy.

Did our Lord intend such confusion when he inspired these words through the apostle Paul? I think not. No New Testament issue has racked the church with more confusion than this, and our Lord is not the author of confusion.

The apostle Paul said we are to "rightly divide" the word of truth. The Greek expression "cutting it straight" is used here. Paul was a tentmaker. He knew the importance of "cutting it straight." If each piece is not cut to the original pattern, each successive piece becomes more unusable than the last. The issue has become more and more bizarre today because we have failed to correctly see the original pattern.

The best thinking today from Greek scholars is that it is impossible in the Greek for this expression "husband of one wife" to refer to a status. It cannot be a *status*. It must be a *trait*. It is not what one *is*, (i.e., married or divorced); it is what one *is like*, (i.e., faithful to his wife).

Commentator John MacArthur writes: "'The overseer or elder must first be above reproach in relation to women. He must be *the husband of one wife*. The Greek text literally reads 'a one-woman man.' Paul is not referring to a leader's marital status, as the absence of the definite article in the original indicates. Rather, the issue is his moral, sexual behavior. Many men who are married only once are not one-woman men. Many with one wife are unfaithful to their wives. While remaining married to one woman is commendable, it is no indication or guarantee of moral purity."

This is not a reference to a mistake made in high school when a boy got married for six weeks and then divorced. God never intended that we try to split the hair that finely.

And what, after all, is marriage? Some people have taken vows that were never sexually consummated and then signed divorce papers. Does this apply to them? What about the bigamist? What about the man who was divorced before he became a believer? What about the innocent party? What about homosexuality? What about a man who never legally divorced his wife but left her a week after they got married, or one who lives in pornography? Are they qualified to be pastors and deacons? Bizarre to the point of the ridiculous are the extremities to which we may go when we don't *cut it straight*.

The Greek does indeed mean a "one-woman man." Not only the Greek but also the simple principles of hermeneutics demand such an interpretation. Contextualizing the passage, you find that every other qualification is an "inclination toward." It is not "hard and fast." It is not a status but a character trait of which Paul writes.

The text doesn't say the prospective deacon never once failed to be watchful; it says he is vigilant. It doesn't say he never once had a belly laugh at a good joke; it says he is sober or serious. It doesn't say he never once misbehaved; it says he is of good behavior. It doesn't say he never once turned down a request to let the visiting preacher spend the night in his home; it says he is given to hospitality. It doesn't say he never once messed up a Sunday school lesson; it says he is apt to teach. It doesn't say he never once had a drink at the senior prom; it says he is not given to wine. It doesn't say he never once lost his patience; it says he is patient. It doesn't say he never once got into a fight in grade school; it says he is not a brawler. It does not say he never once really wanted another's possessions; it says he is not characterized by a covetous spirit.

Let me let you listen in on a conversation I had recently while discussing this issue with some pastors. "Well," one said, "it's all right under certain conditions—that is, he's the innocent party or it was before he was converted—to employ a staff member who has been divorced. But you can't ordain a deacon who has been divorced because staff members come and go, but deacons are here to stay."

One even said, "Well, it might be that Greek scholars today are saying this means a one-woman kind of man, but those King James scholars were five hundred years closer to the fact, so they surely knew more than scholars today." Sound absurd? It happened! Remember our premise: The further you get away from the original pattern, the more and more bizarre become the extremities. The original pattern is, "a one-woman kind of man," not a divorced man. His character, not his marital status, is in view.

In my denomination and probably yours, traditions die hard. We hear sermons on the tradition of the elders and the immovability of the Pharisees whom Jesus criticized because they set tradition above truth, and we say *"Amen."* But when our traditions are challenged, it can be most difficult for us.

I fear we have hurt many good men and lost potential service to the kingdom of God by clinging to this unbiblical position on divorce.

Far too often, unqualified deacons and other church leaders remain in office, while good and godly men who have proven their faithfulness to their wives for thirty and forty years are excluded from service. This should not be. I encourage you as pastors to help transform the thinking of your people at this point from tradition to *truth*.

Chapter 10

Church Discipline

S ad but true, the reality is that it is necessary occasionally to carry out discipline within the church. In Paul's epistles, it is clear that discipline was necessary in the early church. From our experience, we know the problem is still with us. For both pastor and people, nothing is more difficult than this.

Fortunately, we have biblical instruction for dealing with the sins of church members as well as conflict between individuals within the church. The disciplinary measures carried out within the structure of the church are normally separate and apart from civil and criminal measures carried out in secular society. Unlike the secular world, church discipline must be administered with a view toward redemption and with a spirit of grace. The goal is never to *destroy* the offender but to *restore* him to fellowship in the church.

Unless it becomes absolutely necessary for you as pastor to become personally involved in matters of church discipline, I encourage you to use selected staff and lay leaders. They can coordinate and investigate charges and countercharges between church members.

Resist the urge to reach a negative conclusion quickly against a church member who has been accused of wrongdoing. Remember the admonition of our Lord who taught us, "As you would have others do unto you, even so, do ye unto them." Instead, ask your disciplinary committee to explore the matter fully, interviewing all parties involved in the dispute. This can be a lengthy and burdensome task, but it must be done to assure fairness to the accused party. And beware of persons who accuse but are unwilling to have their names associated with the accusation.

Let me reemphasize the importance of you as pastor attempting to stay separate and apart from the disciplinary process. In our church our deacons wisely established a policy designed to insulate the pastor against having to deal with these difficult circumstances. Our procedure has been to have a designated staff member, such as an associate pastor or minister of counseling, join two or three mature deacons in forming the disciplinary committee.

Perhaps the most difficult problem you will encounter is dealing with the person who is viewed with a sense of discomfort within the body, but against whom there is no hard evidence. Foreseeing these kinds of situations, the Holy Spirit wisely placed within the body of Christ those believers who are gifted with the gift of spiritual discernment. Select those kinds of persons for the committee.

Through the years I have forbidden service to individuals about whom there was a spirit of "dis-ease" within the heart and soul of my most mature and sensitive people. Give serious heed to the spiritually discerned church member who says, "Pastor, I just don't feel good about this individual or that situation." That which is not of faith is sin. When in doubt, don't do it. The Quakers call it "minding the checks."

When there is a "check mark" within the spirit of your most mature people, you need to listen and take heed. The wives of your board members may be of great assistance here. Mature Christian women often have a heightened sense of spiritual discernment.

Several years ago the deacons of First Baptist Church Houston adopted a "morals and ethics policy." The policy is based on the Matthew 18 model, and it deals with accusations and responses to accusations within the church. It contains the following elements:

1. The accuser is asked to go to the accused and to seek his repentance. This encounter is then reported to the disciplinary committee referred to earlier.

2. If the accused refuses to respond to the accuser, the matter is referred to the disciplinary committee which, in turn, manages the matter as designated authorities for the church. Our policy is to

officially authorize the committee to act on behalf of the church rather than dealing with the matter before the entire congregation.

3. If the accused is determined to be guilty, he is removed from any place of service or leadership in the church until such time as the disciplinary committee determines that restoration has occurred.

4. In the event the accused is determined to be guilty and is resistant to disciplinary guidelines imposed by the committee and, further, if he continues in his sin or wrongdoing, the guilty party may be asked or directed to leave the church.

5. A second part of the "moral and ethics policy" relates to "unsavory" reputation in the church. The scriptural qualifications for church leaders require that they not only be good people, but also "of good report" or "of good reputation." Should different spiritually discerning members of the church, independent of one another, report a general feeling of "dis-ease" regarding an individual member, such situations should be reported to the disciplinary committee for prayer and counsel. If the feeling of "dis-ease" persists, it may be assumed that God is speaking in a delicate and sensitive area through his body, the church.

In such cases, direct accusation and confrontation might not be wise. The disciplinary committee should communicate with key church leadership quietly and privately about persons who are objects of concern toward the end of not utilizing such persons in places of visible leadership. There is no need to remove parties with questionable reputations from the congregation; rather, the goal is to keep them from holding visible leadership positions.

In an effort to minimize the potential for church discipline problems, it is wise for both staff and committee on committees recommendations to be reviewed by the pastor and senior staff. Sometimes the pastor or another minister will know something in confidence about an individual that would make his appointment to a leadership position inappropriate.

I pray the wisdom of the Father, the love of the Son, and the discernment of the Holy Spirit for you as you undertake the task of dealing with these difficult situations.

Part 2

The Pastor as God's Man

Chapter 11

The Call to the Ministry

In 1959 I was in Belfast, Ireland, leading the music in a citywide crusade for evangelist Hyman Appleman. Speaking engagements at civic clubs, radio stations, shipyards, street corners, church meetings, as well as the rigor of the evening services left us exhausted. When we finished, God allowed us several days to rest. We retreated to an old castle that had been converted to a hotel on the Irish Sea in Colraine, Ireland.

It was just the right time for me before our next crusade. Not only did I need the rest, but I was struggling with the decision to leave the music ministry and become a preacher. I called Dr. Forbes Yarborough, beloved former professor at Oklahoma Baptist University, and he mailed me a chapter from a book by Charles Haddon Spurgeon.

The famed Spurgeon lectured to his students in chapel each week at the school that bears his name. Those lectures comprise a book called *Lectures to My Students*. One chapter, "How to Know the Call of the Ministry," was just right for me. The chapter gave five ways to know if you are called. I read the chapter in fifteen minutes, closed the book and said, "I have the call." That was more than forty-eight years ago, and I've never looked back. Here are the ways:

Desire. Psalms 37:4 says, "Delight thyself also in the LORD; and he shall give thee the desires of thine heart." If we truly do delight in the Lord, our desires will become the same as his. If our passion is to love him and to please him, as two streams converge into one river so will our desires become one with his. If you are truly trying to know

God's will and have a burning desire to preach that will not let you go, you have a call from God.

There was a time when I was passionate about the music ministry, but simultaneously that passion began to fade and a new passion to preach began to grow. I wanted it more than anything else, and I knew it to be the call of God. He will put the desire in the sincere heart to do what he wants done. It is not a fleeting thing. It is an impression, a burden, a passion that will not let you go.

I call it a "holy hunch." How do you know when you're in love? You just know. How do you know when God is calling you to preach? You just know and know and know. If you can do anything else except preach, by all means, don't preach. But if the passion burns, then you must preach. If it is your all-consuming, magnificent obsession, then do it.

Ability. This is not to say you will be the greatest orator in the history of mankind. It is to say that God gives us some natural abilities and gifts to do what he wants us to do. He doesn't call blind men to be truck drivers. If you have the ability to organize your thoughts and express them, let alone some special skills in communication, and this is reinforced with a passion to use them, then the call of God is indicated.

Opportunity. Where God leads us to serve and gifts us to serve, he provides opportunity to serve. Open and closed doors are important in reading the hand of God in our lives. The more I considered preaching, the more opportunities I had to preach. And I was faithful to every one of them—street corners, jails, retirement homes, Sunday school classes, everything. God will open the door for you to do what he wants you to do. A closed door is usually an indication of wrong timing or a detour.

Blessing. The confirmation of God comes upon a person who is walking within his will. Again, this does not mean you will have a hundred decisions every time you preach. Conversely, it does mean if you preach a hundred times with no apparent results, you might need to rethink driving that truck.

Many a man has seen a burning sign in the sky that said "GPC." He interpreted this to mean "Go Preach Christ," when it actually meant, "Go Plow Corn." There should be some degree of visible affirmation of your ministry as you pursue it.

A gift is best determined by what you do naturally, what you do well, and what God blesses. I have not been called to the counseling ministry, because I don't particularly enjoy counseling, and I'm not very good at it. No one has ever come back to say, "You changed my life" after I counseled with them. But many persons have greeted me at the door after a sermon I had just preached and said, "That really impacted my life."

The Opinion of Others. Talk to the saints of God. Discuss your decision with those in whom you have great spiritual confidence. Ask their advice; seek their counsel. Let them hear your heart, and listen to them. Stephen was a great lay preacher as a deacon. Someone said, "It's hard enough to preach if you know you're called without *trying* to preach if you're not sure."

While that might be true, I think it is also true that God doesn't get upset with us for trying to do what we *think* we should do. But seek counsel and watch for the hand of God as you do so. He will make clear his way for you. If these five tests add up to a yes, don't wait a minute more. Start preaching.

Chapter 12

Various Kinds of Ministry

When we think of the call to the ministry, we normally think first of a preaching ministry as pastor of a church. Today, however, there are hundreds of opportunities to serve the Lord in full-time Christian service beyond being a preaching pastor at a local church.

Ministries abound—youth, music, education, counseling, missions—to name a few. In the First Baptist Church of Houston, many dedicated men and women serve in support roles as secretaries, assistants, and associates. On the church staff is an orchestra director, a program coordinator, an activities director, a prayer coordinator, a retreat ministry director, a full-time sound technician, a reprographics person, a missions director, a day care director, and many others.

I have the privilege of being part of a denomination that probably has the most expansive and most effective worldwide international missions ministry anywhere. To ensure minimizing turnover and maximizing longevity of service, we have a very high standard. Frankly, the majority of people who apply to be Southern Baptist International Mission Board missionaries are declined for various reasons.

My counsel is always this: "If you are turned down by our board, unable to meet the standards, and are firm in your call, then go some other way. Go with an independent board, raise your own support, move overseas and get a job, but get there somehow."

There are a thousand ways to serve the Lord in full-time ministry—architects, church planters, missionary aviation pilots, television producers, tentmakers, etc. If you are called of God, somewhere in the world there's a place to use your gifts; somewhere a need that only you can fill. Don't give up because you might not fit the stereotype of a preacher.

Find God's tailor-made will for you and do it. My own son Timothy was called into full-time Christian service at age fourteen. He spent the next ten years of his life in frustration because he did not fit the mold of the traditional eight-to-five church staff member. Tim had a passion for his generation—not just those who happened to be age fifteen to thirty, but particularly those Generation X-ers with green hair and rings in their noses—the unreached, unloved untouchables that "business as usual" ministries will never reach.

So Tim started a Christian rock band, because rock music is the language that X-ers speak. For four years he worked as a foreign missionary with "Youth with a Mission" in Amsterdam, Holland, and in Auckland, New Zealand. They traveled throughout Eastern and Western Europe playing in nightclubs, concerts, brothels, street corners—anywhere anyone would listen. And it wasn't contemporary praise and worship. It was "smash nose," "in your face," "you're going to hell," "you need to quit your drugs and get saved and do it right now" kind of music. Yes, they were beat up, cursed at, and thrown out regularly, but they won hundreds of kids to Christ. Tim didn't do it just his way but God's special, unique way just for him.

Don't be deterred. If God has called you, God will use you. If you can't find a ministry, create one. Just don't drift from your call. Better to be on a side street in Calcutta in the will of God than in the White House in Washington, D.C., out of his will. If you're called to be a servant of the king, don't stoop to be president.

The body of Christ has many parts and many different kinds of folks, and the toes are just as important as the hands.

Chapter 13

The Question of Formal Education

A call to preach is a call to preparation. A call to serve is a call to prepare to serve. Unquestionably, Moses is the overpowering figure in the pages of Old Testament Scripture. Moses earned two Ph.D.'s. His first was in the secular culture of Egypt. He learned literature and history, law and warfare, leadership and the arts. But these things do not a prophet make.

These experiences constituted the first forty years of his life, but Moses was not yet ready to serve. A forty-year Ph.D. in the arts and humanities must be followed by a forty-year Ph.D. in spiritual maturity. Moses had to unlearn much of what he had learned. He had to learn to depend on what God would teach him more than what men could teach him. So it was off to the back side of the desert for forty years. There he tended sheep and learned to wait on God.

Finally, toughened in the steel of his soul, Moses was ready for service. But the Exodus from Egypt and the forty years in the wilderness that followed were only the last phase of his life. Leading two million people through the wilderness journey from Egypt to Canaan was only the tip of the iceberg of the eighty years that preceded it.

The apostle Paul was a member of the Sanhedrin, a master in Israel, a Hebrew of the Hebrews, a Pharisee of the Pharisees, *but* he had a lot to learn. Only after the years in Arabia was he ready to confront the scholars of the Roman Empire with the message of the cross.

And what of our Lord? Jesus had the greatest earthly ministry the world has ever known, yet it lasted only three years. What was Jesus doing the first thirty years of his life? We need to remember that though he was God, he laid aside all that he naturally was and restricted himself to the limitations of a man. He did not just study as an example; he studied because he had to. He did not confound the teachers of the law by accident. Yes, God empowered him; yes, God spoke through him; and, yes, he was God in the flesh, but still he prepared. He searched the Scriptures. He grew in favor and stature with God and man. He grew in every way.

No, he was not, as liberal scholars often suggest, only coming to an awareness of his Godhood. He was God and he knew he was God. But he chose to lay aside what was inherently his for thirty years to study, pray, and fast, and prepare himself for ministry. Think of it, thirty years of preparation and a three-year ministry. But what a ministry he had!

Today we go to seminary for three years and set out on a thirty-year ministry. I wonder if we've "got it right." I have often wondered whether Jesus was tempted to begin his ministry early. What a tremendous youth evangelist he would have made at twenty-two or twenty-five. But he wasn't in a hurry. He knew the value of preparation. The call to serve is a call to prepare to serve.

The question, then, is the importance of seminary education. To be sure, there are those whom God has greatly used who did not attend seminary. Billy Graham did not; Wendell Estep, longtime pastor of the great First Baptist Church of Columbia, South Carolina, did not; and certainly there are numbers of others. But for every person like them—uniquely gifted to gain their education outside the traditional channels of seminary classrooms—there are a thousand who are not.

By all means, do everything possible to secure a seminary education. But if that opportunity eludes your grasp, seek God with all your heart, serve him in the beauty of holiness, be faithful to every opportunity, and he will still use you in a wonderful way.

Through the years I've had the joy of personal study with gifted seminary professors. The private study of the right books can make accessible to you much of the information you will find in the class-room. Good preparation does not ensure great usability. But the chances of great usability are severely limited when formal education is lacking.

Chapter 14

Essential Integrity

D oes it even need to be said that integrity is inseparable from Christian ministry? Unfortunately, I'm afraid the answer is yes. An infinite number of things define Generation X. One of the most prominent is this: They have been let down by virtually everything in the world and have little confidence in anything but themselves.

There are three basic institutions of society: the home, the church, and government. In the home, 60 percent of those who once said, "I do," don't. The divorce rate is growing at an astronomical rate.

In the government, the Nixons, Harts, Kennedys, and Clintons cause us to question their integrity. In the church, the Tiltons, Bakers, and Swaggarts disappoint us. And the end is not yet. Continuing disappointment in leadership is inevitable.

Integrity, and the lack thereof, might well be the most important issue in America today; certainly it is in the ministry. Few persons whom God has greatly used were greatly gifted, but they were persons of integrity. Listen again to the words of the apostle Paul in his letter to the church at Corinth:

> For ye see your calling, brethren, how that not many wise men after the flesh, not many mighty, not many noble, are called: But God hath chosen the foolish things of the world to confound the wise; and God hath chosen the weak things of the world to confound the things which are mighty; And base things of the world, and things which are despised, hath God chosen, yea, and things which are not, to bring to

nought things that are: That no flesh should glory in his presence (1 Cor. 1:26–29).

You don't have to be highly educated, talented, or attractive to be greatly used of God, but you have to have integrity. God can drive the ball a long way with a small club but not with a crooked club. At no time in history has the world so closely examined the integrity of ministers. Circumstances beyond your control have created a stage upon which you must act out your life under tremendous scrutiny.

Remember this: When new people come to your church, they are checking *you* out long before they check out your message. It is unspoken, often even unrealized, but virtually every unbeliever goes to church with a question about the credibility of the person speaking to the congregation.

Statistics gathered by First Baptist Houston when I was pastor there indicated that the average guest used to visit three to six weeks before he or she joined. Today that length of time has grown to three to six months.

Your integrity relates to your finances, your moral life, your word—everything. People will love you and forgive you your faults if you admit them and are honest about them before the congregation. They can accept fellow strugglers who are still on the way, but they will reject the leader who pretends to have arrived when, in fact, they know he hasn't.

Keep your word, keep pure, stay on your knees, and do what you say you'll do. If you don't, apologize, explain, and ask forgiveness. Above all, be open, transparent, and honest. Integrity is the rudder that guides the ship of successful ministry.

Chapter 15

Leading Out of Your Character

W hen I read a book or hear a sermon, I consider my time well spent if I come away with one good idea. In 1996 Dan Webster, president of Authentic Leadership Inc., spoke to the staff of First Baptist Houston at a leadership retreat. It was a wonderful experience and really too much to take in in just two days. However, out of every good thing he said—and there was much—one idea stayed with me and impacts my life virtually every day. Dan Webster: said, "The first part of your ministry, you lead out of what you can do. The last part, you lead out of who you are."

What does Mr. Webster mean by "leading out of who you are"? For one thing, it means you have stayed long enough for your congregation to establish confidence in your leadership. It means that personhood is more important than programs; truth is more important than goals; and spiritual confidence is more important than spiritual plans.

Again, this takes time. When you have introduced several programs that have been successful, you gain a certain degree of credibility with your people.

But the time should come in the life of the pastor when the willingness of the people to follow has been created not out of a proven track record of successful programs. Rather, they have a quiet confidence that their pastor has been with God, heard his voice, and may be trusted not to lead them astray.

It is leadership of being more than doing, of personhood more than programs. In my ministry, I found that the longer I stayed and the larger the church became, the easier it was to pastor. First Baptist Houston grew to have many ministries—missions, schools, child development center, wellness program—more than two hundred persons on the payroll. And yet the church was easier to pastor than when we had twenty-five employees.

There are, of course, layers of leadership and good generals who organize the captains and lieutenants who oversee the sergeants. But though there's much more responsibility, there is a parallel increase of ease as I learned to trust the people and they learned to trust me.

Of course, neither my methods nor my leadership style remained stagnant. But it became much easier to lead because our people sensed, at the helm of the ship, a leader who was not easily rattled, who stayed the course, and who enjoyed the composure of a Spirit-controlled life. Don't sweat the small stuff. Don't lose your cool. Don't get rattled. Lead out of your quietness, your character, your spiritual maturity—and your leadership will become easier as the years go by.

Good words by Dan Webster, "The first part of your ministry, you lead out of what you can do; the second, out of who you are."

Chapter 16

A Touch of Charisma

Charisma. What a fascinating word that is. Most often it is used in the secular sense with a gifted leader, movie star, or singer. What do we mean when we say, "This woman has charisma; that man has charisma"?

The dictionary defines *charisma* as grace or favor, a special quality of leadership that captures the popular imagination and inspires allegiance and devotion.

Let me go beyond that and attempt to define *charisma* as it relates to the ministry. Charisma is a God-given gift, a God-given presence about you that makes people want to please you. They want to do what you want them to do.

Unsanctified charisma in the hands of a lost man can be devastating. A charismatic young man can persuade a young woman to participate in an affair in order to please himself. In the life of a man of God, charisma is a special touch of the Holy Spirit that makes the persuasion of the gospel easier when the anointing of the Holy Spirit falls upon a gifted and charismatic leader.

Every spiritual gift may be prostituted. A gifted leader can use his God-given gift to sing for the Lord or sing in a bar. He can use the same gift to run a business or run a Sunday school department. A good persuader can persuade you to buy a car or, sanctified by the Holy Spirit, to accept Jesus. Good salesmen make good soul winners. The danger comes when we prostitute the gift and use it for secular purposes, or perhaps even worse, use the gift in spiritual things while not depending on the power of the Holy Spirit.

Can a person develop charisma? Perhaps. Certainly the anointing of the Holy Spirit on a person's life enables him to be a more effective channel through which the Spirit can convince people to follow Christ. The ability to convince a person to accept Christ, live a holy life, join the church, give his money, develop a prayer life, or do anything is ultimately done only through the power of the Holy Spirit. But the wise minister will enhance every tangible faculty with which God has endowed him by that Spirit to maximize the effectiveness of his ministry.

Certainly we can prepare our best, educate ourselves, have a pleasing appearance and a heart that is filled with the love of Christ and the power of the Holy Spirit. Yet it is still true that there are those whom God has endowed with an extra measure of charisma. The bad news is that it might be used for secular, even evil, purposes. The good news is that when all the faculties of one's personhood are honed to a fine edge and the Spirit of God anoints the ministry, that person to whom God has given special charisma as a grace gift has awesome potential for usefulness in the kingdom.

Chapter 17

The Pastor's Personality

Preachers can be downright obnoxious people. Someone ought to write a book entitled *Games Preachers Play*. The first chapter could be entitled, "Don't Act like a Preacher." Most ministers have a preconceived image of how a clergyman should act, dress, walk, talk, and live. Trying to fit the mold and fulfill the image often takes a person completely out of his own personality and into something very unnatural.

The phrase "I have never met a preacher that I felt confident around or felt I could talk to," has been said too many times by laymen and laywomen. "Dr. Holy Joe," "Professor Bottletop," and "The Right Reverend Whistlebritches" can turn off more people than all the good gospel preaching in the world can turn on.

Preaching is truth through a personality. It is God's word entrusted to human instrumentality. But if that same personality turns off the hearers, they may never get beyond *him* to the *truth* he is trying to say. Don't try to fit the image. Throw away the mold. Quit playing "Reverend Minister." Don't hide behind a clerical façade. Be yourself. Act natural. Act like a human being. Dress like you want to dress. Smile. Lay off the high-sounding ecclesiological phrases. You are probably scaring away three-fourths of your potential hearers.

See this scene. It is repeated a thousand times every Sunday in the hallway, on the street, and in the parking lots of our churches. The preacher greets the people with a warm and sunny "good morning." He is cheery and natural. He is himself. But when he walks out on the platform, he is someone else. His voice gets a holy quiver and his vocabulary is strictly "high church." After church he is a normal human being again, with a natural style and a normal vocabulary. The people have seen him turn it on and turn it off.

The preacher tells the people their religion should be a part of their everyday lives. They are to be a witness in the home, in the school, and on the job. But the old Sunday morning "switcheroo" belies that idea. He plays the religion game for an hour on Sunday and then steps back into the real world for the rest of the week. If the preacher separates the two worlds, how can the people be expected to make the adjustment?

And so from Sunday to Sunday, no discipleship, no witness, no nothing. Perhaps there is so little penetration of the gospel into the secular world where people really live for this very reason. And is it really any wonder?

To emulate the preconceived universal image of the preacher is to further frustrate the will of God. Remember, he made you like you are. He put you where you are because there are more people at that time and in that place who can relate to you than anywhere else in the world. When you attempt to become someone else other than who you are, you thwart what God wants to do through you. Don't act like you think a preacher is supposed to act. Act like yourself.

Do you think there is no universal preacher image? No movie or television program ever shows a sharp, successful-looking businessman type in the role of the preacher. Never! He is always a Catholic priest; an Elmer Gantry (wolf in sheep's clothing); a hick from the sticks; or a Tweedle-dee, Tweedle-dum Milquetoast. These are the world's images of a preacher.

As a pastor, it is most important to be approachable. Shortly before their fatal trip to Dallas, Jackie Kennedy reminded her husband to be warm and gracious with the huge crowds they expected to encounter. "Dear," she said, "don't be in a hurry. Take plenty of time and give the people your undivided attention one at a time. Walk slowly through the crowds."

Good advice for a president or a preacher. As his servants, we must never be so interested in reaching masses of people that we give the appearance of being aloof, busy, disinterested, and generally carried away with our own importance. Jesus preached to the multitudes on the mountaintop and at the seaside, but he was never better than when he preached to Nicodemus and the woman at the well. You can be busy, without giving the appearance of "busyness." Take time for people. Multitudes of people are made up of individuals with individual problems. To each, his is the most important in the world.

When you stand in the midst of a large group, give one person your undivided attention until he is through speaking to you. Better to let fifteen walk away, unwilling to wait because you were genuinely interested in one, than to give partial attention to fifteen. Take time for individuals, classes, and small groups, as well as large groups. Arrive early. Be relaxed. Listen well. Don't talk to one person while staring over his shoulder to see who else is waiting. Be genuinely interested in the individual. Never make a grand entry. If you cannot arrive on time, get there early—but never late.

In a busy world of blasting horns, flashing lights, and screaming voices, people deserve to have an island of tranquility—at least one place where a little solace can be found. As God's undershepherd, you can provide that place. An early start on the day and an extra prayer in the morning will ensure the smooth flow of the day's activities and will greatly aid you in having time to show genuine interest in people.

Don't be boisterous or make a show of your own importance with one eye cocked to see what kind of impression you are making on the crowd. Genuine humility and sincere Christian sweetness are a rare combination in the personality of far too few. Be a man of God among the people. Speak softly; look straight into their eyes. Give them warmth and genuine attention. Walk slowly through the crowds.

Chapter 18

A Teachable Spirit

T he day you think you've "arrived" is the day your ministry will begin to decline. Few things are more important to know than that you don't know much. A teachable spirit is inseparably linked to humility, and humility is an absolute essential in usefulness. Don't ever think a teachable spirit is a side issue to effectiveness in the ministry; it might well be the heart of it.

Since Charles G. Finney began mass evangelism over two centuries ago, there has always been a world-class evangelist with an heir apparent on the scene. Through the Finneys, Moodys, and Sundays, this has always been true until now.

Let me put it bluntly. Where is the next Billy Graham? Dr. Graham is over eighty years old and not in good health. Obviously, at the most critical juncture of history, perhaps the greatest prophet since apostolic days is in the sunset of his ministry. Why, after all these years, has the cycle been broken? Why is there no heir apparent to Dr. Graham, compelling him to go on and on?

For years I have believed the reason is that someone missed it! Further, I think I know who that someone was, or at least one of the two whom it may have been. Years ago I had the privilege of organizing a great citywide evangelistic crusade in a large midwestern city. In spite of ice storms, the arena was packed night after night. Hundreds made decisions for Christ as the Spirit of God moved in a tremendous way. We asked the local newspaper to cover the crusade, to no avail.

The evangelist said, "I'll get the coverage." The next day he went to the editor and placed his scrapbooks on his desk. "See the front page coverage I've had in other crusades," he said. The editor was obviously agitated. "All right," he said, "we'll cover you."

That night a reporter attended the crusade and took pictures. The problem was that he took them from the back of the platform, showing only the evangelist's back and the one empty spot in the balcony. That picture was on the front page the next afternoon. The evening the reporter and photographer were present, the evangelist had called down some teenagers for moving around. The headline of the article read, "'Shut up and sit down, or we'll throw you out' Evangelist Tells Local Teens."

Rather than being broken, the poor man came to the pulpit the following night and held the front page up before the crowd. He said: "Look at the coverage we got. The preachers couldn't get it, but I got it." I don't think he was smart enough to figure out that he had been insulted. I have grieved over this man. He was so full of pride.

One night after the crusade, we invited him, his team, and the steering committee to our home for a dinner. He looked over the buffet as my wife said, "I hope you like it." He responded, "Lady, I don't like a thing you've got." Although I never knew a man with more authority and power in his preaching, today he has only a small ministry and preaches no citywide crusades at all. The reason? Pride. No humility, no teachable spirit, no long-term ministry.

Consider Dr. Billy Graham. In contrast to the preacher above, Dr. Graham is the most humble man you will ever meet and the most famous preacher of our lifetime.

Let me tell you about another evangelist who may have been "the man who missed it." Years ago I worked with an evangelist whose ministry I helped to birth. I taught him to outline sermons and to preach. I taught him how to set up a crusade and give an invitation. I never knew a man who had the magnetic, charismatic hand of God upon his life as he did. When he walked onto the platform, the room was charged with spiritual electricity. I've seen him give an invitation without a sermon and watched people pour down the aisles. Young and old came under the convicting power of the Holy Spirit through his ministry. But he was a novice. It was too much too fast, and he never learned the great lesson of humility. Before he was twenty-five years of age, he "knew it all."

I've seen him fly across the country to spend an entire day with me, to seek my counsel about decisions in his ministry, and then argue with me the whole time, saying what I was telling him was wrong, only to go back and do what he wanted to do in the first place. Today he also enjoys only a limited ministry and holds no citywide crusades. One of these two men, I believe with all of my heart, may well have been the "next Billy Graham." Meanwhile, that great saint of God goes on and on, while the man whom God might have prepared to follow him apparently remains in his shadow.

I don't intend to write a book on *Humility and How I Obtained It,* but let me tell you with all candor that to this very hour, it is regularly my pleasure to seek counsel and advice and not only to welcome correction but to invite it.

A teachable spirit is an indispensable part of effective ministry.

Chapter 19

You and Your People Skills

Someone once said, "The ministry would be easy if it weren't for the people." Leaky roofs and broken pipes are more easily fixed than broken relationships. The answer obviously lies in not letting the relationship get broken in the first place. Few things are more important in the ministry than the ability of the pastor to get along with people.

Perhaps the best place to start in relating to others is to put yourself in their shoes. I think our Lord had that in mind when he said, "Whatsoever ye would that men should do to you, do ye even so to them" (Matt. 7:12). Treating others as you want to be treated, caring enough to know where they are coming from, and respecting it, is the heart of getting along with people.

Everyone is "coming from some place." Each person thinks as he does for a reason. Take the time to know him. What's going on in his world? What forces have shaped his life? What was going on around him when he was about age twelve? We tend to get locked in to the attitudes and perspectives that shaped our lives at that age.

As pastor, you don't always have to be Mr. Right, but you do have to be Mr. Gracious. Surprise, surprise, dear pastor friend, you just could be wrong. Someone else's opinion might be the right one. Listen more than you talk. Be open to the other person's view, and when he differs, be gracious in your response. "Mary, have you considered this?" "Joe, let's look at it from this perspective." "Sue, could it possibly be that . . ."

Montaigne, the French philosopher, said, "My life has been filled with terrible things, most of which never happened." May I add, "My ministry has been filled with terrible conflict, none of which I allowed to materialize." That person who seems to be your enemy may just be a friend you haven't nurtured. As God's children and certainly as his spiritual leaders, we must be the initiators of reconciliation and the encouragers of friendship.

Within the membership of First Baptist Houston was a highly regarded man who for years was a great encourager and supporter. The introduction of a style of music into our worship services, to which he objected, seemed to turn him into a critic, at best, if not an opponent.

One night I called to ask for an appointment. Visiting him and his wife in their home, I began by saying I had obviously offended them. I knew they were upset with me, and I wished not only to apologize, but also to have the opportunity to quietly share our views and see if we could make at least some progress toward a meeting of the minds. While we made only slight progress in our differences about music, we made great progress in our friendship.

The wise pastor will speak his mind with firm conviction, yet with latitude for the opinions of those who disagree. When people do a poor job, lovingly show them a better way and encourage their potential. When they do a good job, commend them personally and publicly. When they are down, encourage them; when they are wrong, teach them.

Years ago Billy Graham arrived in London to preach at Harringway Arena. Tired and caught by surprise, Dr. Graham was immediately whisked away to an "interview" on public television. It was, in fact, an ambush. Four liberals were waiting to debate him. Dr. Graham did not pretend to be an intellect, but the kindness and humility of his spirit was disarming. The next morning the *London Times* carried an account of the debate. "Dr. Graham," the *Times* said, "lost the debate, but he won the hearts of England."

Even when you are wrong—and you will be—even when you lose—and you will lose—you must ingratiate yourself to your people and live to fight another day. Tenderness of spirit and genuine humility are always in order. When you are wrong, admit it. When you blow it, acknowledge it. When you don't know, ask for help. When you are corrected, take it.

Perhaps no element contributes more to developing good people skills than a true love for people. Ask yourself this question: Do I see people as an object, a prize to be won, a statistic to be added that my denominational paper might write an article about my growing church, enticing a larger church to call me as pastor? Or, do I see people as sheep in need of a shepherd?

A real shepherd never sacrifices the feelings of his sheep for his own; a true shepherd lays down his life for his sheep. A self-serving shepherd drives his sheep; a true shepherd leads his sheep. A hired shepherd compromises for the sake of popularity; a God-called shepherd speaks the truth and defends his sheep at any cost. Our heavenly Shepherd gave us the perfect example in every personal relationship. The successful undershepherd will learn to follow it.

Chapter 20

The Pastor's Prayer Life

At age twenty-five, I wrote a book on prayer that has "enjoyed" worldwide success: *The Power of Positive Praying.* Over two million copies are in print in six different languages. Looking back, I think, "I didn't know I knew that much." Surely God had something to do with writing that little book.

I still have much to learn in the school of prayer. But let me share something new and exciting that God has been teaching me. He doesn't necessarily respond in the areas about which I have been praying; he often moves in apparently unconnected areas. How is it that when I increase my prayer life, God starts to move in areas I wasn't even praying about or thinking about?

The answer is at once simple and beautiful. He is blessing me simply because I am trying to be a man of prayer. My whole world changes when I am serious about prayer. Everywhere there is blessing as I spend serious time with God. A hundred other things are still developing in my soul about prayer, but I can tell you this: *It's important to pray.* In fact, it's most important to pray. Above everything else, be a person of prayer.

Somehow it seems God doesn't necessarily want us to bring him our petitions and our praise because he needs it but because he knows we need it, and he has our best interest at heart.

Let me give you two simple principles about the preacher and his prayer life. First, when you pray, things happen. Second, you have to pray a lot. Yes, the Bible says we are not heard for our much speaking, but far too often that is simply an excuse not to pray very much. God-blessed prayer takes time.

Yes, it's important to stay in an attitude of prayer. To think that our hearts can be silently praying to God while our lips are verbally addressing another in conversation is an awesome thing. Constant prayer is commanded and commended, *but that doesn't let you off the hook in the matter of longevity in prayer.* Every pastor should spend at least an hour a day, seven days a week, on his knees before God in prayer. You will be amazed to see how regularly and how easily that hour turns into an hour and a half and then two.

The time you spend in early morning prayer is time that shortens your time the rest of the day. You will find that you don't spend nearly as much time running around, solving problems, blowing whistles, and pushing buttons. When you spend that early morning time in prayer, there will be less problems and fewer obstacles. When you get to the problems you have feared and situations you have dreaded, you will often find God has already been there before you, and your day is easier and shorter: "And it shall come to pass, that before they call, I will answer" (Isa. 65:24).

How much should we pray and when should we pray? Let me repeat: At least an hour, seven days a week, and early in the morning. How often did Jesus arise a great while before dawn and go into the mountain place alone to pray? If the Creator of the universe, incarnated in a man, found it essential to pray, how much more should we.

I believe God has a special time to meet each of us in the quietness of the day. Your time might be 4:00 A.M. or 6:30 A.M. For me, it is 5:00 A.M. No, I don't make it every time. Far too many evenings until midnight can make it most difficult, but 80 to 90 percent of the time, that's *my time* to meet God. Find yours. You will know it when you find it.

Early in the morning the world is quiet and our thoughts uncluttered. Early in the morning you can sense his voice, feel his touch, know his mind. Whatever you do, cultivate the habit of early morning prayer. This is not a time for sermon preparation, rambling thoughts, study, or idle daydreaming. It is a time to talk to God and listen to God talk to you.

Prioritize God's needs. Pray about the things he is interested in, his glory, his body on earth, a lost world for whom he died. Pray for your family, pray for direction, and then listen.

When you wait upon God, he will speak to you in the quietness of your own soul. His voice will come not with heavenly vocal cords or crashing thunder but in the still, small impression of the Spirit deep in your heart—a language without words, louder, clearer, more distinct than any you will hear from another person. The hymn writer said it so well:

> I come to the garden alone
> > While the dew is still on the roses.
> And the voice I hear falling on my ear,
> > The Son of God discloses.
> He speaks and the sound of His voice
> > Is so sweet, the birds hush their singing.
> And the melody that He gave to me
> > Within my heart is ringing.
> And He walks with me and He talks with me,
> > And He tells me I am His own.
> And the joy we share as we tarry there,
> > None other has ever known.[1]

He waits there for you in the garden of prayer, and he will be waiting every morning. Don't disappoint him.

1. From the hymn, "In the Garden," words by C. Austin Miles.

Chapter 21

The Pastor's Home

The pastor's relationship to his family is a vital part of his ministry. Naturally, the pastor and his family are subject to the same trials and temptations as other families. Being in the ministry is no guarantee of rearing a perfect family. To the contrary, it is often a detriment. This, of course, in no way suggests a pastor should not have a family, although many single persons have been effective pastors.

Our Lord and the apostle Paul, to name two, were incomparable shepherds of the flock. And certainly the qualification (the husband of one wife), addressed elsewhere, does not restrict the pastorate to those who are married. There is, however, something very warm and special about a pastor with a good family. The love and care he receives from them and the nourishment he gives to them are important to his spiritual development as undershepherd of the family of God. And, of course, there is a certain degree of credibility added when a married pastor speaks on matters of marriage and family life.

Perhaps no other factor has the negative influence on the family as does the feeling of "having to perform." The daily pressure of life in the spotlight brings added stresses to family life—and this on top of those already existing in our culture.

My wife is the dearest Christian I know. She is the perfect example of how a pastor's wife should view her role, and she was adored as the pastor's wife by our congregation. To their credit, I must say that our people never placed undue expectations upon Uldine simply because she was the pastor's wife. She graciously served the Lord with a beautiful and holy spirit, not because she had to, but because she chose to do so.

In over thirty of my thirty-five years as pastor, she has consistently, Sunday by Sunday, taught a Bible class. Sometimes she has taught elementary children and sometimes married young adults. But most of the time she has taught college seniors. My scrapbook is filled with letters from young adults whose lives she touched when they were students. There have been periods when she did not teach simply because she chose to serve in other ways, but never has she felt the pressure that she must teach every Sunday without an occasional sabbatical.

For 99 percent of the Sunday mornings and Sunday nights in my two pastorates, Uldine was comfortably seated in the worship center, hearing the Word of God and worshiping with our beloved congregations. But there were a few times when she felt the total freedom not to come to church at all. No legalistic formulas for attendance were imposed by her husband or her church, and that is as it should be.

She was not the church fashion trendsetter. She neither underdressed nor overdressed. Sometimes she was casual, sometimes dressed up, but she always looked like a million dollars and she was an encouragement and inspiration to the women of the church. Uldine's father was a pastor, and he and her mother did a terrific job rearing her. In a sentence, they gave her the freedom to be herself. She always served the Lord because she chose to, never because it was "expected" of the preacher's kid.

Dear pastor, be exceedingly clear with your family and your congregation that neither your spouse nor your children are ever to feel any pressure to do or to be anything for any other reason than their love for the Lord Jesus. When you deal with a pastor search committee and they ask if your wife will be president of the mission society or play the church piano, let them know lovingly but firmly that it will be her decision if she so chooses and senses God's leadership. The church must understand they are not calling two staff members. They are calling a pastor whose wife graciously serves at her pleasure and God's bidding.

The same applies to the pastor's children. They are all different, aren't they? Our daughter Ginger was exactly like her mother, happily serving the Lord with no sense of pressure because of who she was. Our sons, however, were quite different. Both felt a self-imposed sense of real pressure. They chose different routes to find their "way." But the Lord is gracious, and his promises are faithful.

Proverbs 22:6, "Train up a child in the way he should go: and when he is old, he will not depart from it," is not just a promise to good parents that consistent spiritual nurturing assures our children will ultimately be godly. It is also a warning that leaving a child to his own willfulness is the path to destruction. Parenting involves a process of making disciples of our children. We teach obedience in the home as a pattern of authority in order to bring them to salvation and discipleship. Godly discipline provides an umbrella of protection under which a child learns to obey God during the days of vulnerability.

Both our sons detoured, but both are now on that glorious "highway to heaven," and are fine Christian men, happily serving the Lord. Their own testimony is that it was a self-imposed pressure that most caused them trouble in their teens and early twenties.

Relate to your children the same way you relate to your wife. Let each be himself. Train them, teach them, and guide them, and then let them make their choices, take their knocks, and learn responsibility for their own actions. They will usually test the boundaries. But when you have raised them in the things of God to the best of your ability, you have to release them to the Lord to find their own way.

As pastor you will have constant tension between the time required to meet the needs of your congregation and your family. The answer? Family first! You can always find someone to help you do the work of the church, but no one can love your wife and raise your children except you. Someone else can make a hospital visit for you, but no one else can go to the Little League game. That church committee can meet without you, but your daughter must never perform in the school play without you being there.

Date nights with your spouse and family times with your kids must be scheduled as priority in your week. How many times have I declined an engagement by saying, "I am sorry, I have another appointment." That appointment was often with my family, and I still consider it to be more important than any other. God's people are gracious and forgiving and, yes, I have known a few instances where a pastor survived divorce during his pastorate; however, those situations are few and far between. Lose your family and you may well lose your ministry.

Let me close with a challenge about family vacations. You are not a hero if you never take a vacation. In fact, you are not even smart. Take every day you have coming. Our Lord regularly drew apart from the pressures of his ministry, and so must you. It is best not to take three or four short five-day minivacations through the year; take it all at once. Get away three or four weeks. Change locations, change pace, don't call back to the office, and don't preach on your vacation. You and your family need a real vacation and your church will be better for it.

I couldn't count the times I have returned from vacation to hear my people say, "Preacher, you were really on fire today. You ought to go on vacation more often!" Surprise your family. Do fun things. Let your family know you are a regular dad and they are first in your life. Of all the things we have done together, my sons love the following story best.

One cold February day I bought a ski boat and trailer and three wet suits. Parking the boat and trailer out of sight of the principal's office, I got the boys out of school in the middle of the day, telling the principal we had a "very important" engagement. Imagine their joy as we drove off with a smile. What a treat to "skip school" with dad. Our bodies nearly froze to death, but our hearts had a warm glow that lingers to this day.

Give priority to your family. I am not at all sure there is such a thing as quality time without quantity time. The Lord who gave you your ministry gave you your family as well, and you must balance both.

I want you to hear the testimony of my beloved helpmate of forty-five years, written to the wonderful women of God who stand by their husbands:

"The share of the man who stayed with the supplies is to be the same as that of him who went down to the battle. All will share alike" (1 Sam. 30:24 NIV).

A thousand volumes could not contain my gratitude to God for choosing me to be a preacher's daughter and a preacher's wife.

Serving Jesus as a "partner" has been my life from the beginning. My parents were totally committed to Christ and the work of his church. Dad pastored churches in ten states; seven while I was still living at home. I had fun being a "P.K." In fact, I always thought it was very special. I even liked the silly jokes and sly remarks about preachers' kids and deacons' kids. It is and has always been good to be with God's wonderful people. And now being a minister's wife is like graduate school; a bigger challenge and greater blessing.

A minister's wife is not something you do; rather, someone you are. As I look back on my life, I have focused on Jesus and who I am under his teaching in the Word of God. I do not search for temporary significance in something in which I am presently involved at the church or in the workplace. I find total satisfaction of my significance in who I am in Jesus, and the joy of becoming more like him every day.

He fills my life with warmth and color. He fills it with light and life.

"The fruit of righteousness will be peace; the effect of righteousness will be quietness and confidence forever" (Isa. 32:17 NIV).

Isaiah's prophecy is about end times. But we can also have the fruit of God's Spirit in us now, for all that he is may be ours through Jesus Christ. Peace, quietness, and confidence are ours today.

The congregation is looking to us to lead the way to victory. I believe our relationship with our husband is a mirror of our relationship with Jesus. How can we lead God's people if things are not right at home? Communion with Jesus through reading his Word, through prayer, through rest and proper nutrition, according to Genesis 1:29, are basic. Our life's purpose as seen in the life of Jesus is to love one another, to be kind, to be tolerant, and to give generous service.

Loving Jesus, our husbands, and ourselves will be our foundation for loving his people and his work.

Years ago the wife of a youth pastor asked me some questions about praying for my husband. "Yes darling," I said, "probably ninety percent of my prayers are for my husband." She said, "I don't pray for mine at all." I am sorry to say, they are not married today. Pray!

Love the Lord with all your heart, soul, and mind, and love one another as you love yourself. Love your man with all your strength and purpose and passion, and no matter what comes against you, don't weaken. Stand against the darkness—and LOVE.

Whatever your hands find to do, do with all your heart and do it to the glory of God. Surrender your hands and lift them to the resurrection power. What you cannot do, he can and will.

I thank Jesus for coming to live in my heart early in life, for keeping me on the WAY instead of moving down some pointless path. Thank you, Jesus, for the road of grace and thank you for calling John and me into the ministry.

Let's tell everyone about his redeeming love!

—Uldine Bisagno

Chapter 22

Managing Your Time

No one will control your schedule for you but you! The increasing demands of a growing church consistently increase the pressure to choose priorities. As pastors, we are not first of all administrators, pulpiteers, or executives. We are first and foremost shepherds of the flock. As such, nothing tears at our hearts more than to have to say no to even the smallest need of the least-recognized member of our congregation.

Two or three times during my ministry, I have spot-checked the number of demands upon my time, calls for attention, and decisions made in the course of an average day. That number is usually around 150. In my only other pastorate, the First Southern Baptist Church of Del City, Oklahoma, I came to a crisis late in the second year of my five-year tenure. The church had grown from about six hundred to a thousand in attendance, and I was quickly coming to grips with the reality that I couldn't do it all.

I couldn't grant every request for an appointment. I couldn't visit every prospect. I couldn't see everyone in the hospital. I couldn't make every meeting, and I couldn't accept every speaking invitation. "What to do, what to do?" My heart was truly torn. How could I balance the passion in my soul to be a true shepherd to the flock, with the demands on my time for study, prayer, family, and relaxation?

Most pastors go through the same battle as their churches approach eight hundred to a thousand in attendance. The answer is obvious. Like it or not, we must prioritize. Here are some things that have helped me.

1. *Find your security in Christ.* We all want the approval of our people and recoil from their criticism, but frankly, that's life in the fast lane. If you can't take the heat, stay out of the kitchen. You cannot pastor a growing and developing church without going through crisis and criticism, as you begin to move from "one-to-one" ministry to the necessity of touching people in broader strokes and larger groups.

People's commendations and approval are nice but not essential. Our priority must be pleasing the Master. When we do that, he will enable us to live without the need to please everyone in the church. Find your security in Christ. The applause of men is fleeting, but *his* gentle approval is forever.

2. *Expand your efficiency by expanding your morning.* If you start at 8:00 A.M., it will take you until midnight to get finished. If you start at 5:00 A.M., you might be finished by 4:00 or 5:00 P.M. The principle is simple. The early morning hours are the best. Give them to God. That hour or two in your prayer closet will facilitate God's going before you, smoothing the way and working in your behalf. If you are too busy to pray early, you will spend from 8:00 A.M. to midnight struggling alone to fight unwinnable battles.

If you seek him early, he will go before you, working in your behalf so that when you tackle those problems you will find many have already been resolved. Every fifteen minutes in early morning prayer may well save you an hour or two through the day.

3. *Determine your priorities.* Through the years I have been blessed with numerous invitations. I have come to learn that preaching at a seminary or conference of pastors multiplies my ministry and allows me to touch many more church members than I ever could by accepting every invitation to preach directly to their churches. As you develop leaders within your church and learn to delegate authority to them, you will multiply yourself through those whom you empower. Work with your deacons, your staff, and committee chairmen. Then sit back and evaluate which projects and decisions need your personal attention.

First Baptist Houston normally had ten to twenty members in the hospital at any given time. The M. D. Anderson Hospital in Houston is the leading cancer treatment center in the world. For this reason, calls came from across the country to visit loved ones and friends, often expanding the list to thirty or forty. Which of them should I visit? This might not be best for you, but it is the plan God gave me and it served me well.

First, I visited the seriously ill. Second, I visited our leaders and their families. Third, I visited those who specifically requested me. A lady once asked, "Pastor, how sick do I have to be before you visit me in the hospital?" "Ma'am," I replied, "you don't want to be that sick." We both had a good chuckle, but seriously, ministering to God's people at any point in their lives is both our calling and our joy. Pragmatically, however, I do have to stay in control of my time and that often means making choices.

4. *Learn to control your telephone.* The wise church will provide a telephone for the pastor's car. This normally unused time can be turned into profitable time. Hopefully, God will give you a great secretary like I had to help you with returning phone calls. Often I would tell her, "I am looking for a call from 'so and so'; please put him through." Through the years my secretaries learned that for various reasons some people should be "put through" immediately. However, there is always that volume of borderline calls that might be worthy of your attention, just not at that particular time.

If there is any question, the secretary will say to Mrs. Jones, "The pastor is in but unavailable right now. May I help you?" My secretaries found that in the majority of cases, they could either answer the question or transfer the caller to a staff member who could. When the need still exists for a return call, she should say, "Thank you; we will call you back before long." Notice I said, *we* will call you back, not *he* will call you back. Within an hour, an associate pastor or assistant can return the call, saying, "The pastor is still busy and asked that I call you back." If the matter lingers, return the call as soon as you are able, from your office or car. You will, of course, find God's special method for you, but this worked for me.

You can't attend every class meeting, but you can attend gatherings when several classes are together. You might not visit every seniors Sunday school class, but you can attend the monthly seniors dinner. In other words, touch your people in large groups. Walk slowly among them. Be casual. Don't hurry. Give them your time and attention. Don't rush into the services or rush out. Get there early and visit with your people. Stay until virtually everyone has left and greet them as they leave.

Touch the people. This, too, is a part of staying in control of your schedule. If you don't control your time, your time will control you and destroy your effectiveness as a leader.

Chapter 23

Your Weekly Schedule

The best train goes nowhere without well-prepared tracks on which to run. The pastor's weekly schedule should be well thought out and tailor-made just for him. To arrive at the Sunday terminal of a "week well spent" means having run Monday through Saturday on a disciplined track. There is no right way or wrong way to do this. God's leadership must be sought and your own personality must be taken into consideration. Through the years, you will experiment and make many changes before coming to the approach that is best for you.

I cannot overstate the importance of this, however: People are never an *interruption* of our ministry—they *are* our ministry. It is not necessarily a compliment for a church member to say, "Our pastor is always available." One must wonder when he spends time with God, time with his family, and time in sermon preparation.

On the other hand, nothing is so important as to never allow interruption. Urgent needs must be met with urgency. Crisis must be handled immediately. What might seem like "just another interruption" to your day might be life and death to the person on the other end of the line.

Jesus was never too busy for people, and the servant is not greater than his Lord. When you talk to people, look at them. When you hear people, listen to them, and don't just give the appearance of looking and listening. Really look. Really listen. Really care.

The earliest part of the day is always the best, and, as with the "tithe off the top," always belongs to God. The psalmist said it beautifully and well, "Early will I seek thee" (Ps. 63:1). Before the phone rings, before the distractions of the day, before the morning television news, before the sunrise—these are God's hours for you. Meet him in the morning and he will walk with you through the day.

Again, any schedule is a good schedule as long as God leads you to it, as long as it works for you, and if it is subject to interruption. But generally speaking, I have found the following schedule to work for me:

    5:00 A.M. - Prayer
    6:00 A.M. - Personal devotional Bible reading
    6:30 A.M. - Breakfast
    7:00 A.M. - Exercise
    7:30 A.M. - Study
    10:30 A.M. - Dress
    11:30 A.M. - Arrive at the office for staff luncheons, meetings,
                 office work, dictation, phone calls, etc.
    4:00 P.M. - Hospital visitation and other visits
    6:00 P.M. - Dinner

The question of evening priorities is not an easy one. There will always be tension between time for your family, time for yourself, time for meetings, and time for visitation of members and prospective members. Interruptions will abound. The only thing of which you can be sure about your daily schedule is that it will not be sure. There will be interruptions: sickness, crises, speaking engagements, committee meetings, travel, etc. But the majority of the time, I have found it possible to generally maintain the above schedule.

Two of the special gifts God has given to facilitate our ministry are cell phones and answering machines. Use those hours in your car to make and return phone calls, particularly on the way home from the office. Once you enter your home, it is important to do everything possible to maintain the sanctity of family time. This is where you can use your telephone answering machine to a great advantage. This is particularly important during meal times, which should be unhurried and relaxed. A call back a bit later normally will suffice.

Occasionally I am asked, "But what if it's an emergency?" In my ministry, I can recall few, if any, true emergencies. It is your responsibility to determine what is and what is not an emergency. If you do not stay in control of your schedule, no one else will do it for you. There is a delicate balance between accessibility to your people and responsibility to your family and yourself. Our Lord is willing to help you determine the balance.

Chapter 24

Outside Speaking Engagements

Which of us has not attended conferences and seminars, crusades and conventions and wished we were the person doing the speaking? At such times there is a thin line between our pride and a true God-honoring desire to serve. Early on, the young pastor must learn to deal with the issue of his "outside" speaking engagements. There is something very heady about the wine of popularity, and it is not completely unlike Satan's subtle whisper, "Ye shall be as gods."

When I am invited for any type of preaching engagement, I am immediately flattered. Newly introduced into this kind of opportunity, the young preacher will be tempted to take everything that comes along. These invitations normally come because your church is growing rapidly. This usually happens because you are good in the pulpit. But if those engagements begin to take you away too often *from* your pulpit, your church will begin to suffer from neglect and your time away will be counterproductive.

In my first pastorate I succumbed to the flattery of many such invitations. One day the Lord gently spoke to me, "John, if you spend all your time traveling and preaching about what is happening in your church, it will quit happening." Customarily, pastor and people will have some general understanding about "time away." For example, three weeks for vacation, two conferences or conventions, two evangelistic crusades, and eight one-night speaking engagements out of the city per year. Speaking engagements outside your church but within your city should not be an issue.

Few churches are legalistic at this point, and seldom will a personnel committee be looking over the shoulder of a pastor to monitor his time away. Flexibility on both sides is always appropriate, but the wise pastor will be sensitive to the church's needs and the leadership of the Holy Spirit in this regard.

A word of caution: The church must be sensitive to the financial needs of the pastor and his family. No true man of God wants to live like a king, but pastors have the same financial needs as others and often more. Are you as a church providing adequate insurance and retirement? Are you aware of special medical needs or schooling needs of your pastor's children? Often the pastor is caught in a financial trap because of an inadequate salary, and feels pressured to accept speaking engagements that he would have otherwise declined, just because of the honorarium.

Pastor, don't let yourself get caught in that trap. Never accept a speaking engagement because you need the money. Only go because the Spirit of God has clearly impressed your heart that it is his time and place for you. If you are experiencing excessive financial burdens, tell the Lord and share your heart with your most trusted leadership. The needs of God's people and the opportunity to minister to them will be limitless. Your first responsibility, however, is always to your own people. Strive for a delicate balance between time at home and time away. But remember, first things first.

Chapter 25

Faithful Over Small Opportunities

" **W**ell done, good and faithful servant. You were faithful over a few things, I will make you ruler over many things" (Matt. 25:21 NKJV). What more beautiful words did our Lord ever speak? While this precious promise is likely for eternity, it certainly applies to the present.

The persons I know who have been greatly used in large places have this in common: They were faithful to the little opportunities.

Let me tell you a story. In 1952 I became a Christian and enrolled in Oklahoma Baptist University. Immediately I was faced with a conflict. I had committed my life to serve the Lord. Because I was a former jazz band leader, I had a small reputation among my classmates as well as the churches around the state. Instantly there were opportunities to play the trumpet and give my testimony, even leading the music and preaching in every conceivable kind of place.

My dilemma was the attractiveness of campus life. The girls were not only beautiful; they also were godly, Christian young women making them doubly attractive. There were parties, social clubs, movies, homecoming parades, basketball games, and sock hops.

I opted for the service of the Lord. I had met my bride-to-be and fallen in love, but for every date we could squeeze in, there were a dozen other engagements. She was so supportive. She agreed God's service should be priority, and it remains that way today. God has blessed me with a wonderful, wonderful wife. Her attitude is much like Ruth Graham's.

A reporter once asked Mrs. Billy Graham how she could stand to be married to a man who was gone virtually all the time. She responded, "I'd rather be with Billy part of the time than be the wife of any other man in the world all the time." So it has been easy for me because of Uldine's great support. The opportunity to serve the Lord is always priority with her.

Pastors often amaze me with the limitations they put on the Lord. "I want a church to pastor, but only one right here." "Oh, no, I couldn't leave the Bible Belt for Nebraska or New York, let alone the foreign mission field. My family and relatives are here in the South."

Churches are filled with unemployed pastors. There are lots of "almost" pastors, "used-to-be" pastors, "want-to-be" pastors and "gonna-be" pastors, but it is often surprisingly difficult to get them to take a Sunday school class, speak at a nursing home, or work in a small mission.

Of course, there comes a time in your life when you must prioritize. Later in my ministry I found myself at the other extreme of the problem. Too many invitations made it necessary to prioritize and choose in order to have time for my own family and ministry.

But when you're first starting out, don't forget the importance of those small opportunities. Go anywhere. Pay any price.

During my first years of ministry, I was a full-time student in college. I conducted fourteen revival meetings out of every eighteen-week semester going through Oklahoma Baptist University. These were weekend revivals, week-long revivals, and two-week revivals in small towns and country churches across Oklahoma, Texas, Arkansas, and Louisiana. In the average day, we would get out of class at 2:00 P.M., drive until 6:00 or 7:00, conduct services, get back in the car at 9:00, return home, studying by flashlight in the back seat, arriving home at 2:00 A.M. We would get up at 7:00 the next morning, go to class, and repeat the process at 2:00 P.M.

Week after week, we did this. Sometimes I didn't have a car. Sometimes I didn't have any money. Sometimes I hitchhiked to Alabama or Mississippi on Thursday, skipping class on Friday to be at some small church for a weekend revival, only to use most of the love offering to get on a bus Sunday night and ride all night to get back to class on Monday.

Chapter 26

About Those Greener Pastures

Country singer Johnny Lee said it well in his popular song, "Looking for Love in All the Wrong Places." Perhaps Al Jolson had the answer for Mr. Lee's futile search: "The birds with feathers of blue are waiting for you—right in your own back yard." The thesis of Mr. Lee's song applies to far too many pastors who are looking for personal and professional fulfillment in all the wrong places.

The happiest, most fulfilling, most productive place for your ministry is potentially right where you are. Quit looking around. Stop glancing over your shoulder, and bloom where you're planted. God wants to bless you in a powerful way, and it is not in that greener pasture across the fence.

I write of one of the most common pitfalls of the ministry. I am told that through the years, I have developed a reputation as a "friend of pastors." If that is true, it is a reputation justly deserved. I do, indeed, love pastors—particularly pastors of small churches and pastors with big problems.

Jesus did not enlist us as kings to sit on thrones but as warriors to fight battles. The hymn writer said it well:

> Must I be carried to the skies
> On flowery beds of ease,
> While others fought to gain the prize
> And sailed through bloody seas?

The call to the ministry, particularly the pastorate, is not set to the strains of "At rest in Jesus, safe at last," but "Onward Christian soldiers, marching as to war."

For the young pastor, not yet battle-hardened by the realities of life in the ministry, the first reaction to problems is usually to run. Problems, opposition, criticism, misunderstanding, and conflict will be part of your daily fare. But that's what you signed on for. Our Lord spent his entire earthly ministry being misunderstood, and the servant is not greater than his Lord. Jesus did not simply say, "I send you forth as sheep," but, "I send you forth as sheep *in the midst of wolves*" (Matt. 10:16). It's tough! Expect it. God's grace is more than sufficient.

Your supporters will always outweigh your detractors, and your blessings will far surpass your heartaches. When you hit your first snag in that new pastorate, remember to slow down for the speed bump. Don't fight it. Don't run and don't try to go around it. Slow down and take it easy.

In these forty-seven years of ministry, I have received hundreds of "panic calls" from young pastors. "When you hit a rock," I tell them, "keep on drilling; there is probably a pool of oil just below."

With or without the problems, however, most of us live with the illusion of "greener pastures." Let me assure you, that larger church down the road has the same problems as yours. Just add a few zeros to every equation, and you have the only real difference between a small church and a large church. Some of my dearest friends through the years have been possessed with the desire to move. Every time a large church becomes available, telephone calls begin, "Recommend me here, and recommend me there."

I fear the secular world has placed an unreasonable pressure on young pastors to "succeed." Success is not measured by numbers. The size of your congregation and the percentage of growth that is so important to the world, and far too often to our peers, is not the measure of success in the eyes of God. Integrity. Holiness. Commitment. Faithfulness. These are the qualities dear to the heart of God in the lives of his servants.

Do you want to pastor a larger church? Let me tell you how to do it. Quit looking over your shoulder, put down deep roots, double your prayer time, and go to work building a great church where you are. Too many young men, consumed with a secular understanding of success, have driven themselves to distraction, reaching people for "numbers sake," trying to move to a larger field. Every large church was once a small church that God built by the faithfulness of a godly pastor. And you can do that, right where you are!

Some of the world's greatest churches have been built in some of the least likely places. Who can ignore the incredible accomplishment of Pastor Jim Cymbala, who built the great Brooklyn Tabernacle Church in the most unlikely part of inner-city Brooklyn. Pastor Cymbala's secret: "Bloom where you are planted." Plant your life and put down deep roots of prayer. Rome wasn't built in a day, and neither was any great church in history. If you are looking for God's best for you in those green pastures across the fence, you are likely looking in all the wrong places.

Chapter 27

Dealing with Pastor Search Committees

F ew pastors spend their entire ministry serving one congregation. Virtually every undershepherd will be confronted at some point with responding to the opportunity to move to another field of service.

No more important matter will face the young pastor in particular than determining the will of God regarding the invitation to pastor a new congregation.

Many years ago I received some wonderful advice. As I considered a move from First Southern Baptist Church, Del City, Oklahoma, to First Baptist Church, Houston, Texas, God put on my heart to call an old friend for counsel. Dr. W. T. Furr, pastor of the great Queensborough Baptist Church of Shreveport, Louisiana, was happy to help. "John," he said, "when God moves you from one place to another, two things will happen. There will be a release from the old and a passion for the new. These will not necessarily occur in any particular order, but both will happen."

Pragmatically, God's man or woman will always *seek heavenly wisdom and godly counsel* in making these important decisions. Dr. Furr's counsel has served me well through the years, as well as the large number of friends with whom I have shared it. Additionally, I offer you my own counsel.

1. *Don't try to move.* Don't ask your friends to recommend you anywhere. Put down deep roots. Give your heart to the people you now serve and let God move you to his new place in his own time.

2. *Don't close the door on God.* Give him the opportunity to do something new and unique in your ministry. Thirty years ago I moved from First Southern Baptist Church, Del City, Oklahoma, to First Baptist Church, Houston, Texas. The Del City church was three times as large. Though this is opposite the normal progression, I saw a vision of what First Baptist Houston could become and sensed the tug of the Holy Spirit to try to fulfill it. Above all, look for "the tug," that deep abiding impression in your heart that "this I must do."

3. *Don't get in a hurry.* Good decisions are made carefully.

4. *Don't try to sell yourself.*

5. *See the potential.*

6. *Ask the hard questions.* The committee will want to know everything about you. Try to ascertain everything possible about them as well. When I was considering the church in Houston, I asked for the minutes of the last twelve months of deacons' meetings. Ninety percent of their meetings had been spent discussing whether to repair the roof garden in order to continue playing basketball on top of our nine-story downtown building. I knew immediately that the church needed to reexamine its priorities.

7. *Don't play games with the heartstrings of the committee or their church.* You should not agree to come for a "trial sermon" and preach "in view of a call," unless you have virtually made up your mind to accept. Nor should the committee extend such an invitation unless they are confident of the church's call.

8. *Remember the pulpit committee has been selected as a cross section of the church and represents them to you.* Get a feel for who they are, and you will know who the church is.

9. *If possible, have a meeting with the full deacon body of the new church before you agree to come in view of a call.* This will extend the process. The relationship of a pastor and his people is like that of a man and his wife. There is a trusting and intimate relationship between two who will come to love each other more and more

through the passing years. Take the time to have a sweet, open courtship, and sweeter will be the marriage.

10. *Involve your family in the process.* The pastor's spouse should be involved in the initial meeting with the committee and be urged to enter into the conversation, asking and responding to questions. The couple should participate in all visits to the new church field with their children accompanying them at least once. Even though the children may be very small, they should be made to feel it is a family decision and be comfortable with their new home.

11. *Be yourself with the church as you were with the committee.* Don't try to impress them with an old "sugar-stick" sermon. When I preached in view of a call that first Sunday in February 1970, I said to the church, "In my own pulpit in Del City I am in the midst of a Sunday morning series on the Ten Commandments. Were I at home today, I would be preaching on the fourth commandment. I am going to preach that sermon to you because I want you to hear a good example of what you would hear on an average Sunday in my church in Oklahoma."

At the conclusion of the evening service, you and your family should leave the sanctuary while the church votes on extending a call. You should then be prepared to accept that call on the spot. Why wait? Once you have come that far, it's time to propose, accept, rejoice, and celebrate the future.

12. *It is customary for the church to pay all moving expenses and related costs, as well as a relocation allowance.*

Look forward to that first Sunday, the beginning of a great new ministry. The committee should arrange a reception for the pastor and his family and be as diligent in helping them settle into their new home and new church as they were in bringing them to it. When the process is completed, invite the committee to your home for an appreciation dinner. They have been God's special instrument in your life and that of the church, and they will be deeply grateful for a genuine expression of appreciation from you and your family. Pray for yourself and pray for the committee. The time spent in the marriage can and should be as sweet as was the courtship.

Chapter 28

Faithful to the End

M y father-in-law, Dr. Paul Beck, is in heaven. Dr. Beck was a wonderful and special man. An ordained minister with three earned doctorates, he preached the gospel faithfully for sixty-five years. When I became engaged to his beautiful daughter Uldine, he gave me his blessing and admonished me to be faithful in the ministry to which God had called me.

"John," he said, "it has been my observation that only one in twenty-five men who begin in the ministry at age twenty-one are still in it at age sixty-five." I didn't believe it at the time, but I believe it today. I made a list of the names of twenty-five of my peers and wrote them in the back of my Bible. Through the years, I have crossed them off, and today there are only three.

Some fell through discouragement. Some quit because of opposition within their own churches. Some had affairs. Some became obsessed with making money. Some became liberal in their theology, hence, ineffective, and quit the ministry.

It is not important whether you have five hundred members or five thousand. It is important that you be true to the Lord in matters of prayer and integrity, that you love the Lord and His people, live a clean life, do the best you can with what you have, where you are, and do it for the glory of God. "Faithful to the end!" What a testimony.

What more could you want as an epitaph across your life than these words, "Well done, good and faithful servant."

Guard against things that can trip you up. Never be suggestive or flirtatious. Tithe to your church. Don't live above your means. Be prudent in your investments for retirement but not obsessed with it. Tell the truth. Do your best and leave the results to God. The single most important thing about your life will not be how many people you won to Christ, how much money you raised, the size of your church, the number of books you wrote, or the offices you held. The single most important factor of your life is that you are faithful to the end.

And don't feel compelled to retire at age sixty-five. Retire when God tells you to. The pressures of a large pastorate are extremely heavy, and they will need to be eased at some point in your life. But remember other ministries await you in your later years that can greatly profit from your experience. Always look forward to tomorrow. The best is yet to come.

One of the great dangers of the ministry is giving up about age sixty or sixty-two and just "hanging on" until retirement. We all begin with hopes and dreams and ambitions. We all want to be special!

But somewhere about age forty-five to fifty, reality begins to set in. "I'm not special." "I'm not being used in a great way." "I'm not going to make it big." And so we try desperately to make a move to that greener pasture.

Ambition has no place in the ministry. God knows your phone number, and he has a wonderful plan for your life. Don't try to move and don't ask anyone to recommend you anywhere. Put down deep roots and just let it happen. It's a long, long way to the finish line, and faithfulness is its own reward.

"I have fought a good fight, I have finished my course, I have kept the faith. Henceforth there is laid up for me a crown of righteousness, which the Lord, the righteous judge, shall give me at that day: and not to me only, but unto all them also that love his appearing" (2 Tim. 4:7–8).

Part 3

The Pastor as Spiritual Leader

Chapter 29

The Pastor and His People

O n a recent trip to the Holy Land, we again enjoyed seeing the relationship between the shepherd and his sheep. No more beautiful illustration exists of the relationship between God's pastor and God's people. The shepherd is always in front of the sheep. He is out there alone. He is the leader and enjoys the privilege of leadership. But he is always the first to lay down his life for his sheep, to fight and even die in their defense. Far too often, words like *authority* and *leadership* are criticized by those who do not understand the concept of "servant leadership." But leadership, remember, is deserved, not demanded; granted by the people, earned by the pastor.

The ideal pastor is very much like his people. In all great growing churches, there is, among other things, the common denominator of a homogeneous mix between pastor and people. They are comfortable with him; he is comfortable with them. First Baptist Church, Houston, is a good reflection of that. I had never been comfortable with just the poor or just the rich, with just the illiterate or just the educated, just the black or just the white. As such, this church was extremely eclectic, a good cross-section of our city—not racially, as much as I would like—but certainly socially and professionally. We had bankers and homemakers, old and young, short hair and long hair. We became all things to all people that we might by all means win many.

It is important to be like your congregation. To be like them, you need to know them. To know them, you need to spend time with them. To spend the time, you need to love your people sincerely. The highlight of my week was to attend the services early as people gathered and to linger as they left. I loved to walk up and down the aisles and greet our people. I loved it when little children came up and hugged me and the older children told me about their Little League baseball games.

I loved it when our folks invited us on a trip with them or when they asked us to come to their homes and play softball or cook hamburgers. It was not a game I played. I really did love it. I was comfortable with our people and they were comfortable with me. You can't simply appear to love people; you have to really love them. You can't play the game on Sunday morning; you have to live the reality seven days a week.

Every wise minister will protect his time for personal devotions, study, sermon preparation and prayer, but accessibility is still important. People don't want a pastor who is available twenty-four hours a day. They want their pastor to be alone with God and alone in his study. But that's not all day, every day. The rest of the time, take time for people. Remember these words: The people's needs are never an *interruption* to your ministry. They *are* your ministry.

Chapter 30

Casting the Vision

I t was business as usual. Prayer meeting night in a little suburban church. Five hundred seats, 475 empty and 25 faithful souls. The organ cranked out, "Day is Dying in the West." And, unfortunately, that's not all that was dying in the west, and the east, and the north, and the south! Regrettably, many churches are dead and just don't know it. Why? There are a hundred reasons why people stay away in great droves. Ninety-nine percent of America will not be in church next Sunday night. And it is only a little better on Sunday morning. And why should they go?

Too many services are dead, dull, despondent, and depressing. Any ball game, concert, movie, or street fight has more life than the average church.

One reason is the absence of vision. There is no life because there is no hope. And there is no hope because there is no expectancy. There is no expectancy because there is no vision. There is no vision because the pastor has not instilled vision, and the result is death. "Where there is no vision, the people perish" (Prov. 29:18).

Vision, like expectancy, always hopes for something better, always expects it, always believes it will happen. "Can do" is its motto; "The Impossible Dream," its theme song. I like this statement: "The difficult we'll do right now; the impossible may take a little while."

For five years at the First Southern Baptist Church of Del City, Oklahoma, people in large numbers came to Christ and joined the church every Sunday. For several months during the first year at Houston, that intangible something I wanted, and to which I had become accustomed, was not there. I did not know what it was, but I knew what it wasn't. Sunday after Sunday I would go home from church and say to my wife, "It was a good service, but it is not the same. It's not right, but I can't put my finger on it." That elusive "something" was missing.

One Sunday morning, fifty-seven people made decisions for Christ and joined the church. The next Sunday there were thirty-nine. The following Sunday it happened! That special "something" I had missed was there. I did not know what it was I was looking for until I reviewed that service over and over again. The thing that made the difference? Expectancy! An atmosphere of expectancy—hope, vision, excitement—filled the church.

I knew that we would probably never win everyone in Houston to Christ, but I didn't want anyone telling my people that. They were almost convinced that they could! They were expecting to do it. They were expecting a packed worship center, souls saved, lives changed, and fire from heaven every Sunday.

Sunday after Sunday, I told them that because we bore the name "First," it was our responsibility to lead the way, to set the pace in evangelism. Three million persons live in greater Houston. It is the crossroads of the nation, heart of the Americas, gateway to outer space. Revival here would affect the world. Slowly it began to dawn on them that our church must be one of God's great bastions of the gospel. It must be a mighty lighthouse in a mighty city. He had placed us there for a purpose. We must set the pace. We must launch out. *Houston must be won for Christ—now!*

They began to believe it could happen. The raindrops began to fall. Faith became sight. Dream became reality. Then there was expectancy. They prayed, worked, and expected it again and again.

It is the place of the pastor to be the vision-caster. He first must get alone with God and stay until he hears from heaven. Once your soul is stirred about the direction of your church, call your leaders together and share it with them. Listen to their response. Massage your dream, refine your focus, and then take it to the pulpit. It might not be popular, it might not be easy, but God will always bless the person who has a vision and follows it. If you would lead people, you must get out in front of them. Deep in the heart of every child of God is the natural desire to follow an earthly shepherd whom he believes is following the heavenly Shepherd. God has called you as the spiritual leader of his people, and the purpose of leadership is to lead.

The front of ancient sailing ships was called the "pulpit." That small protruding portion extending beyond the bough was where the "lookout" watched for rocks and other dangers. Standing there was called "riding the pulpit." In times of danger, a volunteer allowed the captain to tie him to it. If he died, he died. But he pointed the way and gave the vision to the crew. Go to God, get the vision, ask your heavenly Captain to tie you to it, and lead his people by his grace. "Without a vision, the people perish!"

Chapter 31

Hospital Calls

Our Lord was the master at touching hurting people. How often have we watched "television healers" and said in our hearts, "If they are really doing what they claim, why don't they walk up and down the halls of the hospital and heal everyone?" Although we readily admit that few of our prayers for healing appear to be answered on the spot, a healing touch occurs just because you cared enough to come. How often the gospel writers remind us, "Jesus had great compassion upon the people."

I acknowledge that the hospital ministry was not easy for me. Searching my soul, I think the reason is that I felt so inadequate. I wanted to do so much, but was able to do so little. Though having made thousands of such calls through the years, I admit to occasionally having tried to find a reason not to go. But of this I have become confident after thirty-five years of pastoral ministry: Of most importance is not *what you said*, but *that you came*. I doubt that many of our people will remember what we said, but they will remember that we came.

As your church grows larger, you must come to grips with the tormenting decision of whom to visit, whom to see, which invitation to accept, etc. The struggle for priority of time in a day with only twenty-four hours is never easily resolved. In a larger church, your staff can help visit the hospitals. Additionally, in First Baptist Houston, retired deacons did a wonderful job, often even visiting the same person three or four times in a week. But what of you as pastor? How are you to confront the reality of too many visits and too little time?

First, determine your priorities. I visited the critically ill first. Those who are in and out of the hospital in a day or two for an operation on their finger would probably not get a visit from their pastor. Second, you must pastor your leadership. All other things being equal, the staff member, Sunday school teacher, deacon, or members of their families will get a visit from the pastor before another church member with the same need. This is simply a part of learning to pastor your leaders, who in turn pastor others. Remember the principle that Jethro taught Moses, and organize that army into divisions and companies.

When you are unable to go, send a card. Better yet, make a phone call. In a city the size of Houston, I spent at least ten hours a week in my car. I was constantly on the phone calling shut-ins, calling hospitals, calling prospects, dictating letters, and returning telephone calls. This is an ideal time to call those persons in the hospital. They will be deeply appreciative that you remembered they were there. Don't forget to use that telephone.

As you enter the hospital, be certain you have the right person and the right room. Remember, bed "A" comes before bed "B." Knock gently before entering. Ask permission to come in. Be certain your presence is appropriate. If it is not, offer to wait a moment.

Upon entering the room, call the person by name and greet him or her with a smile. Let the person talk. Be encouraging. Assure patients that they are in a great hospital with a wonderful doctor. People are in the hospital because they are sick, and sick people have neither the need, energy, or time for small talk. Stay ten minutes or less, hold their hand, pray, and leave. Assure them of your continuing prayer and interest and ask them to feel free to call if the need arises.

Remember, a warm smile, a friendly touch, and just that "you were there" will leave the lingering fragrance of our Lord, who said that in visiting those who were sick, we visited him.

Chapter 32

Death Calls

T he most difficult part of the ministry is ministering to a person whose loved one has just passed away. But it must remain at the top of your priority list. The membership of First Baptist Houston congregation was scattered across a wide area. The majority of the people drove at least ten miles to church, and hundreds drove twenty to thirty miles.

The first reaction that usually comes to mind upon receiving notice of the death of a member is, "Oh, but I'm so busy, and their home is so far away." That thought comes from Satan. That which most always immediately follows comes from the Lord. "But think how many thousands of times they've made the trip to church. Surely you can make this one trip to their home."

People, particularly in times of crisis, are never an *interruption* to our ministry; they *are* our ministry. As our churches grow larger, we must guard against becoming high-powered executives, cloistered in luxurious offices, barricaded by two or three secretaries and assistants. Your church might have fifty thousand members, but never forget that you are not an executive, but a pastor—and pastors care about people. Even interrupting your important morning study time to make an immediate death call is always appropriate. I cannot count the times I have received such a call on my car phone on the way to another engagement. Immediately I turned the car around and went to the home of the bereaved.

If at all possible, I quickly picked up a staff member or friend and took them with me because I needed their support. It may be easy for you, but it never became easy for me.

When you arrive, go quickly to the door and ring the bell. Often the individual will fall into your arms weeping. What you say is relatively unimportant. Through the years, they will remember little, if anything you say, but they will remember your love and your presence.

Once inside the home, ask all the members of the family to gather in the living room. Be seated next to the nearest relative, normally the parent or spouse. Put your arm around this person, allowing time for him to grieve and talk, and as he does, listen—really listen. Don't be thinking about what you're going to say or the questions you need to ask quickly about funeral arrangements in order to hurry off to your next engagement. And don't just *act* as if you care. Care—really care.

As the family begins to allow you time to speak, ask them to tell you more about the deceased person, about his childhood or about his marriage and occupation. Ask them to share with you when and how this person came to know Christ and became a member of the church. This is not the appropriate time to discuss funeral arrangements. That will come later on in the day or, more likely, the next day. All suggestions about the memorial service—when, where, pallbearers, music, etc.—should come at an appropriate time and only as tender suggestions from you. You must not try to manipulate the scheduling of the service for your convenience, but encourage the process of finding the best time for their schedule *and* your schedule.

I normally spent about forty-five minutes in the home. Encourage all members of the family to talk. When you feel the need has been satisfied, ask the family if you may read from Scripture. The appropriate passages are always John 14 and/or Psalm 23. Others will come to mind. When you finish, bow your head and pray. Leave your home, office, and cell phone number with the family, suggesting they place it by the telephone. Assure them they may call you at any time.

Later that day or early the next, call to see if they need any assistance in making arrangements for the memorial service. Offer the services of your office to help contact pallbearers, florists, musicians, etc. There should never be any charge to the family of a church member for these services or for the use of the building.

Often the funeral director will offer you an honorarium in the fifty to one-hundred-dollar range at the conclusion of the funeral. I have never been comfortable keeping this and have often given it back to another family member, particularly in the case of a family of low income. Through the years, however, I have learned that while we don't need to receive this honorarium, the family needs to give it. Be tender and sensitive at this point. God will lead you in this decision.

Very often there will be a "wake" or "viewing of the body" the evening before the day of the memorial service. The viewing is usually held for two to three hours. It is not necessary for you to attend the wake unless you choose to do so or the family specifically requests you to do so.

Another important call is made after the funeral. By telephone or preferably in person, contact the family within three days after the burial for additional ministry, comfort, and support. If you're unable to do so, be certain that a staff member, deacon, or elder does so in your behalf.

Encourage other church members to give ongoing support to the family. Nothing is more lonely than a home with an empty chair. Your most tender and meaningful ministry can be done in touching those who have been touched deeply by death.

Chapter 33

Conducting the Funeral

When the time and place have been determined for the memorial service, contact the funeral director to be certain you are in agreement about every detail of the service and subsequent burial. Advance planning will save confusion and resultant embarrassment.

I say this kindly but firmly: Assume leadership in planning the service. You are in charge of the funeral—not the funeral director. He serves at your bidding, not you at his. Don't ask him what he wants. Tell him what you want. I have never found a funeral director to be uncooperative. Funeral homes conduct many types of funerals for various religions and denominations throughout the year. They expect to be adaptable, and they await your direction.

A call to the home of the family on the day of the funeral is a special, warm touch and will take only a few minutes of your time. Ask if they have any questions; tell them you are praying for them and that you will meet the entire family just a few minutes before the service begins. Be sure to pray with them over the telephone. The family will never forget that prayer.

In most communities, the funeral home will pick up the family members of the deceased and transport them to the place where the service is being held. Normally, the coach provided by the funeral home will arrive at the home of the deceased about an hour before the service begins, depending on the distance to the church or other site of the service. Determine the approximate time the family will arrive for the service and coordinate your arrival at the funeral site with theirs.

Family members will have come from many places, and there will be those whom you have never met. As you enter the room, embrace the widow and other close family members whom you know and ask everyone to be seated. Address the entire family and relatives by first introducing yourself, then expressing your sympathy and a word of deep appreciation on behalf of your congregation for the loyalty and service this person has provided your congregation through the years. Assure the family the service will not be long, and see that it is not. Nothing is worse than an hour and a half funeral service. Thirty minutes is ideal, and forty-five is maximum.

Tell the funeral director that you and others assisting you—such as another person who might read the obituary, read Scripture, sing, or pray—are to be seated with you on the platform before the service begins. You must already be seated before the family procession is led into the chapel or worship center by the funeral director. As they enter the room, rise from your seat and take a step forward, gently lift both hands a few inches, palms upward, indicating that the congregation is to rise. An area will have been reserved by the funeral director at the front of the room near the casket, which may or may not be open at the family's discretion. This will, of course, have been determined in advance.

Fifteen minutes before the service is scheduled to begin, the organist should begin playing softly and continue until the time for the message begins. Two solos or other specials are normally sung in a memorial service. They should, of course, be appropriate and, as with weddings, approved by you in advance. A good general order of service is as follows:

- Solo
- A welcome, including: (a) A simple statement of purpose, "We are gathered here today in memory of our loving friend, John Smith, etc." (b) An expression of thanks on behalf of the family for the many kindnesses shown to them.
- The reading of the obituary

- Scripture
- Prayer
- Solo
- Message
- Closing prayer
- Viewing of the body, if desired by the family
- Family recessional and exit

On occasion, there will be a eulogy or testimony by a family member or friend about the deceased. It is important that these be few and brief. A ten-minute eulogy is seven or eight minutes too long. If eulogies are given at all, there should be no more than two, one by a family member and one by a friend. Where the person has been a member of the military, that portion of the service—folding of the flag, presenting it to the widow, and playing of "Taps"—should be done at the graveside.

Remain standing with the congregation throughout the entire procession of the family into the room. Once they are seated, reverse the process, palms down, hands lowered, to indicate the congregants may be seated. Let the service immediately begin with brevity, grace, and dignity. Fifteen minutes is the maximum for your message; ten to twelve is better. Speak warmly and tenderly. Speak from your heart. Try to speak without notes so you may look compassionately into the eyes of the family as you speak. Every funeral, including the message and the entire service, should do three things:

- Honor the deceased
- Comfort the family
- Glorify the Lord

When the service is complete, close your Bible, pray, and step to the head of the casket. If it is open and the people are going to file by, stay there until they are finished. Do not extend your hand to shake hands with each person who passes by, but do respond to any who extend theirs to you. Some will pause longer than others. Some will be weeping. Some will embrace you. Be tender and supportive in your response.

After the congregants have filed by, the family will come last, normally led by the nearest relative (i.e., the widow or parent). As they approach the casket, move from the head of the casket to the side of the persons, put your arm around them or take their hand, support them, and give them the time they need to weep. Do not pull them away. They often will be leaning over, touching or even kissing the face of their loved one. When they are finished and have straightened up, take their elbow and walk gently with them, placing them in the loving care of other family members. Step a few feet down the aisle and pause, then lead the casket to the waiting funeral coach.

Walk very slowly. Don't get ahead of the pallbearers. Once you have arrived at the coach and the casket has been placed inside, step with the pallbearers to the rear of the coach and await the instruction of the funeral director to the people to go to their cars. You may ride with the director or drive your own car. I choose to drive myself.

Once you arrive at the cemetery, return to the rear of the funeral coach, wait for the pallbearers to remove the casket, and walk slowly ahead of it and them to the grave. *Do not* have a second service at the graveside. This should be no more than five minutes. One service is enough. You might wish to pour sand or perform some other rite customary to your denomination or church. I normally lead the people in one verse of "In the Garden," "What a Friend We Have in Jesus," or "The Old Rugged Cross," read 1 Thessalonians 4:13–18, and pray.

After the graveside service, it is not necessary for you to shake hands with every family member. Normally there will be two rows of chairs, four to five per row, seated in front of the casket, with everyone else standing. The nearest relative, such as parent or widow, will always be seated on that front row. Walk by slowly, grasp the hand of each person seated on the front row, tell them you love them, and assure them of your prayers.

Normally the funeral director will tell the people, "This concludes the service." Those at the graveside will naturally move toward the family to express their condolences. It is not necessary to remain until everyone has left. Move among the people ten to fifteen minutes, and then you may leave. And don't forget that follow-up call or visit to the home.

It is acceptable to conduct the memorial service and allow someone else to conduct the graveside ceremony. If this is done, make arrangements in advance with family and funeral director as well as the person chosen to conduct the graveside service. Encourage them to be brief.

The most tender side of Jesus' ministry may be seen with the sick and hurting. This is our opportunity to be his hands and his feet, loving people with his heart, touching them in his name.

Chapter 34

The Counseling Ministry

T he gift of exhortation is one of the prominent gifts of the Holy Spirit given to edify the body of Christ. Contrary to much opinion, the gift of exhortation is not so much the ability to exhort people from your pulpit as to encourage them in your office. One cannot overstate the importance of good seminary and other professional training for those who would counsel, but few of us will ever have a Ph.D. or be licensed by the state as certified psychologists. Let me encourage you in two ways: Not only is the best counseling done from a listening ear and encouraging heart, but that counseling which truly changes lives is biblical counseling.

As a pastor, you can and you must be a counselor. It is not what I like best or do best, but it is something I have learned to do better as I have learned to listen to counselees and encourage them from God's Word.

Let's talk about the mechanics of counseling. Many persons who request a counseling appointment can be dealt with without an appointment. Very often I call a person who has requested a counseling appointment and say, "Bill, my schedule is rather heavy for a couple of weeks, but go ahead and share your heart with me, and let's see if I can help you right now over the phone." Many needs can be met in this manner. Listen, understand, respond with Scripture-based suggestions, and pray.

Counseling should always be done with an open door or with a large window in the door. Be cautious here. It is very easy to be made aware of the personal details of a person's life and begin to get emotionally involved. A word to the wise is sufficient. Pastors ought not to do ongoing counseling. The person whose needs cannot be met in one session should be referred to a professional. God-called and well-trained family counselors abound. Take every opportunity to refer.

When a counseling appointment is made, ask your secretary to inform the counselee that you have a thirty-minute slot available at a given time. If the time is running beyond that duration, the secretary should enter the room and say, "Pastor, don't forget your next appointment." Gently control the conversation so the person is encouraged to get to the point. You really don't need a forty-five-minute family history to grasp the problem and give a biblical answer.

Some of the best counsel ever given is already in print. Books by John Trent, Gary Smalley, Chuck Swindoll, Robert McGee, to name a few, are an invaluable help. Recommend an appropriate book to the person you are trying to help. Needs are generally in a few predictable categories, such as family, guilt, depression, spiritual direction, financial, call to the ministry, broken relationships. There is always an appropriate book to be recommended and an appropriate passage to be read. Listen, offer biblically based suggestions, recommend a book, and pray.

I like the counseling technique of Dr. Charles Allen, beloved former pastor of First United Methodist Church, Houston, Texas. Dr. Allen used to say, "I ask every counselee two questions. Number one, 'What is your problem?' Number two, 'What are you going to do about it?'" The bottom line is: Seek the Lord, get to the point, show the person how he can help himself, pray, and move on.

I do not wish to sound uncaring at this point, but pastors who spend hours a week in counseling should go into the full-time counseling ministry. Twenty hours a week invested in counseling will leave little time for your personal spiritual development, study, and family, let alone any time to meet the expanding needs of a growing church and a lost world.

Most experienced pastors will acknowledge, "I have spent over half my time trying to help the same five or ten persons." When Jesus said, "The poor you have with you always," he wasn't speaking contemptuously of the poor. He was simply saying there are some things that will never change. And there are some persons who will not be helped. I do not say they *cannot* be helped; I say they *will not* be helped. If some people didn't have a problem, they wouldn't have anything to talk about. Sometimes people unknowingly create problems to have a purpose not only for their appointment but for their very existence.

As pastors, we will do some counseling, but that must not be the priority of our ministry. If it is, do it full-time. Better to try to help several people once, with a strong sermon, than to allow a few to dominate all of your available counseling time.

The counselor must always keep confidences. As pastors, we know things about people that we must carry to the grave. Nothing is more despicable than a counselor who cannot be trusted to keep the confidence of the counselee. Urge the counselee to get in the Word of God and seek the Holy Spirit, who is the consummate Counselor. In the Word of God, with the help of the Spirit of God, that dear one will find the answer to his problem.

Years ago a Christian psychiatrist in our church made an insightful statement. "Pastor," he said, "the problem with psychiatry is, we can take them apart, but we can't put them together again. We are long on analysis but short on therapy." Simply understanding one's problem affords some help but provides virtually no long-term solution. Help is found when the problem is brought to the light of God's Word. The counselor has the power of insight and encouragement. God alone has power to heal.

Chapter 35

Preparation-for-Marriage Course

T he strength of any society lies in its moral strength; the moral strength of society is a derivative of the strength of the church; the strength of the church depends on the strength of its marriages; and marriages depend on the strength of the believer. If the church is to make a difference in society, it must equip believers to have effective, healthy, biblical marriages. It is part of the call to make disciples.

The pastor or relevant committee should set a list of criteria for the leaders/director of a preparation-for-marriage program. In larger churches, it might be advisable to separate the leader from the director roles. In such cases, it is best to have a couple to serve as leaders.

Qualifications include, but are not limited to, committed, active and growing Christian; strong marriage; strong administrative (director) and teaching skills and gifts; strong people skills; and a good understanding of the issues facing young couples. The person or persons selected should agree to serve a minimum of two years in order to provide adequate time for follow-up of the engaged couples. Training should be provided for both the leaders and director. Good training is available in virtually every denomination. It is, of course, also possible for the leader/director to attend a preparation for marriage program at another church such as First Baptist Church of Houston.

The leaders/directors should familiarize themselves with church policies in the areas of interfaith marriages, couples living together before marriage, remarriage after divorce, and the right of refusal. Pertaining to right of refusal, there might be circumstances in which it is prudent not to condone a marriage (i.e., a convicted child molester wants to marry a woman with young children). The church needs to set the policies, and the leaders or directors need to have a clear understanding of policy and procedures in this area.

After an engaged couple contacts either the minister or person responsible for scheduling weddings, they should be directed to the person in charge of the marriage preparation program. A series of individual, couple, and group meetings should be scheduled as soon as possible. These should conclude at least four weeks before the anticipated wedding date. This allows for additional counseling before the wedding if deemed necessary by joint recommendation of the program leaders and director.

A record of the meetings should be kept and forwarded to the minister or church wedding coordinator to verify completion of the program. Once the program is in place, no couple should be allowed to marry in the church until they have completed the entire course. Since First Baptist Houston adopted this policy, the percentage of divorces has dropped dramatically. If a situation prevents completion of the program before the wedding and the minister consents to marry the couple anyway, the couple should commit to completing the program upon return from their honeymoon.

The format for the sessions should be informal and relaxed and be scheduled in a consistent and well-publicized manner.

In addition to meeting with the leaders as a couple, the participants should have an individual meeting. If there is only one leader, caution should be exercised in meeting with the participant of the opposite sex. A large group meeting to discuss relevant topics encourages the development of camaraderie, normalcy, and openness. This approach is encouraged. Follow-up sessions should be conducted by the leaders at three months, six months, and twelve months after the wedding.

The content of a preparation for marriage program can be summarized by three *P*'s: the purpose, priority, and plan of marriage.

The purpose of marriage includes the biblical origin of marriage and the biblical roles of husband and wife. The biblical view of partnership should be emphasized in contrast to the world's view of need-based relationships.

On the matter of priorities, contrast the biblical view of marriage as an unbreakable covenant with the world's view of marriage as a legal contract, binding only as long as both partners are perceived to have met the demands of the other. Also discuss that the marriage relationship comes second only to the individual's relationship with God: before work, school, children, or even church.

In the plan for marriage, address communication, conflict resolution, emotional intimacy, extended family relationships, financial management and stewardship, sexual intimacy, and spiritual intimacy. The application of these principles will involve:

- commitment to sexual purity before marriage,
- development of a budget and debt reduction plan,
- discussion regarding the number and timing of children, as well as birth control issues, and
- identification of potential conflict areas (the Prepare/Enrich inventory is an excellent resource for this).

While other issues will surface, these represent the basic areas of discussion necessary for every couple. The leaders should continue to meet with the participants until all basic areas have been covered and all questions by the couple have been resolved. It might become necessary during these sessions to refer one or both of the participants to professional counseling. A list of community referrals should be maintained, and a working relationship should be established between the leader of this program and professionals in the community.

A preparation-for-marriage program is an essential component of the discipleship ministry of the local church. It is vital to the establishment of biblical marriages, which form the basis for sound families, churches, and societies. The world's model of marriage is not simply *different from* the biblical model; it is directly *opposed to* it. While the biblical model is one of sacrificial love, the world's model is based on the hedonistic pursuit of self-gratification.

If the tide of divorce is to be turned and its devastating effects on children and society reversed, the church must take a proactive role in preparing members of its body for the biblical covenant relationship of marriage. Build great marriages and you build a great church. A correct relationship with one's spouse enriches understanding of what it means to be part of the bride of Christ.

Chapter 36

Weddings

The celebration of marriage is one of life's greatest events. There is no greater joy in the life of the pastor than being invited to participate in the life of a young couple who love the Lord, love each other, and have come to commit themselves to each other in marriage.

After an initial appointment to set the date on the church calendar and make preliminary plans for the wedding, direct the young couple to two different persons in the church for help.

The first is the wedding coordinator. This person may be a volunteer, a part-time employee, or full-time employee of the church. She will assist the couple with music, decorations, candles, flowers, invitations, etc., and will represent the pastor and the church in every detail.

The second is a person (or committee) that will lead them through a preparation-for-marriage course. This person may be a volunteer coordinator or a part-time or full-time employee.

You might not have time to attend the rehearsal dinner. If not, simply say so. I attend very few and have the blessing of having a full-time wedding coordinator who does the rehearsal as well. Our church in Houston had more than one hundred weddings each year. Each wedding had a preliminary meeting, a preparation-for-marriage course, a meeting to discuss arrangements, a rehearsal, a rehearsal dinner, a wedding, and a reception. If I had tried to do all of this for every wedding, I would have had time for little else. Do as much as you can, but don't forget the principle of delegating. There are talented women in your church who will be happy to serve their Lord and their pastor by doing many of the things connected with a wedding.

Be certain to find out whether it is appropriate for you to wear a dark suit, tuxedo, or robe. This will vary from wedding to wedding and church to church.

There are two reasons I did not normally conduct rehearsals. For one thing, I didn't have the time. For another, I didn't need the practice. I always knew what I was going to do. I shared with the coordinator and the couple that the wedding has two basic ingredients. The first is the "pomp and circumstance," the processional and recessional, and this is rehearsed with a coordinator. The second is the ceremony. That's the part I conducted once we arrived at the altar.

You may use a wedding manual or other plan for the ceremony as prescribed by your church or selected by you and/or the couple. But I told each couple that I was going to be a bit spontaneous, trying to make each ceremony uniquely personal and individual. I wanted them to be able to hear a recording of the ceremony twenty-five years later and be able to say, "Now that was *our* wedding, not everybody else's wedding." I always told the couple, "When you arrive at the altar, relax. I will tell you precisely what to do, when to hold hands, when to look in each other's eyes, when to kiss, when to kneel, and what to say." All my instructions were worked into the ceremony.

Relax at the wedding. Weddings ought to be a great time. Jesus' first miracle was performed because a good wedding celebration had gone bad. Have fun. It's not a funeral; it's a wedding. If something goes wrong, laugh. It is very easy to change the mood in a moment from serious to joyous and back again at a wedding.

The wedding coordinator knew that while I was personalizing it as I went, I generally followed a very predictable pattern in the order of service. Before the wedding began, I asked her to inform me of anything out of the ordinary, such as: Is there a unity candle or is there not? Will they kneel or will they not? Is there only one song or are there two?

Numerous handbooks on weddings are available. The following procedure is generally how I conducted a wedding:

1. Mothers and other family members are seated to music.

2. I led the groom and groomsmen in from the side.

3. Processional of bridesmaids down the aisle, each joined at the altar by a groomsman who escorts her to her place.

4. Flower girls and ring bearers enter.

5. Entrance of the bride.

6. Opening sentence "Dearly beloved," etc., with a short welcome.

7. Prayer.

8. "Who gives this woman to be married to this man?"

9. Step from floor up to the platform and stand behind the kneeling bench.

10. Five-minute sermon on marriage.

11. Ask each person, "Do you take_____ to be your lawful wedded _____?"

12. Instruct them to turn to each other, join hands and, looking into each other's eyes, I again asked each to repeat after me, "I _____ take you _____ to be my lawful wedded _____."

13. Ask them to turn and face you again.

14. "May I have the ring for the bride?" Say a few words about the ring, give it to the groom, and ask the bride to extend the third finger of her left hand to him. Instruct the groom to place the ring on her finger and repeat these vows, "With this ring, I thee wed and with all my worldly goods I thee endow."

15. Repeat the process with the groom.

16. Ask the couple to kneel on the kneeling bench.

17. Normally I liked to have someone sing "The Lord's Prayer" at this point. If they do, it is not necessary for you to upstage "The Lord's Prayer" with your own prayer. When the music is finished, simply say "Amen." If a different song is sung while the couple is kneeling, pray your own prayer.

18. Ask the couple to stand. Say, "Now, by the authority vested in me by the laws of this state and by this New Testament church, it is my pleasure to pronounce you husband and wife," or say "Mr. and Mrs. _____," as they choose. (Determined in advance.)

19. Say, "You may kiss the bride," at which time the groom will raise the bridal veil and do so.

20. Take each of them by the outside elbow, turning them all the way around to face the congregation and say, "Ladies and gentlemen, we present Mr. and Mrs. _____."

21. They proceed out the middle aisle, the bride often stopping to give a rose to her mother, and perhaps, her new mother-in-law.

22. Observe the reverse order of processional of the bridal party—i.e., mother was seated last, mother exits first.

23. Step to the front of the platform and say, "This concludes our ceremony. _____ and _____ have asked me to invite you to the reception that follows in fifteen minutes in the parlor. Thank you, and you are dismissed."

You may choose to add, "Or you are invited to remain seated for the taking of the pictures." In any case, the couple will always exit the center aisle, reentering from the side for the taking of pictures. A word of caution: Do not let the photographer control the ceremony. He must submit to your authority and will often ask when he is allowed to take pictures.

Do not allow the taking of posed pictures at the conclusion of the ceremony to exceed fifteen minutes. The photographer must be prepared and have adequate assistants to help him arrange the bridal party and take the pictures quickly. The reception will be spoiled if the people have to hang around for forty-five minutes to an hour, waiting on the photographer to finish taking pictures in the sanctuary.

Someone asked, "What do you like best about the ministry?"

"That's easy: the preaching, the kids, and the weddings."

Part 4

The Pastor as Organizational Leader

Chapter 37

So You Want to Be a Leader

Our world is dying for lack of moral and spiritual leadership. Deep in the heart of every pastor lies a God-given desire to be the true spiritual leader of his people. But beyond the bounds of your own congregation, both your denomination and the secular world yearn for respected, authentic leadership that only you can provide. Someone is going to provide special leadership in the world around you, and it might well be that our Lord has chosen you to be that person. The apostle Peter lays down some marvelous principles of leadership.

First Peter 5:1–4 reads:

> The elders which are among you I exhort, who am also an elder and a witness of the sufferings of Christ, and also a partaker of the glory that shall be revealed: Feed the flock of God which is among you, taking the oversight thereof, not by constraint, but willingly; not for filthy lucre, but of a ready mind; Neither as being lords over God's heritage, but being examples to the flock. And when the chief Shepherd shall appear, ye shall receive a crown of glory that fadeth not away.

Let's talk about five biblical principles of pastoral leadership from this text that are applicable to every pastor.

1. Don't even think about being a leader unless you are certain God has called you. When it really gets tough, the only thing that will sustain you is a deep conviction: "I *must* do this because God has called me."

Peter begins by addressing a group of people he calls "elders." These words are used interchangeably in the New Testament: *elder, pastor, shepherd, presbyter,* and *bishop.*

When great decisions are made, study groups are organized, committees are formed, conferences are held, and studies are made. But through the years I have found the people of God will ultimately turn to their pastor and say, "Pastor, we want to know if you have been with God. Have you sought the mind of the Lord in this matter? What do you feel God would have us do? What do you feel to be the leadership of the Lord?" And dear pastor friend, you had better have been with God and have a deep conviction that you are doing what he wants.

If your plan is God's plan, a deep affirmation will develop within the hearts of the people. Pastoral leadership is an honest effort to discern God's leadership and lead the people to follow God's plan. First and foremost, be certain of God's call to lead.

2. It is better to do a few things well than many not too well at all. Verse 2 of 1 Peter 5 says, "Feed the flock of God which is among you, taking the oversight thereof." The apostle Peter has been giving direction to specific groups of people in the church: In chapter 1, he says, "And you servants," and gives them directions. In chapter 3 he says, "And you wives," and instructs them. "And you husbands," he continues, and instructs them.

In chapter 5, Peter begins, "And you elders." When I saw those words, I could not wait to read what followed. How would Peter instruct me as a pastor to go about leading my congregation? To my amazement and delight, Peter stated only two things for the pastors to do: feed the flock of God, and take the oversight thereof. How simple yet comprehensive. I take this to mean the primary responsibilities of my ministry are: (1) be prepared to preach and teach the Word of God every time I stand in the pulpit and (2) give general direction to the work of the church.

You can hire someone to do everything in the church for you except studying for your sermons and seek God's direction for your church. You must do these two things well. Fail in these, and little else will matter.

3. What you do may not be as important as how you do it. Peter says only two things the pastor is to do but several about how he is to do them. Humility, motivation, character, attitude—these are the qualities that make for great leadership. Style is never a substitute for substance, but substance apart from this kind of style is not authentic biblical leadership. The pastor's leadership, although focused primarily in only two areas, must never be done grudgingly or unwillingly. Nor is it to be done for the sake of money, prestige, or influence.

He who would inspire others to serve must demonstrate an eager spirit of service himself. The shepherd must be a sheep, not lording it over others, but humbly serving alongside them as an example to the flock. Leadership, especially spiritual leadership, must be earned and not demanded. The pages of this and a hundred other books could not contain the names of those who have disqualified themselves from service because of their lack of these qualities.

4. Leadership holds sacred the trust of another. Verse 3 tells us it is *God's* flock, *God's* heritage. We have nothing in the way of leadership and influence that is not given to us by God and granted to us by his people. How many times have we said, "Let me tell you about *my* church." It is not your church but *his* church. He said, "On this Rock, I will build *my* church." We owe every privilege that leadership affords to someone who gave it to us, to One to whom we are totally responsible and accountable.

5. The rewards of leadership are later and greater than the price you pay. When you pass through deep waters in your leadership, you will probably want to untie yourself from the "pulpit." Verse 4 says, "*When* the chief Shepherd shall appear, ye shall receive a crown of glory that fadeth not away," and he has not as yet appeared.

Dear pastor, I cannot promise you that you will have an easy time. In fact, I can promise you won't. The road will be rugged, but the rewards will be great. As someone said, "The ministry is a tough job, but the retirement plan is out of this world!" A special crown is promised to the faithful undershepherd. What a joy it will be to lay it at his feet one day.

In review: Don't even think about being a leader unless you know God has called you; better to do a few things well than many things not very well at all; what you do might not be as important as how you do it; leadership holds sacred the trust of another; and the rewards are always later and greater than the price you pay.

To lead, one must be led. To have authority, he must be under authority. Jesus had all authority because he was under the authority of his Father. We are but undershepherds; he is the chief Shepherd. Love him, follow him, and obey him. As you do, your dear people will follow you as you follow the Lord, and great will be your reward.

Chapter 38

Community, Cause, Corporation

Ayoung seminary graduate set out to establish the perfect church. He set three parameters: (1) never talk about money, (2) never act upon a decision that's not unanimous, and (3) never own buildings. The utopian church went "out of business" within the first year. In recounting the lessons he learned from that experience, Jim Dethmer determined the balanced New Testament church must include community, cause, and corporation.[1]

To ensure the growth and health of the church, we must maintain balance between these three New Testament paradigms.

Community. We rightfully think of the church as family (Eph. 3:15). Seen in this light, our core values are love and care (1 John 3:11). We give priority to helping those who are physically weak: infants, members in the hospital, and the elderly (1 Tim. 5:8). People expect the church to provide love, security, and a sense of belonging (1 John 3:1). Most people think of the church primarily in these terms.

Cause. Many New Testament passages describe the church in distinctly military terms (2 Tim. 2:3). The core value is winning the war (Phil. 3:14). Here the emphasis is upon commitment and sacrifice (2 Cor. 11:22–28). The person who sees the church primarily as cause is looking to be involved in a world-changing endeavor.

The implications for you as pastor are profound.

1. Biblically, we must accept all three: community, cause, and corporation, as valid views of who we are.
2. Typically, a church member will lean heavily toward one of these dimensions, accept another, and reject the third.
3. Disharmony occurs when we fail to appreciate the value of all three aspects of the church.
4. Sunday school both defines these values and drives all three in the church.

Corporation. God's work is also described in business terms (John 15:15). Great emphasis must be placed on effectiveness and efficiency (1 Cor. 16:9). Sunday school is a great example of corporation. Bible classes have directors, teachers, secretaries, in-reach leaders, and outreach leaders are organized into groups and keep extensive records. Churches are also corporations in that they have budgets, employees, facilities, calendars, and programs. The corporate view tends to see the church primarily in terms of "the bottom line."

Consider the Church as Community

Church growth expert Peter Wagner argued decades ago that every growing church needs some sort of cell-group structure in addition to the larger structures of congregation and celebration.[2] Perhaps the most significant contribution of the Sunday school to the life of the church is the sense of belonging that accompanies the small, cell-group experience. Even in large classes, the more effective organizations assign members to smaller care groups. Contributions of this small-group identity include sociability, support, and significance.

Sociability. Lifelong friendships in a church often begin in a Sunday school class. We like to believe that participants attend Sunday school solely for great Bible study. My advice is, "Never force a choice between coffee and donuts *or you!*" Rather than opportunities for fellowship being treated as unspiritual, they should be magnified. The larger the church and/or the larger the urban setting from which it draws, the fewer the opportunities for Christian fellowship. Sunday school must then become the "meeting place" for church members to feel part of a community of faith.

Support. A prime characteristic of "community" is the desire to rally to the support of the weakest family member. In our increasingly anonymous society, times of illness, bereavement, birth, or catastrophic change can be overwhelming. When my dear friend Jake Self, former associate pastor at First Southern Baptist Church of Del City, Oklahoma, died and his home was destroyed in the Oklahoma City tornadoes in May 1999, his wife Galelia chose to remain in her home church, First Southern Baptist of Del City, rather than move to one of her children's cities. Faced with the loss of almost every earthly possession, she chose to stay and rebuild her life primarily because of the tremendous support shown by her Sunday school class.

Significance. Sunday school is the place where people know your name and miss you when you are absent. Sunday school membership provides both accountability and security. More important, perhaps, it is a place where somebody "knows my name."

Sunday school has proven to be an enduring institution because most members accept it as their community, but it is much more.

Consider the Church as Cause

The "cause" component is often called being "purpose driven." Perhaps the biggest difference between growing churches and declining ones is the presence or absence of a sense of "cause." "Cause-driven" churches focus on the Great Commission; they produce "cause-driven" leaders who reach people, equip the saints, and instill the vision to begin new classes and new churches.

The greatest barrier to church growth is resistance to change and reluctance to get outside our comfort zone. *Community* is comfortable; *corporation* is necessary. And to our great loss, *cause* is often nowhere to be found.

As Rick Warren writes: "There is no single key to church health and church growth; there are many keys. The church is not called to do one thing; it is called to do many things. That's why balance is so important. I tell my staff that the ninth Beatitude is 'Blessed are the balanced; for they shall outlast everyone else.'"[3]

Consider the Church as Corporation

Few members like to think of their church primarily as a "business." We much prefer the "warm fuzzy" view of the church as community. The organization and accountability of Sunday school units, however, provide perhaps their most significant contribution to the local church by providing stability and structure. Over the years, Sunday school-based churches have been able to adapt better to a change of pastors, for example, without significant decline during the interim.

Just as a business strives to increase its "product line," so the Sunday school expands its structure and varies its offerings:

- Varied class sizes ranging from smaller classes graded by age to large multiage classes.
- Varied groupings—men's, women's, and coeducational.
- Varied target groups—single adults, senior adults, newlyweds, and new parents.
- Varied locations and times. Bible study classes now meet in various churches on every day of the week, both morning and evening. Off-site classes and "Saturday schools" have revolutionized how we offer Bible study.

1. Jim Dethmer, "Cause, Community, Corporation," taped message, Fuller Theological Seminary, 135 Oakland Ave., Pasadena, California 91182

2. C. Peter Wagner, *Your Church Can Grow* (Glendale, Calif.: Regal, 1976), p. 97.

3. Rick Warren, *The Purpose Driven Church* (Grand Rapids: Zondervan, 1995), p. 128.

Chapter 39

Making the Tough Decisions

I n the vernacular of the business world, "It's windy at the top." Leadership is a risky, dangerous, and lonely business. You have to go before God and stay in your prayer closet until you can come out with a firm and settled peace that you know the way God would have you lead the church, and then do it. Talk to the people, explain the options, solicit input, and take them with you. But there are times when that process brings you to the point where not everyone is on board, but you must go forward.

In 1995 in First Baptist Houston, I came to the crossroads of six years of discussion, deliberation, conferences, think tanks, and prayer about the decision to start a new contemporary worship service in our traditional church. After all of that time, I came to three convictions: (1) it was the right thing to do; (2) it would not be supported by everyone and therefore would be controversial and costly; and (3) I had to do it. I was not prepared for what followed. Yes, the service grew from five hundred to nearly two thousand in attendance in just two years. But somehow, some of the people with whom I was closest strongly opposed it.

And yes, I would do it again, but it was done at a great price. Two years later, our young singles and married young adults were booming. Hundreds of new people were attending the church, and the preschool/nursery division enrolled seventy new babies in one month.

When you come to the end of the road and have to make a decision, the results and the fallout are in the hands of God. Remember, every great decision is made with an element of risk. We do not claim infallibility. We may be wrong, and perhaps often are, but we go forward in faith, doing the best we can to follow the will of God as we understand it. Great progress is accomplished at great cost.

Change is always difficult, and the only thing that will see you through is a deep, settled conviction that you have been with God, heard his voice, and know his will. Take your time. Everything must be done on God's schedule. Sometimes God's answer is "yes, but not now." Timing is everything, and the battle is the Lord's.

Chapter 40

Dealing with Opposition

T he bad news is that some people will oppose you. The good news is that it's not as bad as you think. Ninety-nine percent of the time, if a situation becomes serious enough to go to the floor of the church in a special-called Sunday morning business meeting, the people of God will stand with you.

Frankly, some churches can be very difficult to pastor. First Baptist Houston was not. I know of several churches with a long history of "running off the pastor" every year or two. Often the reason is that there are three or four people in places of leadership who are frustrated preachers. Deacons and committee chairmen who heard the voice of God as youth, disobeyed it, and live in a state of rebellion against God are hard people to shepherd.

This does not mean that everyone who opposes you is such a person. It does mean that many times the church with a pattern of pastoral opposition is a church with a history of frustrated, disobedient people in places of leadership.

At a recent conference, I heard an exceptional statement: "Remember, *the devil can make one sound like a thousand.*" Things are seldom as bad or as widespread as you are led to believe. "Everybody's saying" or "everybody thinks" usually means "me and my brother-in-law."

As pastor of one of the more recognizable churches in our city, I probably received at least a hundred letters a month about people's opinions. Ninety percent were most encouraging and supportive, but ten in a hundred were negative and critical. The first thing to do when you receive such a letter is absolutely nothing. Whatever you do, don't react and don't answer the letter. Put it aside a week or ten days, settle down, cool off, and wait. At first, your emotional response will be as great from those ten letters as from the ninety. But after a while, it will subside.

Several days later, read the letter again. Read it objectively and fairly. The writer has the right not only to hold the opinion he does but also to express it. Everyone thinks as he does for a reason. Everyone is the product of something.

Circumstances have shaped people. Their parents have affected them. Life has formed them. Everybody's coming from some place. Older people don't like to change. They don't like the new music; they don't like to sit in a different place in the auditorium—and that's fine. Consistency can be closely connected to security, and rare is the person who can gracefully accept change in his or her older years.

Perhaps they lived through the Great Depression. Those things that were happening in our world at age nine to twelve tend to lock us in attitudinally. Was there a divorce, a world war, a tornado, a family death, a depression? Estimate the age of your critic. Backdate to what was happening in their lives when they were between nine and twelve, and you will likely understand the frame of reference from which they are coming. People who were that age at the time of the Great Depression are extremely cautious. They don't like to borrow money; they don't like debt. Something deep inside them says, "It can happen again."

Understand the person, take your time, and be gracious in your response. Carefully write the letter, set it aside a few days, pray over it again, think about it some more, rewrite it, and mail it. Your letter should be kind, gracious, and conciliatory. I always thanked the person for writing, told him I was glad he felt the freedom to express his views, and assured him that I would respectfully consider his opinion. Finish the letter with a word of appreciation for who he or she is as a person and what he means to the kingdom, and ask her to pray, as you together seek the Lord in the matter under consideration.

Take very seriously what your critics have said. They just might be right. There is almost always something valid in the opinion of a critic.

There's a fine line between being a leader and not totally making unilateral decisions. If your committees and your leadership know you want their input, opinion, advice, and prayers and if they are satisfied that you have sought their counsel, they will normally support you in your ultimate decision, whether it is what they would have preferred or not.

There will also be those difficult times when letters go beyond differences of opinion to outright anger.

Years ago, I received a letter from a former church member. He said I had made the statement, "If God doesn't prosper you when you begin tithing, I will give you your money back." He demanded the return of some $7,000 in tithe gifts. My response did not address his demand and was instead an outpouring of genuine concern for his needs and those of his family. I never heard from him again.

God's people are good people, and some are certainly easier to pastor than others. But if we respond in love, our Lord will always help us find a way to deal with them in grace.

Chapter 41

Don't Use Up Your Leadership

J ust because you don't sweat the small stuff doesn't mean you don't have to sweat. If you get involved in every brush fire, fight every battle, worry about every little problem, you will use up your leadership, and you won't have it when you need it. Whatever you do, don't use up your leadership. Don't go to war over small issues. Don't even get involved. Let your leaders handle them.

In my ministry, I have only had one or two serious problems. By God's grace, I was able to address both with complete success. The secret? I saved the authority and influence of the position of pastor until something major was on the line.

Let me tell you a story. In the late 1970s, a plethora of strange doctrine began to invade our church from certain sources. I talked to all the people—church members, deacons, and teachers—who were caught up in and perpetuating it to our membership. It was a serious issue, and no one could address it but the pastor. I went straight to the pulpit on a Sunday morning and confronted the issue head-on. The sermon was comprised of ten aberrant doctrines being taught in our church and the biblical answers that refuted each.

Then I finished the message by saying, "Henceforth, the teaching of that doctrine will no longer be tolerated in the Sunday school classes or meetings of this church. It is the responsibility of the pastor to articulate the historic doctrines of the church. If it's not, then tell me whose responsibility it is. Is it the custodian's? Is it the minister of music's? I think not. It is mine, and I will accept it."

Pointing to our brick walls, I said, "See those bricks? See that mortar between those bricks? That's not cement. That's blood. That's Baptist blood. When I came here ten years ago, I came to a Baptist church that had been built by the blood, sweat, tears, and sacrifice of Baptist people for more than a century, and when I leave here, it will, by God's grace, still be a Baptist church. And if that's not satisfactory to you—there's the door."

You can't stand up on your haunches and talk that way and know that the people will support you if you're always haranguing about secondary issues. Save your leadership.

As a friend so insightfully says, "I'm going to choose the hill I die on." That afternoon I walked into the deacons' meeting, and our men gave me a standing ovation.

Another such incident happened in the early 1970s. A man in our church began to follow the teachings of Herbert W. Armstrong. During one morning service, he put literature under all the windshield wipers in the parking lot, attempting to refute the deity of Jesus. I called him on Monday morning and said, "You have until Wednesday night to give me your answer. You have three choices: You can stand before our church next Sunday morning and apologize and refute this doctrine; we can vote you out of our membership at the conclusion of the morning service; or you can leave the church and never come back." He chose the latter.

I am willing to die on the hill of the historic doctrines of the faith. Jesus Christ is God in the flesh. Salvation is by grace through faith. It is by the blood that we are saved. I am willing to die on those hills.

These are nonnegotiables. Don't use up your leadership on small issues. You will have a major battle to fight some day, and you will need all the leadership you have saved up in the bank.

Chapter 42

Staying above the Fray

Nothing is more important in a church than the unity of the pastor and his leadership. At all costs, you do not want to become confrontational with your own leaders. They can and must be your best supporters.

For nearly three decades, at nearly every monthly meeting, I reminded our deacons of the importance of staying together. We finished each meeting with an open dialogue in which I not only allowed but also encouraged questions, comments, criticisms, and suggestions. I wanted to know what our people were saying. I wanted to know what our deacons were hearing. What do the people like? What don't they like? What's going on in the hallways? What's the spirit of the church? What don't I know that I need to know? The reverse side of this is that they can then be your defenders, your helpers, your explainers, and your legitimizers.

I admit that committees can be cumbersome. As I look back over my ministry in Houston, we were probably at thirty years where we should have been at about twenty-nine and one-half. Committees might have slowed us down a total of six months over the last three decades. But we arrived at just about the same spot at just about the same time. And, the good news is, we made the journey together, and they helped me greatly. They were insulation for me. Yes, I had the right to fire any staff member when I chose, and I did fire some. But most of the time I brought the personnel committee into the process. When they helped make the decision, they helped absorb the heat.

I occasionally met with the personnel committee and the finance committee and one or two other key committees, but most of the time, I didn't. I assigned staff members as liaisons to every committee in the church. I told them what I was thinking, and they told me what they anticipated before each meeting. They then reported, and if problems existed, we met again, together. But I didn't get involved in every committee meeting and every decision.

Bringing your leadership along with you in the good times builds a bond. This helps them stand with you in the hard times. Stay above the fray. Don't get involved in the battle over small issues. Don't sweat the small stuff. Frankly, I don't really care whether the bathroom doors swing in or out or whether the nurseries are pink or blue. There are more important issues to deal with than these.

The deacons should fight your battles for you. From time to time, there may be accusations about a staff member, confrontations between members, disturbances in a class, teachers who need to be replaced, or other distasteful disruptions in the fellowship of the church. Ask your deacons to handle these issues. They should never even get to you. If the leaders are earning their salt, they should be handling most of the problems in your behalf.

The privilege your leaders enjoy has a price, and a part of that price is sweating the small stuff for their pastor. At this writing, I could name hundreds of men in First Baptist Houston whom I believe would die for me and protect me as pastor from having to worry about those agitations that would drain the concentration and passion from my ministry. Most were deacons; many were not. I was blessed and our church was enriched because of these people.

In any important decision, it is critical to bring along your legitimizers. Committees, deacons, elders, church leaders, the respected, the influential—these should be in your corner when important decisions are announced to the church.

For the past twenty years during my pastorate in Houston, we conducted two morning services—at 8:15 and 11:00, the 11:00 service obviously being the larger. The overwhelming success of a third, contemporary service at 9:30 begun three years before, led to the cancellation of the 8:15 service and commitment of all our best efforts to just the 9:30 contemporary service and the 11:00 traditional service.

For some years I had felt it best to discontinue the 8:15 service and ask the people who attended it to join the 11:00 worshipers—but how to do so? Some people would be hurt, some would disagree. Worse still, some would probably leave the church. I could simply have announced that the service was coming to an end, but I needed to "bring along those legitimizers."

I took the time to go through channels and allow God to bring the people along. First was the appropriate committee. In this case, it was our Vision 2000 Committee, an ad hoc committee appointed to review everything the church was doing, with a view toward maximizing our effectiveness as we approached the twenty-first century. To my surprise, the committee was ahead of me. All fifteen members began urging me to drop the early service and put all our effort into just two great services.

The next step was to have a gathering of all the leaders in our church who attended the 8:15 service. I did not force it upon them. I simply gave them the thinking of my own heart and that of the committee. A second meeting followed with the same group. Finally a consensus was built, and both committee and leaders agreed it was the right decision.

When I introduced the decision to the church, I shared with them that the Vision 2000 Committee and attending leaders joined with me in recommending the cessation of the early service.

I could have simply announced the important decision on my own. But through the years, I have learned it is much easier if you bring along the support and influence of those lay leaders in whom the people have confidence. It will slow you down a bit, but it will be well worth it. Remember these words: Work with your committees and bring along your legitimizers.

Chapter 43

Principles of Motivation

I nformation plus motivation equals action. Is there action in your church? Is there growth, purpose, and direction? Are there results? Is there conquest and achievement? If not, and you are preaching the truth, if you live among prospects, and if you are a man of prayer, one of two things is true: either there is no information or there is no motivation. In other words, people must know what to do and want to do it.

The problem is that most of us *know* to do more than we *want* to do! We are the best-informed people in history. We have more education, information, conferences, conventions, clinics, and colleges than our forefathers. Multitudes of us have covered our walls with seals representing completed courses of study. We learn, but we do not accomplish. We comprehend, but we do not do. We are hearers of the Word, but not doers. Too many have won a seal but have never won a soul!

While we continue to use new methods, new witnessing ideas, and new ways to teach our people how to be soul winners, the truth of the matter is that most of them simply do not want to be soul winners. We have *information* but not sufficient *motivation*. If they had to, most Christians could probably tell a person how to accept Christ as his personal Savior, but few there be who really do it. It is obvious that the reason we do so little is that information—knowing what to do—is not being coupled with motivation—the desire to do what we know. To know what to do is human. To do what we know is divine.

The first ingredient in motivation is *enthusiasm*. Years ago I flew to Florida. On the plane I chatted with Darryl Royal, University of

Texas head football coach. I asked him to choose one word that in his opinion was the major contributing factor to his unparalleled success as a coach. The word? *Attitude!* Centuries ago it was said the same way, "As [a man] thinketh in his heart, so is he" (Prov. 23:7).

A mediocre football team can beat a better team if it thinks it can. You can do, and your people can do, what you dream and plan to do. If you approach a situation with failure in mind, you will fail. Expect, plan, hope, and dream. Attitude is all-important. If you want to do it, and if you believe that God wants you to, get your people excited about it and you can do anything. Motivation begins with *enthusiasm.*

A preacher awoke in the middle of the night to find his church building ablaze. And who was leading the bucket brigade, throwing water on the fire, but the town atheist! "Atheist," said the preacher, "I've never seen you at church before." "Preacher," said the atheist, "I've never seen your church on fire before!" Let the church get on fire, and the world will come and watch it burn!

Enthusiasm builds empires. Enthusiasm makes successes of common men. Enthusiasm wins the day. Enthusiasm does the impossible. Enthusiasm is half the battle. He who would excite must be excited, and a leader must excite his people. Lest you think I speak of a hollow, claptrap kind of emotionalism, I would remind you the word *enthuse* comes from two Greek words *en* and *theos*. That means simply, "in God" and "God in you." "God in you" carries the picture of the lesser containing the greater. It is like two wildcats in a gunnysack. The result: enthusiasm, excitement, and action!

Second, motivation is *repetition*. Wrigley built an empire on five-cent packages of gum. But he sold an awful lot of those packages. His business philosophy was repetition. Over and over and over again, keep before your people the urgency of outreach, the imperative of evangelism. At every gathering, every committee meeting, and every assembly, talk about winning the world to Christ. Repeat it again and again. Make it the driving, burning, consuming passion of your people.

Years ago I walked into a drugstore in Ohio to buy some razor blades. The store was having a sale on peach sundaes. Hundreds of flyers hung from the ceiling. They were everywhere—"Peach Sundae,

19 cents, Peach Sundae 19 cents, Peach Sundae 19 cents." I went to the counter and took out a dollar to buy razor blades. The clerk said, "What will you have?" I said, "Give me a peach sundae!" I didn't want a peach sundae. I wanted razor blades! But they had convinced me that I wanted a peach sundae. Repetition had won the day!

For years the First Baptist Church of Amarillo, Texas, led the entire Southern Baptist Convention in mission giving. I asked the pastor, Dr. Carl Bates, for his secret. He said, "For many years, I have never preached a sermon on Sunday morning, Sunday night, or Wednesday night without at least mentioning tithing." Repetition. Repetition. Repetition.

Third, motivation is *illustration*. Every time I preach I try to mention the name of one of our people who has done what I am attempting to get them to do. When a new convert is introduced, and you know one of your people has led him to Christ, call that person to the front to stand by the new convert when he is introduced. Illustrate soul winning to the people. Show them what others are doing. Suggest they can do the same.

Fourth, motivation is *example*. Do it yourself. People are not naïve. If you go Sunday after Sunday without conversions, the people will justifiably begin to ask why you as pastor cannot win someone once in a while yourself. Lead the way. Set the pace. Show them how. Jesus said, "Let not thy left hand know what thy right hand doeth" (Matt. 6:3). But he also said, "Let your light . . . shine before men" (Matt. 5:16). How do you reconcile the two? Simple! He added, "that [you] may . . . glorify your Father which is in heaven" (Matt. 5:16).

We motivate others when they see us do it, and only you know in your heart whether it is for God's glory or yours. If you know it and the Lord knows it, that is all that is important. You need not tell the people; they will know it without being told. Be a living example. Lead the way. Set the pace. Do it yourself.

Motivation is getting people to do what they already know they ought to do, and it is probably 75 percent enthusiasm and 25 percent repetition, illustration, and example. Get excited! Say it again. Talk about others who are doing it, and do it yourself. In a few months your people will begin to follow!

Chapter 44

Streamlining the Organization

Without exception, the great Sunday schools and churches of America have established priorities and eliminated less important activity. Busy-ness is often the death knell of the modern church. While it is good to be organized and active, it is possible to relegate the primary into the role of the secondary and organize yourself out of business.

Wednesday night must be centered in preparation and outreach for Sunday's day of harvest. Through the years as pastor I discovered that any week that has a special activity, such as an extra one-night service, banquet, or fellowship, will likely be a week in which other regularly scheduled activities will be affected. People only have so many hours in a week, and they do have more to do than go to church.

Christian families must have time to be a family. Home life, recreation, and other outside interests are important, too. Parents should attend their son's debate contest, or their daughter's volleyball game. It is imperative that parents take interest in the activity of their children. All activities should not be centered in the church. A well-rounded life is important. The family that is involved in church activities five or six nights a week might well become a family with burnout.

Because a particular church activity has met on a particular night at a particular time for a long time does not make it hallowed. The hour meeting could be cut to forty minutes. With proper preparation and efficiency, the thirty-minute meeting could be cut to twenty. Consolidate Wednesday night activities. Go over every activity with a fine-tooth comb. Streamline and reorganize, plan, add, and eliminate.

In the most ideal situation, everything churchwide is accomplished in two nights per week—Wednesday and Sunday. In a neighborhood church, it might be possible to have all auxiliary meetings, including officers' and teachers' meetings, and a Wednesday night meal from 5:30 to 7:00, churchwide visitation from 7:00 to 8:00, and prayer meeting from 8:00 to 8:30. If you would involve your peripheral members in visitation, make it easy. Give them the opportunity to visit prospects on nights when they will already be at church. It is better for two hundred people to visit two prospects each on Wednesday night than for the faithful fifteen to visit five each on Monday night.

Give your organizations a boost with quarterly dinners or monthly prayer breakfasts. But, by all means, find a way to streamline the organization.

Take one-fourth or one-third of the time off each activity and try to consolidate it all into a streamlined, swiftly moving Wednesday night program. Don't drag your people to church four or five times a week. They will be better for it, the kingdom of God will prosper, and you will have time to be a better husband and father as well as pastor.

Doing less and doing it better is always right. No church can be a "jack of all trades," and certainly not every pastor can meet every need. Bigger is not always better. Great buildings and great crowds of people do not necessarily mean great success in God's eyes.

It is still true, however, that when my team wins, I win. When my church wins, I win. Nobody likes a loser. Your people will not witness and attend, will not bring their friends and talk up the church if a negative attitude of despair, pessimism, and defeat permeates your church. It is important to instill pride in your people. Clean up the buildings. Paint that old sign. Mow the grass. Shine your shoes. Sharpen up the service. Make your people proud to be Christians, proud of the church, and proud of their pastor. They will relate, they will want to come, and they will bring their friends.

Yours might be a small church, but in the heart of your people it should be the greatest little church in the world. Forget your problems and major on the majors. Do a *few* things and do them well and do *some* things better than anyone else in town.

Chapter 45

Things to Control

The pastor of a church, large or small, is not a dictator or an emperor. There is a special combination of leadership and servanthood combined in the office of pastor, which we often refer to as "undershepherd."

On one hand, we are leading the people, shepherding the flock. On the other hand, we ourselves are servants of God and servants of the people. Leadership is never demanded; it is always deserved. It must be granted by the congregation but earned by the pastor as well. Jesus referred to this when he said, "He that would be greatest among you, let him be servant of all."

One day a centurion, commander of a hundred Roman soldiers, came to Jesus. His request to Jesus to heal his servant was met with a warm response: "I will come down to your house and heal him." "No," said the centurion, "you needn't make the journey. Just speak the word (right here) and he will be healed."

Then the centurion made a very insightful statement. "For I too am a man under authority. I say to this one, go and he goes and to this one come and he comes." The centurion was saying, "I understand how authority works. I have authority over my soldiers because I am under the authority of the Roman government." He recognized that Jesus had authority to heal his servant with a simple command because he was under the authority of his Father. Jesus responded, "I have not found so great faith, no, not in Israel" (Matt. 8:10), and the servant was healed at Jesus' command.

Pastor, you have the responsibility and authority to lead your congregation only because you stay under the authority of God. And there is a sense in which you are, as well, under the authority of your people. The apostle Paul said, "Let each esteem the other better than themselves" (Phil. 2:3). Yes, your congregation is accountable to you as you speak for the Father on the basis of his Word. But you, in turn, are accountable to them. It is a system that is virtually impossible for the secular world to understand, but it does work within the body of Christ.

When I came to the pastorate of First Baptist Church of Houston, I assured the pastor-search committee that it would be my joy to work with the deacons and other leadership in making major decisions. But I also told them there were four things that were not negotiable—four areas in which I must have absolute control—to which they wisely agreed:

1. It was my responsibility and mine alone to articulate the doctrines of the church. I will speak from the pulpit and say, "This is what this church believes." If not the pastor—who?
2. I must have control over who preaches in our pulpit and when.
3. I must have control over what special offerings are received, when, and for what purpose.
4. I must have the right to hire and fire staff.

In the higher levels of our staff structure, I always made those decisions in concert with the personnel committee. To the glory of God, in thirty years we always agreed on the decision that had to be made. But I reserved the right to make the final decision. Our committees wisely followed this procedure, and the results were more than satisfactory.

Again there is a tender and delicate balance between leading the people and being their servant. Another chapter addresses the issue of "Don't Use Up Your Leadership." Don't make a big deal out of small issues. Save your influence and authority until major issues are on the line. Some things are worth fighting and dying for. Some issues are worth losing your church over. The integrity of the Scripture, the historic doctrines of the faith, and certain other issues are non-negotiable.

The best time to come to agreement about these issues is when you begin to get serious with the pastor search committee about the possibility of accepting the pastorate of their church. Talk them through in advance. Be certain the committee has the authority to articulate the position of the church in these matters and that they are thoroughly conveying your position back to the congregation.

Let there be no surprises three or four months into your new pastorate. Good marriages are in part the result of good courtships. And good courtships take time. Take your time and work these things through in advance. There are some areas you must control, and it is imperative that they be clearly defined before your installation as pastor. No church wants a "puppet preacher." People respect leadership, and the purpose of leadership is to lead. The smoothness of a leader's path can be greatly enhanced by clearly plotting out the map before the journey begins.

Chapter 46

Publicity and Advertising

People cannot go to a place, attend an activity, or buy a product if they do not know it exists. The importance of good publicity cannot be overstated. The first Christmas angel publicized tidings of great joy.

The two-by-two, person-to-person witnessing taught by our Lord cannot be improved upon. But it is not inconsistent with the principle of mass publicity. The two go hand in hand. As the B-52 bombers soften the terrain for the foot soldiers, so publicizing through the mass media opens hearts to one-to-one personal witnessing and invitation. "Oh yes, I have heard of that church. I'll try to come some time," is a lot more likely to be heard than "Where's that again?" when you publicize.

Bumper stickers do little good. They are too small and move too fast. If they are used, they should contain only three or four words. Attractive wrought iron signs in church members' yards are nice. Radio spots not to exceed fifteen to thirty seconds with repeated exposure are good. Don't quote Scripture passages and don't preach sermons in spot announcements. Take a few seconds, get to the point, and move on.

Billboards are also effective. They should be lighted, on major freeways, on the right side of the road, and not cluttered with too many words. Handbills should be done professionally. Do not distribute homemade mimeographed invitations to anything. Do it first-class. Most newspapers and radio stations will carry announcements about your church's upcoming activities when neatly typed, well-written, concise reports are mailed to them well in advance of the event.

Good newspaper ads should contain pictures and plenty of white space. Again, do not clutter. Get to the point and always request a right-hand page location in the main news section when submitting advertising.

Creative TV advertising is excellent, but it is often prohibitive because of the cost. A live Sunday morning radio broadcast is a good idea, and live TV is even better. Live TV broadcasts will not hurt your church attendance. If you offer a good product, it will ultimately enhance it.

Get a slogan. Our slogan, "A Church for Our Times," spoke about everything we tried to be and do. Have a slogan that is justified and have one that does not belittle any other church or even belittle yourself. "Come, help us grow" or "the littlest church in the city" will not have the result you want. Make it truthful and make it positive.

Major on your assets. Don't advertise your problems, and don't expect publicity to pay off immediately. The effect of advertising is cumulative. It takes time to produce results, but it is well worth the wait.

Chapter 47

The Church Newspaper

Our Lord was far more than the consummate communicator. He was even more than God's communication to us. He was, in fact, God in the flesh, come to communicate the Father's character and love in his life. Nicodemus, in John 3, didn't quite get it when he said to Jesus, "Thou art a teacher come from God" (John 3:2). Jesus was not simply a teacher come from God; he was God come to teach. The living and written Word of God is the very heart of the Christian faith. And, it is about communication. It is God the Father communicating his love to us through his Son Jesus Christ.

Revelation 1:8 says, "I am Alpha and Omega, the beginning and the ending." As the alpha and omega, John was describing Jesus as the full Word of God. Alpha and omega are the first and last letters of the Greek alphabet. As the Word of God, Jesus is the whole alphabet; he is the full revelation, the complete living message of God. Everything the Father had to say about himself, he said in his Son, Jesus Christ.

When you and I communicate God's Word to our people, we do that which is very close to the heart of the Father. Limited and finite though we are, it is the consummate task of his pastors to be his communicators. In our lives, our pulpits, our character, and our relationships, we are always communicating God's love and truth to our fellowman. Let that lofty understanding of what you are doing be preeminent in your mind as you consider the issue of a weekly tool through which to communicate with your congregation.

From one Sunday to the next can be a very long time for your people. How helpful it is when they receive at midweek a message of love from their pastor and his staff. Having a weekly church newsletter, newspaper, magazine, or mail-out is of high priority in the life of your church. You might be limited by a small budget and serving a small congregation, but do your best with what you have. Start small. Write the entire paper yourself, print it yourself, and attach the stamps if you must, but communicate with your people between Sundays.

In various ways, our mail-outs represent us and speak volumes about who we are and how we view our people and the work of our Lord. It is important, therefore, to make the paper as high class as possible. Coated glossy paper is better than uncoated paper. Pictures are better than no pictures; some color is better than all black and white. Make your weekly paper as good as you can, but do start somewhere.

In a large church you might have the luxury of a talented graphic artist, your own print room, and even a reprographics coordinator. If so, you will, incidentally, save a lot of money by being able to meet many other printing needs—stationery, record forms, envelopes, etc. But even in the smallest church, it is very likely that some talented, committed person is just waiting to be asked to help prepare and publish the weekly church newsletter. To start, do this:

1. Get some people together and brainstorm about a name for your paper.
2. Set a deadline, perhaps the preceding Thursday or Friday, by which columns, articles, announcements, and other pertinent information must be submitted for Monday layout.
3. Promote upcoming events three to four weeks in advance with increasing prominence.
4. Edit the material meticulously for accuracy of spelling and information.
5. Use pictures when available and appropriate.
6. Condense. Ask, "Is this as brief as I can say it?"
7. Don't clutter. A paper filled with too much information will not be read.
8. Don't feel you must write every week just because you "have a column." Encourage other staff members to write from time to time. When something is on your heart,

when there is something you want to say, write an article. The pastor's column will always take precedence over other items if space is limited.

In folding, addressing, stamping, and mailing the church news-letter, volunteers may be used. Those wonderful senior adults will do it for you on a regular basis. Perhaps a potluck lunch or morning coffee and donuts can be provided. Make it a fun and positive experience for them. Thank them regularly and publicly and let them know they are important.

And be certain to organize your printing and publication so the church newsletter can be mailed and in the hands of your people no later than Friday. A paper received the following Monday or Tuesday after the fact is of no value. Church newsletters that arrive on Saturday will hardly be read. Put it together on Monday, print it on Tuesday, fold, address, stamp and mail on Wednesday, with the goal of Thursday or Friday arrival in the homes.

Study other newsletters. Clip from here and there. Get ideas. Be short and be fresh. It's a great way for the people to hear from their church.

Chapter 48

Protecting the Church from Liability

In the not-too-distant past, it was virtually unheard of that a church was the object of litigation. Unfortunately, such is no longer the case. In recent years, there has been a proliferation of lawsuits against churches and other community organizations. Not only are churches being sued with regularity, but they are also "losing" virtually every case—either through out-of-court settlements or jury verdicts.

In 1993 First Baptist Houston hosted a seminar helping churches learn how to protect themselves against lawsuits. To my amazement, one of the attorneys stated in his lecture, "In the past five years, more than a thousand churches have been sued; in every case, the church lost." Further, it is commonly reported that seminars are held on "How to Sue Churches." It is assumed that big churches have deep pockets, so the larger the congregation, the more likely the lawsuit.

While such news is discouraging, the good news is that churches can greatly reduce the risk of financial loss and a tarnished reputation in the community. *This is an extremely serious issue.* It is vitally important that you protect your people from individual harm and collective liability.

Understand clearly that the church is generally responsible for everything that takes place in its buildings, on its premises, on rented equipment or property, and almost anything under the influence of staff and other persons whom the court would identify as "an agent of the church." This means the church is legally responsible not only for activities that occur on its property, but could, for example, include incidents that occur away from the church in a vehicle that had been rented to transport students to a youth retreat, as well as at the retreat itself. Therefore, in the same manner you make certain your church is adequately insured against fire and other catastrophic events, make certain your church carries adequate liability insurance. Such insurance should cover everything from broken legs incurred during church-sponsored softball games, to food poisoning at a restaurant suggested by a staff member, to leading an out-of-state mission trip, to sexual misconduct by a staff member—*and everything in between!*

The church's greatest exposure to being found negligent lies in the area of child abuse. It is critical that every pastor lead his church in establishing policies and procedures that reduce the risk of child abuse occurring in the church. After many years of unreported physical, emotional, and sexual abuse of children, such "secret sins" are increasingly being reported to law enforcement authorities. And you need to know that the law *requires* you to report known incidence of child abuse. Abuse can happen anywhere, including at church.

Every New Testament church must make a commitment to minister to children in ways that are scriptural, loving, safe, *and legal.* Children are precious, and anything that threatens them—including physical, emotional, or sexual abuse—is unacceptable and not to be tolerated.

Developing a *children's protective policy* must be done with a broad base of understanding and support from your church's leadership, including staff and laity. Like many important policies, the developmental phase might be quite time-consuming; however, once in place, the policy can be maintained and updated with relatively little effort.

As you develop and implement child-abuse prevention policies and procedures, pay heed to this statement made by an attorney who specializes in defending churches against allegations of child abuse: *"The only thing worse than not having formal policies against child abuse is having such policies and not enforcing them."* It is essential that you lead your people to develop good, sound, comprehensive policies and procedures and emphasize the need for them to be *diligently followed.*

Your children's protective policies and procedures obviously relate to preschool, children, and youth ministries. However, make certain that your policies also include ministries related to music, recreation, missions, and any other programs which involve "children" (defined legally in most states as anyone under 18 years of age).

Listed below are highlights from the "Child Abuse Prevention Policies and Procedures" that we developed at Houston's First Baptist Church. In concert with staff and lay leadership, develop a clear and comprehensive written document that describes policies and procedures. These should then be officially adopted by the church membership *before* their implementation. As the written policies are disseminated, provide an opportunity for church members to ask questions and develop an appreciation for why such "legalistic" measures are needed. Lead the people in diffusing any attitude of "it could *never happen* at this church," to an attitude of "we *won't let it happen* at this church."

(1) Worker Enlistment

    (a) All volunteer and paid workers with children will complete the Preschool/Children/Youth Worker Application form.

    (b) The supervising minister will interview all volunteer and paid workers with children.

    (c) All workers with children will provide personal references.

    (d) No person will be allowed to work with children who has been convicted of, placed on regular or deferred adjudicated probation, received pretrial diversion, pled guilty, or nolo contendre, to any offense involving sexual contact or physical abuse with a child.

    (e) All potential workers with children must sign a "Waiver of Confidentiality," which gives the church permission to do a background check of the potential worker. (This same "Waiver of Confidentiality" form is required of all church leadership, including staff, deacons and all employees, as a preventive measure and to demonstrate the church's commitment to providing a safe environment in all of its ministries and activities.)

(2) Worker Supervision
   (a) A reasonable ratio of adult workers will be maintained in situations involving children, with a minimum of two workers present.
   (b) Corporal punishment of any kind is never appropriate in the church setting.
   (c) Physical affection should be deemed inappropriate.
   (d) Written parental/legal guardian approval will be obtained concerning the sleeping accommodations at any church-related overnight event for children.

(3) Worker Training
   (a) All workers with children will receive written information which describes state laws regarding the definition of child abuse as well as procedures for the reporting of suspected child abuse.
   (b) All workers with children will receive annual training regarding child abuse, including how to identify child abuse.
   (c) Procedures will be developed that document that all workers with children have received and read the information described in sections (a) and (b) above.

(4) Worker Reporting
   (a) A worker who suspects that child abuse has occurred will report the incident or suspicions in writing to the supervising minister immediately.
   (b) If there is cause to believe that child abuse has occurred, such cause will be investigated promptly by the supervising minister and appropriate church staff; such investigation will be documented in written form.
   (c) The person reporting the suspected abuse and/or the supervising minister will arrange for timely reporting to Children's Protective Services or to other state law enforcement agencies.
   (d) Should child-abuse allegations occur, workers will:
      (i)   Respond to each allegation in a serious manner;
      (ii) Treat each allegation with confidentiality and respect for the privacy of all involved persons;
      (iii) Cooperate fully with civil authorities;
      (iv) Extend genuine care to all victims of child abuse;

(v) Arrange for professional counseling or other treat-
      ment as needed to persons affected by alleged
      and/or established child abuse incidents;

(vi) All child-abuse allegations will be communicated
      to the church's insurance carrier by the church's
      attorney or administrator.

For complete information regarding the "Child Abuse Prevention
Policies and Procedures" at Houston's First Baptist Church, contact:
Personnel Director, 7401 Katy Freeway, Houston, Texas 77024.

Part 5

The Pastor as Preacher

Chapter 49

Preparing the Message

D r. Manuel Scott, noted pastor of St. John's Missionary Baptist Church in Dallas, may be the premier African-American pulpiteer of our time. Dr. Scott tells the story of an automobile accident. Relaying the account to an insurance man, he was asked, "Dr. Scott, how much did you make?"

"Make?" replied the great preacher, "I didn't make anything. I didn't know I was supposed to make anything."

"Oh, preacher," the man replied, "you ain't no businessman. You can't do nothin' but preach."

With a broad smile and a twinkle in his eye, Dr. Scott replied, "Thank you, sir. Far too many preachers can do everything *but* preach."

Dear pastor, your preaching is your priority. Your time with God, your sermon preparation, the credibility of your life, your personal study, all that you do moves toward that focal point of your public preaching ministry. Our heavenly Father had only one Son, and he made him a preacher. Observe the gospel narrative. Listen to Jesus; he's talking about preaching: "Let us go into the next towns, that I may preach there also: therefore came I forth" (Mark 1:38).

In a sense, we are preparing to preach all day long. As a pastor, early in the week I determined the subject and began to read myself full, watching for illustrations from life, from the media, from every source, praying, mulling over, and meditating about the subject for the following Sunday. By Wednesday or Thursday, the ideas began to crystallize, and I was ready to start putting my thoughts down on paper.

Some of the best preaching is done through books of the Bible. God's Word is alive, and no other primary source for your preaching ideas need be considered. Of course, certain resources will amplify, explain, and augment the topic of the text, but the source is always the Scripture. And, however we approach it, the subject is always Jesus. "Search the Scriptures," he said, "for they . . . testify of me" (John 5:39).

I urge you not to spend your time plowing through a plethora of commentaries. Through the years, you will identify two or three that you like best. Stay with those. Frankly, I have found that many of them are just quoting the others. A good concordance and a good word-study source, such as Pink, Robertson, or Wuest, are important. And, remember, you don't have to make the Scripture relevant. It is relevant. When you explain it to people and apply it to their lives, the Holy Spirit brings it to life in their hearts and produces transformation of character.

And remember that all Scripture is given by inspiration of God. So we have a living book, with a living message, a living author, and a living and vital message for modern man. The source of our material is obviously God's Word. Preach the Word.

A hundred professors might suggest varying ideas regarding steps to the sermon. The purpose of this chapter will be to open my heart and share with you my own personal method, created and refined through many years of trial and error. A teenage boy asked his buddy, "What's the best way to kiss a girl?" His friend replied, "There ain't no bad way."

What's the best way to prepare a sermon? It is *your way* and *God's way.* Don't try to walk in Saul's armor at this point. Be yourself. Find what fits you, determine what is comfortable, and go with it. Following is what's comfortable for me.

Let me say first that narrative preaching is easier than doctrinal preaching. Those great Old Testament stories, including the Gospels and Acts, are unbelievably powerful and rich. We instantly relate to the characters and find our hearts open to the truths their lives teach us. Don't discount the Old Testament, and don't discount preaching from narrative. They are wonderful vehicles on which to hang the truths of the great doctrines of the New Testament. All the truth of God's Word relates to the human experience. When you can teach it from the vantage point of those who actually experienced it, you are miles ahead in the process of communication.

What, for example, could be more relevant than a series on the life of Samson, the product of a dysfunctional home? Samson had relationships with three different women in his life. Each was bad news. Why did Samson never learn to relate appropriately to a member of the opposite sex? Twice at the beginning of the story of Samson, the angel bypasses Manoah, the father of the home, and goes to his mother. This is not the correct biblical order. The man should be the spiritual leader of his home, but the passive Manoah apparently gave no leadership. Looking to his mother as the spiritual leader, Samson developed a distorted view of womanhood, and the result was disastrous. This is relevant, biblical preaching.

As I begin to preach through a book in the Bible, particularly a book that is primarily narrative, as with the great stories of Abraham, Moses, David, Samson, Elijah, Enoch, etc., I first spend several long minutes in prayer, clearing my mind and opening my innermost self to God. Then I open to the passage at hand and begin slowly and meditatively to read word-by-word through the account. I read until the subject changes and there I stop. Usually that particular story will cover anywhere from five to twelve or fifteen verses. It is within the boundaries of those beginning and closing verses that I will preach.

The next step is to determine the central idea and condense it down to a single propositional statement. You are not ready to begin developing the passage into a sermon until you can answer the question that your hearers will be asking. Here's the question: "If I do everything you want me to do, if I buy everything you're selling, if I say 'yes' to everything you're trying to persuade me to do, tell me in one short, simple sentence—*what do you want me to do?*"

You will have to answer the question like this: "You should tithe to your church." "You should be true to your word." "You should develop an early morning prayer life." "You should get out of that immoral relationship."

Once you have determined the central idea and reduced it to a simple propositional statement, go back and find three or four things in the passage that support it. "Why is that true?" "What will happen if I do?" "What are the consequences if I don't?" "Is there any help?" Every sermon must answer the grand "*So what?* How does this apply to me? What are you trying to get me to do?" If you can't answer that, you're not ready to start the sermon. Determine the central idea, support it three or four ways from the text, and then write your outline.

Rick Warren, the creative pastor of Saddle Back Valley Community Church in Orange, California, has given invaluable help in preaching relevant sermons to today's hearers. Simply stated, it is called "principle preaching." Though they might not articulate it precisely as such, analyzing the preaching of Chuck Swindoll, of "Insight for Living"; Bill Hybel, pastor of Willow Creek Church in Chicago; and even Pastor Charles Stanley of "In Touch"; you will find their sermons have this in common with Rick Warren. Could this have any connection to their being among the most widely heard preachers in the world?

I consider this to be a very important part of my preaching ministry. I learned it from Rick Warren some years ago and believed it so firmly that I made a conscious decision to change my preaching style. I consider it simple but profound: *The outline should consist of principles, not points.*

Points are predictable, and the predictable tends to turn off the hearer. Principles, conversely, instantly grab the attention of the hearer. The reason? Any valid principle about life is universally applicable. The Buddhist, the communist, the atheist, the old, the young, the astronaut, the farmer—all are immediately open to valid biblical principles. A principle that is true in one area of life is true in another. If everything that goes up comes down in physics, it does so in the stock market, in athletics, and in business as well.

For example, you might outline the story of Jonah like this: "The Call of Jonah, The Rebellion of Jonah, The Judgment of Jonah, The

Repentance of Jonah." To outline the sermon, however, with instantly relatable principles rather than points, you might outline it as follows:

1. God always waits to speak to those who want to hear.
2. He is a fool who thinks himself wiser than God.
3. You cannot run from God.
4. When you come to the end of your rope, you'll find God is there.

Rick Warren suggests the following approach for each part of the sermon:

1. State the principle.
2. Explain the principle.
3. Apply the principle.
4. Illustrate the principle.

Once you have stated the principle, explain it. You will want to spend a good amount of time here because your explanation will be an exegesis of the portion of the passage with which you are dealing. This kind of preaching is *not shallow preaching*. At this point, you will use many sources to explain the principle from history, from the Greek, from customs, from quotations, etc.

Never assume your hearers understand what you're saying, let alone agree with you. Be the apologist as well as the explainer and the exhorter. Your principle has probably claimed a lot. Prove it, explain it, defend it from every possible perspective. Anticipate disagreement. Anticipate the critic, and answer him in the explanation of the principle before he can even articulate his opposition. The apologetic element of the sermon is what separates the men from the boys in preaching!

Next, apply the principle. It is at this point that the Holy Spirit especially helps us. Certainly he is the one who applies what we are saying to the heart of the listener. Even before we can state our application, God has already opened hearts with a measure of understanding and conviction. But God calls pastors to teach because he needs teachers. We do not help him teach. He helps us, but we *are* to teach.

So explain how it applies to the lives of your people. In most cases, it will already be obvious, but articulating what the Holy Spirit is likely already saying in their hearts reinforces the truth and bears fruit.

Finally, illustrate the principle. I want to caution you about two things most preachers do which I believe to be counterproductive. The first is to reach way back into antiquity for illustrations. When I hear Swindoll, Warren, and Hybel preach, they use illustrations out of their own experience and out of this week's newspaper. These illustrations are fresh and alive; they are relevant and, as such, are instant attention grabbers. But 95 percent of the preachers I listen to are telling me stories from Scotland and England and France about Lord Chancellory, vicar of England, or Baron "Von Whosoever" of Scotland in the seventeenth century.

Get rid of those old sermon illustration books and get into life. Read today's authors. Read modern books of sermon illustrations. Read *People, Time, Newsweek, USA Today,* and your local newspaper. Listen to the radio. Listen to television, particularly the evening news. Get among your people. Get out into the real world and find real, live, relevant illustrations.

A second ingredient in far too many sermons today is the overuse of alliteration. Many preachers really stretch the point with the use of cute alliterations, even double alliterations, such as the "available power," the "awesome purpose," and the "amazing purity."

Further, far too often I hear preachers who keep bringing me up to date with their outlines. For example, "Consider the available power of it." Second, "consider not only the available power of it, but the awesome purpose of it." Third, "consider not only the available power of it, and the awesome purpose of it, but the amazing purity of it." I come away with the feeling that this preacher was so proud of his outline that he wanted me to remember *it* more than what he said *about* it. Guard against these practices. They will help your sermons be more alive and relevant.

There are obviously times when we want to do word-by-word studies of the Bible. But this kind of teaching is primarily done on a Wednesday night or Thursday night Bible study when you are going deeper with your people. The Sunday morning congregation is normally very diverse. People from all walks of life and at all stages of spiritual development are there. The young, the old, the saved, the lost, the backslidden, and the mature—all these are among your hearers. Aim down the middle aisle, and you will reach most of them. Good, relevant, biblically based principle preaching does a great job on Sunday morning. And I want to reemphasize that *it is not shallow preaching.* The element of explanation is where you ferret out the deep things of the text.

Let me give you one additional example of principle preaching. Consider the call of Joshua and God's direction to him as successor to the mighty Moses.

Joshua 1:1: Now after the death of Moses the servant of the LORD, it came to pass that the LORD spake unto Joshua the son of Nun, Moses' minister, saying,

Verse 2: Moses my servant is dead; now therefore arise, go over this Jordan, thou, and all this people, unto the land which I do give to them, even to the children of Israel.

Principle No. 1: *Don't get stuck in life's passageways.* God says to Joshua, "Moses is dead. Stand up and go forward." Far too many people spend their lives stuck between the regret and disappointment of the past and the dream world of the future. They are stuck in the passageways of life. Yesterday is a room forgotten; tomorrow, a room not yet entered. Today is for living. The past is past. Moses is dead. Life goes on. Get up, move forward.

Verse 3: Every place that the sole of your foot shall tread upon, that have I given unto you, as I said unto Moses.

Principle No. 2: *God has already been where you're going.* Don't fret about the future. God is already in your tomorrow.

Verse 4: From the wilderness and this Lebanon even unto the great river, the river Euphrates, all the land of the Hittites, and unto the great sea toward the going down of the sun, shall be your coast.

Principle No. 3: *God has a wonderful blueprint for your life.* Every detail has been planned by our Lord. He is never caught by surprise.

Verse 5: There shall not any man be able to stand before thee all the days of thy life: as I was with Moses, so I will be with thee: I will not fail thee, nor forsake thee.

Principle No. 4: *God himself guarantees the victory.*

Continue through the passage with a creative eye and a prayerful heart and let other principles explode off the page.

Many times a single story will have so many principles that it will be necessary to make it into two sermons or even three. I once preached a chapel sermon at Southwestern Baptist Seminary in Fort Worth, Texas, containing thirty-two principles. *DON'T!*

State the principle, explain the principle, apply the principle, illustrate the principle. When I discovered this kind of preaching, I discovered the real me. Perhaps you, too, have been trying to walk in Saul's armor.

Chapter 50

Delivering the Message

Too little emphasis is placed on the importance of the delivery of the sermon. Again, our friend Manuel Scott tells a classic story. "One day," he recounts, "someone asked, 'Dr. Scott, why do you preach so hard?'" "When your mortar's thin," Dr. Scott replied, "you have to sling it extra hard to make it stick."

Manuel Scott, of course, spoke in jest. His mortar was thick, and he "slung it" with perfection. But the point is that preparing the mortar and applying the mortar are both important. Every baseball player from the Little Leagues to the majors delivers the same size baseball from the pitcher's mound to the plate. But the difference between the Little Leaguer and the professional is the manner in which they deliver it.

The delivery of the message should always be natural. With my discovery of principle preaching came the realization that I had been parroting other preachers in my content and emulating them in my delivery as well. In fact, today I can do a pretty good job of entertaining a crowd by imitating some of the best-known pulpiteers in America. If preaching is the delivery of truth through a personality, and it is, then it is important that the message of Scripture be allowed to be what *it* is and the preacher be who *he* is.

For many years my own identity as a proclaimer was unclear. I would hear this or that famous preacher, and more than subconsciously begin to emulate them in my preaching style. If preaching is a symphony, it should always be played in the key of "B natural." Don't change the message, and don't change the personality.

As young preachers, we all struggled with our pulpit identity. For too many years I found mine in being someone else. But I have come to understand it is imperative that you be yourself. Remember, if they don't buy you, they won't buy what you're selling. If they turn you off, you'll never get a hearing to tell them what God says. People quickly detect a fake. Above all, be yourself.

If the Lord has put you in the right place, with people you can relate to, you are thwarting the plan of God by consciously or subconsciously attempting to be somebody else. Why do we think we have to assume a different personality in the pulpit? Lay aside your preacherisms, your assumed mannerisms, your holy quiver, and get up there and talk to the people.

I've been seated on the platform with preachers from all over the world who would whisper to me, "Boy, this sure is a good crowd tonight." But when they walk to the pulpit to preside, rather than saying, "Boy, this sure is a good crowd tonight," they say something like, "We are delighted with the magnitude of the congregation."

Jesus was a carpenter and he lived in an agrarian culture. He talked to farmers and tax collectors. He won over the prostitute and the thief. Only the phoney Pharisees rejected Him. The common people heard him gladly. He was one of them. He loved them. He related to them, and it drove the religious establishment crazy.

If you want a hearing, be yourself. Don't act like a preacher, don't look like a preacher, and don't talk like a preacher. Someone said, "So live that no one will suspect you're a preacher, but if they find out you are, they won't be surprised." That's good advice, and I commend it to you.

Clearly, television, for better or worse, is the single most important influence on our culture, and it is a medium of one-to-one communication. Television personalities, reporters, newscasters, and commentators do not *yell* at us or talk *at* us; they talk *to* us as if we were the only person in the world.

Talk to the people. Be yourself. Certain things you will say will excite you, anger you, stir you, humor you. Your inflections will rise and fall. Your volume will be varied, and your words will be well-paced. But you should basically communicate not as an orator, but as a friend. I shall always revere the talents of the great orators, but let me tell you frankly that the day of the orator was another day.

On another equally important note, I challenge you to memorize your material. The single most important contribution you will make to your delivery is to master your material and memorize it. Let me calm your fears by telling you it is much easier to memorize than you suppose. When you're using other people's material, simply parroting the words of another, it is difficult to memorize. But when the Holy Spirit has birthed the material in your own heart; when it is your insight, your principles and your application, you will find as you begin memorizing that you already know what you're trying to memorize. It's in your mind, it's in your heart because it came from you.

As you memorize, you will have to work at recalling some of the sermon, but you will discover that you already know it far better than you realize you do, *if* it is your *own* Holy Spirit-birthed material.

When I finish writing a sermon, I immediately close my eyes, visualize my Sunday morning congregation, and see how much of the sermon I remember. I preach it out loud and, to my amazement, find I have to glance back very few times, and that, in fact, I can quote 90 to 95 percent of it.

Good sermons are not written; they are rewritten, and rewritten, and rewritten. And with each rewriting, they are condensed. Consolidate your finished product down to thirty or forty key words. My average introduction is two minutes and contains three or four thoughts. I condense those thoughts into one word each. Then I find a common denominator within each and memorize them. I do the same throughout the message.

If you are following a *state-explain-apply-illustrate* approach to the principles you are preaching, those four ingredients in each of three or four principles will give you only twelve or sixteen key words you memorize. Within the explanation portion, you will have to memorize more words because it contains more background material, Greek word meanings, etc. That portion of the sermon will take you longer to memorize, but you can do it more easily than you imagine.

You will immediately find yourself to be a far better communicator for several reasons. First, when you memorize the material, you have an increased sense of confidence. You are the master of the material. It is your slave. When you are chained to notes, they are the master and you are the slave. Confidence, authority, and freedom occur when you memorize your material.

Second, eye contact is created. It is much easier to persuade people when you are looking into their eyes than when you are looking down at your notes and they are looking at the top of your head.

Third, it is easier to pace yourself. A certain nervousness is omitted when we eliminate notes. A natural pace, an increased naturalness in inflection, good changes of volume—all these occur far more naturally in the relaxed pace that comes from looking constantly into the face of your hearers.

Fourth, it gives the Holy Spirit the opportunity to bring instantaneously to your mind something you hadn't planned to say. It also means he can eliminate something you had planned to say that you needn't say. Any time I struggle for a thought, I assume the Holy Spirit is blocking it out and I move on.

In our Houston church, we had two morning services that were quite different. The congregation tended to be younger at the earlier contemporary service. Often I dealt with certain subjects a bit differently with this group than I did with the older, more mature congregation at the later service. That is not to suggest any compromise with sin or watering down of the message. It is to say that while the truth never changes, the means by which we state it may change, and the Holy Spirit may bring different spontaneity, pacing, augmentation, and creativity to each sermon. Each Monday I had to determine which of two Sunday morning sermons I wanted to send out through our tape ministry, because they were always somewhat different. The uniqueness and freshness that made them different, I attribute to the spontaneity of the Holy Spirit.

Is delivering that baseball important? Indeed, it is. Ask Nolan Ryan, who pitched seven no-hitters, and the thousands of frustrated batters who tried to hit his pitch. Don't underestimate the importance of delivery.

Chapter 51

Extending the Invitation

Our Lord entrusts to us no greater honor than extending his invitation for people to come to him. His last words to mankind were an invitation: "And the Spirit and the bride say, Come. And let him that heareth say, Come. And let him that is athirst come. And whosoever will, let him take the water of life freely" (Rev. 22:17).

While many forms of invitation may be extended, every sermon should be marked by an appeal to persuade the hearer to make some kind of response. The tangible expression of that response is important. It might be filling out a card, raising a hand, moving to an inquiry room, coming forward, or some other means, but it is important that the hearer be afforded the opportunity to make a tangible response.

Virtually everyone our Lord called to follow him, he called publicly. He called Zaccheus to come down out of the tree; Matthew, to leave his tax collecting; Peter and John, to leave their fishing boats. A physical expression of the intent of the heart was normally called for. Indeed, our Lord warned, "Whosoever therefore shall confess me before men, him will I confess also before my Father which is in heaven. But whosoever shall deny me before men, him will I also deny before my Father which is in heaven" (Matt. 10:32–33).

It is not that he needs our public stand as much as we need it. And, of course, the world needs the testimony and encouragement of our public profession of faith. It is for that reason that I am most comfortable with extending a public invitation that calls for the respondents to come to the front of the church and stand before the pulpit. Incidentally, for some years now, I have added a second invitation. Just before the benediction, I invited those who did not come forward publicly to go directly to the counseling room and join those who did.

The invitation of our Lord must never be extended in the flesh without the powerful touch of the Holy Spirit. It must never be manipulative, high pressure, overly extended, embarrassing, or confusing. One of the most important ingredients in the public invitation is the manner in which it is begun. A smooth transition from sermon to invitation is best accomplished with the help of background music and prayer. I finished every sermon by asking the people to pray. Immediately the praise band, organ, choir, or ensemble began. A soloist should never sing during an invitation as it draws attention from the pulpit, the focal point of the invitation.

The one who has delivered the message should extend the invitation. To give an invitation after someone else's message is most difficult. As heads were bowed and music played, I would pray a simple prayer that encapsulated the message with an appeal to God that each hearer would respond with a public commitment.

Few things are more important in the invitation than specific instruction. Exactly what are you asking your hearers to do? I once heard a stirring patriotic sermon with an invitation so confusing and general that I wasn't sure whether the speaker wanted me to join the church or the Marines! Directing people to raise their hands, then look up, then stand up, then come forward approaches the borderline of manipulation. Some people might respond in sincerity to this method, but I have too often seen the response of many confused sheep among the goats. The battle for the invitation is not won in the pulpit. It is won in the prayer closet. It is won in advance. Trust the Holy Spirit to tug at the hearts of the people and bring them to the altar.

It is extremely important to be honest in your invitation. If you tell the people, "We're going to sing three verses," sing three verses. If you tell them, "This is the last verse," let it be the last. We should be cautioned at the extremes of both an invitation too long and one too short. Don't be afraid to sing more than two or three verses. If God is moving, let it go on. And above all, don't limit God by saying, "We'll stand and sing three verses, and if no one comes forward, we'll close." It takes time for people to assimilate what they've heard and get the courage to come forward. Throughout my ministry, I have seen the majority of those who have publicly responded in an invitation come on the fourth verse or beyond.

Conversely, don't extend the invitation beyond the movement of God. Don't preach during the invitation, and do little, if any, continued exhortation. Let the Holy Spirit do the work, and when you sense he is finished, close the invitation.

Don't underestimate the value of a militant invitation. Songs like "Stand Up for Jesus" or "Onward Christian Soldiers" can stir the heart to respond. Plan a simple system of communication between you and the person who is directing the invitation music. You and you alone must determine what songs are sung and when. If, for example, after three verses of "Just as I Am" the invitation hymn is changed to "Have Thine Own Way," it is the preacher, not the choir director, who should determine it is time to change. A simple signal of two fingers, for example, can refer the person leading the music to a previously determined invitation hymn.

To extend the invitation is to extend the love of the Savior, and this must be done with a compassionate heart. Warmth and tenderness are always in order. Harshness and condemnation never are. Don't scold the people or threaten them. And certainly don't try to preach above the music. Let God do the work and warmly welcome those who respond. Unless the attendance is rather large, as in a crusade where the people need to see the evangelist in the pulpit extending the invitation, it is often good to leave the platform and greet the people at ground level, welcoming them, shaking their hands, even embracing them as they come.

What a joy to watch God at work, changing minds and transforming hearts. Who can remain unstirred at the coming of thousands upon thousands during an invitation in a Billy Graham crusade? But as important and moving as that may be, it is just as meaningful that one young child has come to respond to the invitation of Jesus in the smallest country church. With clean hands, pure motives, and a tender heart, offer yourself to our precious Lord as the extension of his love as you invite those for whom he died to come to his waiting arms.

Chapter 52

Doing Good Follow-up

To take new members in the front door is one thing. To keep them from going out the back door is quite another. That they "dip 'em and drop 'em" ought not be said of any church. The process of evangelism is never complete until the "evangelized" become evangelists themselves. The conservation of the converts is of utmost importance.

Building a great church means building great people. It involves making disciples of converts and witnesses of disciples. A good basic follow-up program consists of several principles:

1. The new converts must be well-born into the kingdom; it is impossible to make disciples of unbelievers. For many years at First Baptist Houston, we followed the traditional Southern Baptist method of counseling with those who came to make decisions on the front row of the church as the invitation music continued. They were then immediately introduced to the congregation with an explanation of their decision.

Through the years, I came to believe that not enough time was being given to counseling. We began taking the people to a decision counseling room, followed by presentation to the church at a later date. This can be done in the following Sunday service, with pictures in the church paper, or even from the baptistry at the time of their baptism. The counseling room might, incidentally, best be referred to as the prayer room, the decision room, or the inquiry room. The word *counseling* has connotations that you might not want to project.

In the decision room, a trained decision counselor should greet each individual, couple, or family. The chair of the decision counselor should face those making the decisions and be separated from other groupings around the room. One individual might welcome a couple or a family, but in the interest of time, might determine it best that another person be brought over to talk to an individual family member.

Whether a person is coming simply to join your church from another church or to receive Christ as Savior, begin with the assumption that none are believers and lead them through the process of giving their testimonies in order to validate their conversion. If they are believers, they will not be offended. If they are not, they may be filtered through the process at the time and thus led to Christ.

Counselors should be well-trained, friendly, mature believers, willing to spend extra time after the service is over. Their families might have to wait for them. The person making the decision should *never* be asked to fill out a decision card at the beginning of the conversation. After a person has been led to Christ or adequate assurance has been given that he or she already knows Christ, the record of the decision may then be made. Give the person time to ask questions. Share literature about the church. Get full and complete information on your decision card. Pray, and introduce the person as a new Christian or a new church member to someone immediately.

Good follow-up begins in the follow-up room. Decisions must not be allowed to abort at this delicate moment. Counseling of new members should be done in a room located near the auditorium. This should include introduction of staff, get-acquainted time, and explanation of the contents of the new members' packet.

2. A biannual membership survey should be conducted to check up on new members and find out where they are and how they are doing.

3. Every new family should be assigned to a deacon or other responsible person for follow-up. They should be visited in the home the week they join, with a second visit a week later, a third visit a month later, and a fourth visit six months later.

4. All new members should be told they are being automatically enrolled in Sunday morning Bible study. Their names are entered into the Sunday school register on Monday morning and immediately mailed to their new teacher and director. These persons are now someone's responsibility.

5. A new members' class taught by the pastor, associate pastor, or qualified layman should be conducted on a revolving basis for thirteen weeks during the evening training hour. Membership is automatic and attendance is expected.

Chapter 53

The Meaning and Method of Baptism

C ertainly, we respect the wide divergence of opinions within the body of Christ. Nowhere is this more true than in the ordinance of baptism. Let me share with you the views and practices of our church and denomination. The very name Baptist, of course, implies some unique denominational distinctions about baptism.

In earlier years, Baptists were called anabaptists—that is, the "again Baptists" or "the ones who baptize again." Out of the Protestant Reformation came the reality that some true believers had not experienced authentic New Testament baptism. Baptism is for a believer, not an unbeliever. If a person goes through a baptismal ceremony and subsequently becomes a Christian, he should be baptized again. Baptism demonstrates something. It shows something. And if that something has not happened, it might well be meaningless.

That something, of course, is twofold. First, baptism is a picture of our identity with Christ and what he did for us in his death and resurrection. Our immersion under the water pictures his death. Rising from the water pictures his resurrection.

Further symbolism in immersion baptism pictures the death of our old rebellious nature and the beginning of a resurrected and yielded life. These two beautiful symbolisms have no saving power, but they do have great persuasive power. They visualize to the world what Jesus did for us and the transformation of life that has occurred because we have embraced it.

The word *baptism* is a Greek word *baptizo,* meaning "to cover," or "as a sunken ship submerged under the water." There *is* a Greek word for "sprinkle" which is *rhantizo,* but this word is not used in the Scripture in connection with baptism. As with the Lord's Supper, immersion has no saving grace, but is a beautiful picture of what has happened in our life.

Sprinkling pictures little and is virtually a picture of a picture. If I were to join the Air Force, I would symbolically show my union with this branch of the military, characterized by flying, by placing wings on my uniform. If I am not really a member of the Air Force, simply putting on the uniform doesn't make me an airman. If I really am a member, taking it off doesn't mean I am no longer an airman. Both the jacket and the wings are only symbolic. If I remove my wedding ring, I am still married. If I am unmarried, simply putting on a wedding ring doesn't make me married. It, too, is only symbolic.

The symbolism of wings is flying. The symbolism of the ring is its endless nature; the ideal for marriage. The symbolism of immersion baptism is the cross and its transforming power in my life.

The question arises, "Who can baptize?" Whether in a swimming pool, a church, or a river in Africa, individuals should baptize on the authority of their church. In Acts 2:41, those who were baptized were added unto *them.* The *them* to which the verse refers is the church birthed on that day. The New Testament knows nothing of baptism apart from the authority of the church.

Baptism is not essential to salvation; it is essential to obedience. I cannot believe that if a person receives Christ as his Savior and dies on the way to the baptistry, he will be forever lost.

At the conclusion of Simon Peter's sermon on the day of Pentecost, the people in Acts 2:37 were convicted in their hearts and asked what to do. Note that the question was not "what must I do to be saved" but "what shall we do?" They had heard the Word, believed it, and received it with yielded hearts of faith. Verse 41 says it this way: "They gladly received His word." Believing and receiving the gospel of Christ's death and resurrection brings salvation. These humble hearts simply asked, "What's next?" The answer of Acts 2:38 was "repent and be baptized." When a person says to me, "I have heard the gospel and believe. What do I do next?" My response is, "Repent and be baptized—change the way you live and join the church."

This story is quite different from the one in Acts 16 where the Philippian jailer had not heard the word of God but was under conviction because of the faith and praise of Paul and Silas. The Acts 16 question of the Philippian jailer was not "Sirs, what must I do?" It was "Sirs, what must I do *to be saved?*" The only answer the Bible ever gives to *that* question is, "Believe on the Lord Jesus Christ and thou shalt be saved." In Acts 2, the people received the Word and were therefore already saved. The question was simply, "What do we do next?" The answer was, "Change your life and join the church."

Acts 2:38 further states, "Repent, and be baptized . . . *for* the remission of sins." The word *for* has many different meanings in English. In verse 38, the Greek word is *eis,* meaning "in response to." Repentance and baptism are not the cause of forgiveness but the effect. The people were told to change their lives and be baptized not in order to be saved but in response to having been saved when they believed the gospel.

A further example may be seen in Matthew 12:41. "The men of Nineveh . . . repented *at* the preaching of Jonah." The word *eis* is here interpreted "at" and is used to explain that the Ninevites repented *in response to* the preaching of Jonah.

Read again the first portion of John 3:16. "*For* God so loved the world that he gave his only begotten Son." Did God give his Son in order to love the world or because he already loved it?

Imagine you are seated next to me on a train going from Houston to Dallas. In your pocket is a gun, and you intend to go to Dallas to kill a man. If I ask you, "Why you are going to Dallas?" you will say, "For murder." You mean, "In order to obtain or commit a murder." If the following week I see you on the same train, handcuffed to a sheriff, and ask, "Why are you going to Dallas?" you will again reply, "For murder." But this time you're not going to commit a murder; you're going because a murder has already been committed. The first *for* is a cause—in order to. The second *for* is an effect—in response to.

One of the recurring problems with which I have had to deal through the years is confusion over persons who were sprinkled as infants. Some of my best pastor friends in other denominations observe this practice and do not believe that the child is being saved or that his sins are being washed away. They believe this is simply an act of commitment by the parents. But I have often found this to be confusing to people when they grow up and make their own decisions to receive Christ as Savior. Not only do they often have difficulty making such a decision because "they were really saved back then," but it further clouds the issue of New Testament immersion baptism.

In First Baptist Houston, we regularly had an act of parental dedication in which parents presented their newborns to the congregation. At that time, the parents made a commitment to raise the child in such a manner that their subsequent conversion will one day more likely occur. But we did not sprinkle infants, and I think this helps us avoid confusion later on. Each of us must make the decision of salvation for himself. An infant, of course, can make no such decision, nor does he need to. It seems reasonable that baptism which pictures our salvation is deferred until *after* our personal experience of salvation has actually occurred.

You, of course, will filter these things through your own theology and church practices, but these thoughts will help shed some light on the subject.

Following a public profession of faith by both children and adults, we urged them to go through a brief six-week course on salvation, church membership, baptism, witnessing, and other matters before they were baptized. Some young people and adults, however, come from a strong Christian background and may be baptized more quickly. As completing catechism and being confirmed is not tantamount to salvation, neither is class training and immersion baptism. All these things teach us about salvation, but each person must make that decision for himself.

At First Baptist Houston, we had a baptism committee, a deep pool baptistry, dressing rooms, robes, hair dryers, towels, etc. It will be helpful for each pastor to enlist the services of laymen and laywomen to assist in this meaningful experience.

Chapter 54

Administering the Lord's Supper

T he Lord's Supper is also called "the Table of the Lord," "the Lord's Supper," "the Sacraments," and "Communion." There are as many views and methods of observing this wonderful ordinance of our Lord as there are names. This chapter and the one on baptism reflect the views of my own denomination.

The frequency of the Lord's Supper is optional. Jesus did not say whether to observe it weekly, monthly, or quarterly. He did say, "As often as you do it, do it in remembrance of me" (See Luke 22:19; 1 Cor. 11:24). In First Baptist Houston, we chose to do so approximately once a quarter—four times a year.

This tradition has developed in our denomination partly in reaction to those who take it every Sunday and view it as an instrument of saving grace. All churches, of course, that receive the bread and cup weekly do not believe it plays a role in a person's salvation, but some do. We believe it is a memorial that reminds us visually of the broken body and spilled blood of Jesus on the cross for our sins but is not a medium through which we receive his grace. We reject the doctrine of transubstantiation held by Roman Catholics that the bread and wine literally become the body and blood of Christ.

Certainly, Jesus said, "This is my body, broken for you, and this is my blood shed for you" (see Luke 22:19–20). But time-honored principles of hermeneutics require us to answer the question, "Did Jesus mean what he said, or did he mean what he meant?" When he said,

"If thy right hand offends thee, cut it off" (Matt. 5:30), did he mean take an ax and sever it from your arm, or did he mean remove those things that are an impediment to your spiritual growth?

There is, incidentally, a style of cup with an indenture that holds the bread within the cup. By this means, both elements can be served at one time, shortening the time spent administering the elements. Normally, a person or committee is designated to purchase and prepare the elements, placing them on trays covered with beautiful linens before the pulpit and across the worship center. In many churches, the elements of the Lord's Supper are served to the congregation by deacons or other delegated church officials. They may be served as well by anyone designated by the pastor and approved by the congregation. The beauty and significance of the observance lies not in the hand of the person who administers the cup but in the heart of the person who receives it.

The cups, once received and used, are normally either placed in special holders in back of the seat in front of each worshiper or collected by those who served them. A different set of people, perhaps a committee, normally gathers up the utensils and cleans and stores them in preparation for the next observance of this ordinance.

The serving of the Lord's Supper should emphasize the following four things.

1. An inward look. The people should be challenged to look within their heart, confess and forsake sin, and be forgiven and cleansed before receiving the cup. The apostle Paul said, "Whosoever shall eat this bread, and drink this cup of the Lord, unworthily, shall be guilty of the body and blood of the Lord" (1 Cor. 11:27). Frankly, I really don't know everything this means, nor do I want to.

2. A backward look. Paul said, When you drink this, remember Jesus, for in so doing, "ye do show the Lord's death till he come" (1 Cor. 11:26). The purpose of the cup and the bread is to visually reinforce the experience of the cross and all its wondrous meaning in our lives.

3. An outward look. Our Lord said if our brother has anything against us, we are to leave our offering at the altar and go make peace with our brother (see Matt. 18:15–21). We are not to receive the

Lord's Supper with bitterness and unforgiveness in our hearts. If we have such attitudes, we should make them right before we participate. If that is not possible, pass the Supper by, make peace with your brother, and then take it next time.

4. A forward look. Paul said, In the Lord's Supper, we "show forth the Lord's death till he come" (1 Cor. 11:26).

An inward look, a backward look, an outward look, and a forward look. Taking the Lord's Supper is a serious matter and should be given serious thought as we participate.

In the ceremony at First Baptist Houston, a Lord's Supper table covered with a white linen cloth was placed before the pulpit with covered trays. I stood on the floor behind the middle of the table with our chairman of deacons at one end and a vice-chairman at the other. Normally the associate pastor stood beside me. The two men at the ends of the table removed the cloth, folding it carefully. They then served each of our deacons on the front row a plate, who in turn passed it to their section of worshipers throughout the sanctuary.

When everyone had been served, I read a Scripture passage about the breaking of bread, and prayed God's blessing upon it. Then I said, "Let us all partake of the bread." The process was then repeated with the cup. A prayer was said, and the service either continued or was concluded.

In our church and thousands of others, it has long been a tradition to sing a hymn and receive an offering for the poor when the Table of the Lord is observed. This we did at the doors as our people left. By the way, when Jesus said, "Drink ye all of it" (Matt. 26:27), he was not saying, "Don't leave any; drink it all." He was saying, "All of you are to drink it."

The observance of the Lord's Supper is one of the most beautiful, bonding elements in the life of God's children. Your people will be deeply moved and blessed. Make it a special time for your congregation.

Chapter 55

Calling Out the Called

F ew contributions you will make to the kingdom of God exceed the importance of encouraging and developing ministers and leaders. A regular challenge to your people to use their gifts in the work of the Lord is a high priority; training and actually using them are of equal importance. The wise leader will do this on a regular basis, and develop, with the minister of education, an ongoing program of training workers. But I speak here of extending the challenge and call of our Lord to those whom he has ordained to full-time Christian ministry.

In a very real sense, twentieth-century Christian philosopher Francis Schaeffer was right when he taught that every Christian is in full-time ministry. I refer, however, to the vocational minister whose salary is paid by a church or Christian organization and who devotes his full time to nothing else.

The beauty of the work of the Lord is that no matter how a person may be gifted or employed, there is somewhere in the world the need and the opportunity to use his talents in full-time Christian ministry. Agricultural missionaries, for example, are doing a marvelous work in teaching people better methods of providing for the physical needs of their families and their countrymen, all the while witnessing to them about Jesus Christ.

Often we report the visible results of an outreach event, "There were twenty who accepted Christ, ten who joined the church, plus a few rededications and one for 'special service.'" The obvious inference is that the rededications and special service decisions were somehow less important than the others. Next Sunday morning, ask your congregation this question: "How many of you accepted Christ as your Savior at some point in your life and subsequently recommitted your life to him? And, as far as changing the direction of your life, your recommitment was more significant than your conversion?" You will be amazed to find the latter number is probably greater than the first.

Additionally, too little importance is placed upon inviting people to give their lives in full-time Christian ministry. In fact, it is seldom done at all. In my ministry in Houston, I never recall preaching a stirring message on missions and thrusting the sickle into the harvest without reaping a large response of those who were ready and willing to go to the mission field. Admittedly, not all actually get there, but certainly a number do.

When extending an invitation to full-time Christian ministry, several things should be emphasized. First of all, it is important to be clear. Few people who respond will be able to say, "God is calling me to a particular ministry in a specific place." The invitation should be clearly given for response by men and women who feel a stirring in their soul that this is the will of God. His direction in our lives is an unfolding revelation. Only after we respond in obedience today does he shed light on tomorrow. Emphasize to the congregation that you will help them come to understand and refine God's call on their lives. Little did Saul of Tarsus dream what lay before him when he answered the call of Jesus, "Lord, what wilt thou have me to do?" (Acts 9:6).

Help the people understand that if they can be happy doing anything else, they should do it. A life of full-time Christian ministry is filled with peril and discouragement as well as blessing and joy. There will be times of loneliness, rejection, failure, and despair, but blessed will be the journey.

Help them understand that a call to serve is a call to prepare. God's great servants have always spent long years in preparation. Whether in the classroom setting or the backside of the desert, there is much to be learned. We don't start at the "top." We're not Billy Graham overnight. And the joy of the ministry is not the "spotlight" of man but the "well done" of the Lord.

The Lord puts us in the small places first to develop our faithfulness. After forty-eight years of ministry, I still wake up every morning and wonder how all this could be happening to me. The first five years of my ministry, I preached and led the music in one-room country schoolhouses, county jails, nursing homes, etc., and never saw more than a hundred people together in any one place at any one time. In my heart of hearts, I know that being faithful over these smaller opportunities had something to do with the larger opportunities that came my way.

Sermons that "call out the called" should contain two things. First, they should include the need. A lost world is waiting for Christian workers. It is an embarrassment to the gospel that 95 percent of the world's Christian workers are in North America, which has only five percent of the world's people, while only five percent of Christian workers valiantly minister to the other 95 percent around the world.

Second, the sermon should contain an appeal to listen to your heart. The tug to "respond" and the pull to "go" are not from Satan; they are from God. How do you know when God is calling you? You just know. And if you know, say yes. Take the first step of willingness, and God will take it from there.

When persons respond to the invitation for special service, follow-up on them. The immediate first step will be to lead them to a quiet room where you can spend thirty minutes to an hour talking about what comes next regarding refining the call, educational opportunities, and requirements. Spend time answering questions and urge the person to continue to pray. The second step is a follow-up meeting with representatives from various agencies within your denomination to talk about particular fields of service.

Keep a list and stay in touch. Cultivate those people who respond. Encourage them. Whatever you do, don't let them "fall through the cracks." Their decisions came in response to the stirring of the Holy Spirit in their hearts. Keep fanning the flame until it is burning brightly.

Chapter 56

Great Preachers or Great Pastors

T wo obvious functions are required in the ministry of the pastor. The first is to shepherd the people of God. The second is to deliver God's Word to them. While there are obviously many other duties, these are the most important.

In the smaller church, the pastor must often assume the role of printer, maintenance man, custodian, and a myriad of other responsibilities. As the congregation grows, he will be blessed with the services of other gifted persons who can perform these duties. Obviously, the pastor will be the vision-caster, the motivator, the fund-raiser, and the administrator as well. But in the broadest sense of the term, he is first and foremost a pastor and a preacher.

The ministry of the pastor is to shepherd the flock. This means taking time to know the people and being involved in their lives. At lunch, in the hallways, in their homes and hospital rooms, the caring shepherd will know no greater joy than learning to appreciate each member of his congregation.

But he is the pulpiteer as well. His public ministry of teaching and preaching the Bible, explaining it to the people, and applying it to their lives is his supreme calling. While both of these are distinct ministries, they are inseparably intertwined. A pastor will not endear himself to his people in such a way that they are prepared to hear his heart in the pulpit unless they feel they know him and he truly knows them. His personal ministry to the people will validate the authenticity of his public message. Both threads of ministry are intricately woven into the fabric of the pastorate.

It is at precisely this point, however, that tension might arise not only within the heart of the pastor but between himself and his people. Although it will not be easily developed in the mind of the minister, let alone that of his congregation, pastor and people must ultimately come to accept this insightful truth: *Great preachers are seldom great pastors, and great pastors are seldom great preachers.*

Generally, these two individuals are two entirely different personalities. While human character can be changed, human personality rarely can. We are what we are. The personality and makeup of a great preacher might be described as a "racehorse." This kind of man is not usually comfortable in one-to-one counseling, spending time in the hospital, or visiting shut-ins.

The personality of the person who is first of all a pastor, however, is normally slower, quieter, and more gentle. He is easy to be around and very comfortable in circumstances that are moving slowly. Predictably, when churches change pastors, they tend to seek out one who is the opposite of the pastor they just had. Some will say, "I want a man who is a good pastor. Brother Smith never came to see me when I was sick." After Brother Smith's replacement leaves, they will likely say, "I want a man who is a good preacher this time. His sermons were boring, and I fell asleep when he preached." That great racehorse in the pulpit will likely make you nervous in the hospital room. That great shepherd in your hour of bereavement might put you to sleep from the pulpit.

Ideally, a pastor will have a large measure of both qualities and certainly be growing in both. But never forget that great preachers usually don't make great pastors and great pastors are seldom great preachers. Let me make three observations:

1. Scripture is clear that the body of Christ is filled with people with unique individual giftedness. This makes for good, corporate, well-functioning ministry.

2. The wise pastor will *recognize* and program *to* his weaknesses. The weaker preacher might employ an associate who is a strong teacher. The weaker pastor will enlist staff members who are gifted at

hospital visitation and counseling. By the way, before you terminate the services of a faithful staff member, reevaluate whether he is in the right position. Reassigning an administrator to the pastoral care division of our staff years ago was one of the best decisions I ever made.

3. Teach your people to understand and accept the difference between a pastor and a preacher. God's people, given the facts, may be trusted to do the right thing. Help them to understand what I am saying here. They will be supportive, and you will be better for it.

4. Accept yourself. Each of us possesses a different set of gifts and talents. Do your best to enhance and expand your abilities while accepting your own uniqueness. God has made you a very special person and has placed you in the right church at the right time. Accept who you are, be yourself, and enjoy it.

Part 6

Worship Services

Chapter 57

Multiple Services

B y all means, use your existing building twice or even three times each Sunday morning before you build a new one. Classrooms and worship centers used only an hour or two a week need to be considered for other purposes. Starting schools, scheduling additional services, and sponsoring Bible studies are certainly high priority in that consideration.

The question is, "Do we start new services in order to grow, or do we start them because we are already growing?" The answer to both questions is yes. Prevailing wisdom says that if your existing space is 80 percent full, it's time to build or start a second service. Frankly, I have a problem with that philosophy because another question must first be answered.

Is the facility 80 percent full because you are in a growth mode and have moved from 50 percent to 60 to 70, to 80, and it is apparent that you'll soon be out of space? Or is it at 80 percent because you're not growing or you're running 80 percent while you once ran 100 percent and then 90? In the latter case, factors other than space should first be addressed. Let me say that again. If you are at 80 percent because nothing's happening in your church and you've been there for a long time or because you have declined to 80 percent, starting more services is not the answer.

If, however, you have grown to 80 percent and are still growing, it is time to consider multiple services. Obviously you don't need more room until you reach 100 percent, but a church in a growing mode will be there in a few months, and a great deal of advanced planning and preparation are required.

One of the more appealing factors in starting a second service is that *people like choices.* All other things being equal, I will opt for the church that gives me a choice to come at 8:30 or 10:30 rather than the one that says I must come at 10:30. Something psychological happens here. We do like a sense of control. Perhaps that's good; perhaps it isn't. But for better or worse, we do want the ability to choose.

If your worship service begins at 10:00 or 11:00, you should get immediate growth by adding an "early option." I have found 8:30 A.M. to be the best time for that option. To your surprise, you may find married young adults as well as senior adults will like the earlier time. Seniors are early risers. Sixty to seventy percent of our seniors arrive forty minutes before any morning Bible study or worship service, regardless of the time. They like to get there early, miss the heat of the day, and have a leisurely and relaxed time for coffee and fellowship with their friends. It is also a great attraction to seniors to be able to leave the facilities before the heavier flow of traffic comes in for the later services.

Additionally, many married young adults find the early option to be attractive. Remember, of course, that the nursery must be well-staffed and functioning thirty minutes before the service begins. Little children often wake up early. Babies are sometimes wide awake and ready for that early feeding by 5:00 or 6:00 A.M.

I personally find the early option extremely appealing. In my retirement years, I look forward to visiting other churches. My first act will be to determine the time of their earliest service of the day. That's the one I'll attend. I look forward to having the day free to enjoy a leisurely Sunday with my family.

The same factors enter into the decision on the advisability of multiple Sunday schools. Here are several possible models to consider.

1. Sunday school space is cramped, but a lot of room to grow remains in the worship center. The answer? One central worship service at 10:00 A.M. with two Sunday school options—one before and one after the worship service.

2. Plenty of room to grow in Sunday school with a worship service at near capacity. The answer? A central Sunday school at 9:45 or 10:00, with worship services at 8:30 and 11:00.

3. Both Sunday school and worship center have limited space, both are growing and approaching capacity attendance. There are two possible answers:

Option 1: Flip-flop services: *Schedule A,* Sunday school at 9:30; worship service at 10:45. *Schedule B,* worship service at 9:30; Sunday school at 10:45.

Option 2: A staggered schedule: *Schedule A,* Sunday school at 8:30; worship at 9:45. *Schedule B,* Sunday school at 9:45; worship at 11:00. I personally prefer Option 2 for three reasons: (1) it is easy to understand, (2) it is naturally sequential as everyone goes to Sunday school before they attend worship, and (3) traffic flow is the best.

There are, of course, varying other options. Some churches even have three worship services. Others stay with two but add a Saturday night option. This concerns me a little about what we may be teaching our children regarding the sanctity of the Lord's Day, but each church must determine God's will in this matter.

In multiple worship services, I urge you to consider the possibility of different kinds of music. One service might be traditional and the other contemporary. I think it would be fantastic for a church to offer four services on Sunday: traditional, contemporary, classic, and country.

Before you begin, be certain you are fully staffed with musicians, ushers, greeters, and traffic control personnel. With multiple services, it is essential that you not develop a "herd-the-cattle" mentality. There will always be some people leaving a classroom or the worship center as others are waiting to come in. If you hurry the people, you will develop a shopping mall mentality and lose the opportunity for relaxed, warm fellowship between brothers and sisters in Christ, many of whom see one another only on Sunday morning.

To avoid this, allow more time than is normally provided between services. Spread the schedule out. We offer twenty- to twenty-five-minute turnaround times in our Sunday morning schedule. It is conducive to the fellowship so essential for building a great church.

In multiple Sunday schools, every age should be given an opportunity to attend a class. Never allow a situation in which the young people or any other group can go to Sunday school at only one hour. Survey the people in advance. Determine which schedule they will attend, and then staff the Sunday school appropriately. At the 9:30 Sunday school, for example, you might have four classes for teenagers: One each for ninth, tenth, eleventh, and twelfth graders. If the 11:00 Sunday school is going to be a lot smaller, you will still want to offer a class for all four grades, but it might be only one class in which all four grades are combined together. This concept must be carried out throughout the entire Sunday school.

There is a danger that the quality of teaching might drop when you go to a second Sunday school. Take your time and be certain you have staffed it with an adequate number of well-trained teachers. "Taking your time" is always called for in preparing to go to multiple worship services and Sunday schools. For one thing, it will take people a while to decide which service or Sunday school they wish to attend. Time will be required to take the survey, compile the results, enlist and train workers, and inform the people. If you jump up and start two Sunday schools next month, you'll regret it.

One of the more difficult decisions will involve young people and children who wish to attend a particular Sunday school while their parents choose to attend a certain worship service at the same time. Immediately you are faced with the issue of divided families. Some families will choose to do this, and some will not. But it will be an issue, and you might temporarily lose some numerical attendance. When adults are in worship at the same time their children are in Sunday school, there is a tendency with some people to "get it over all at once." In this scenario, the children never go to worship and the parents never attend Sunday school. However, while that might happen in some cases, the overall net gain in your church will likely be more than worth it. This is a decision you will have to make thoughtfully with your leadership.

Growth by starting missions and building new buildings is valid growth, and starting those missions and going to multiple services are, of course, not mutually exclusive. But at least before you build more buildings, give serious consideration to multiple services.

Chapter 58

The Traditional Music Ministry

O n the last day of 1997, popular Christian talk show host Marlin Maddox arrested my attention with these words: "For the past twelve months the number one subject we have debated on this program is not abortion or homosexuality, but the raging issue of the new contemporary praise music and the older traditional church music." This is an issue you will not sidestep. It is not going away. It is here to stay. The new wave of praise music is everywhere, in virtually every church, and it need not be divisive.

At First Baptist Houston, we were somewhat successful in blending the two. We had two Sunday morning worship services—one contemporary and one traditional. Although the traditional service had some contemporary music, it was still heavily traditional and, over a period of time, became well accepted by our more traditional members.

Personal tastes, however, are not exclusively divided along lines of age. There are younger people who prefer the traditional, just as there are older members who prefer the contemporary. Approximately 30 percent of the people in the contemporary worship service at the Houston church are age fifty and older. But argue either side of the case, and I strongly believe it is largely a matter of taste. There are many ways to do both in your church, and I urge you to commit yourself to finding the one that is right for you.

The wise pastor will not resist the new music. Those who prefer it will leave your church and look elsewhere. And there is a danger of becoming an older congregation much too quickly.

But there is another danger equally important—the mistake of embracing the contemporary music exclusively and throwing out the old. The great hymns of the church are here to stay. It will never quite be said like it is said in "And Can It Be That I Should Gain," "A Mighty Fortress Is Our God," "Come, Thou Almighty King," and "When morning gilds the skies my heart awakening cries, may Jesus Christ be praised." Of course, you can lead your church to sing traditional music exclusively, but you do so at the risk of losing the young. Or you can lead your church to use contemporary music exclusively and lose something of the great heritage of our faith as well as the people who love it. I appeal to you to find a way to do both, and I suggest at least *some* possibilities.

1. Blend your worship services with a fifty-fifty balance.

2. Offer a contemporary service that occasionally adds some of the great hymns. Many of them are embraced by the contemporary worshiper. "Holy, Holy, Holy" is an example of such. Our younger crowd loves to worship our holy Lord with that hymn. And, of course, use some praise songs in your traditional service.

3. Have two services with entirely different music. If you do this, I must emphasize the importance of the pastor preaching at both services. Having a young staff member preach at the contemporary music service while an older pastor preaches at the traditional music service is not wise. It is impossible to maintain the unity of the church with two different styles of services unless the pastor preaches at both.

Let's think together about the value of both kinds of music. Across the centuries the church has loved to worship. The word *worship* is an Anglo-Saxon word, *worth-ship,* meaning the manner in which we express the worth or value of a person or an object. The word *worship* has grandeur about it—a majesty that moves the soul. For decades God's people have worshiped in stained-glass sanctuaries, led by majestic robed choirs, with a spirit of dignity and reverence that is awe inspiring.

I have a deep and abiding love for formal worship. It is, in fact, my personal preference. I especially love the worship of an Episcopal church or a Lutheran or Methodist church, which is often even more formal than the traditional, formal worship of my own denomination. A grand piano and a pipe organ with an orchestra and choir singing the praises of God create a moving and stirring experience. There is grandeur in the great hymns of the faith, a sense of connectedness to our roots that lifts and inspires the soul of the traditional worshiper, and I, for one, love it.

Pageantry, handbells, orchestras, children's choirs—even the lighting of candles and processions at certain special services such as Christmas Eve—are among First Baptist Houston's own great traditions. Others will follow me in the pastorate of this historic congregation. My prayer for them is that they will never allow the loss of the heritage that is great traditional church music, while giving its rightful place to the "new."

The secret is to find God's way to enrich the great musical tradition of your worshipers with the addition of new contemporary music. Let's talk about that in the next chapter.

Chapter 59

The Contemporary Music Ministry

W hat is acceptable worship? Our first response to that question is normally to think of physical things: guitars or organs, loud music or lights, robes or street clothes, choirs or praise bands. Some much-needed light may be shed on our search for the answer to that question by considering the response of Jesus to the woman at the well:

> The woman saith unto him, Sir, I perceive that thou art a prophet. Our fathers worshipped in this mountain; and ye say, that in Jerusalem is the place where men ought to worship. Jesus saith unto her, Woman, believe me, the hour cometh, when ye shall neither in this mountain, nor yet at Jerusalem, worship the Father. Ye worship ye know not what: we know what we worship: for salvation is of the Jews. But the hour cometh, and now is, when the true worshippers shall worship the Father in spirit and in truth: for the Father seeketh such to worship Him. God is a Spirit: and they that worship Him must worship Him in spirit and in truth (John 4:19–24).

Clearly, the woman had it fixed in her mind that worship was about the physical. Where is the right place to worship? Here or there? We might ask, "Where is the right place to worship—in the company of guitars or organs, praise bands or choirs, new music or old?"

Jesus' answer was at once profound and insightful. "Neither," he said, "is Jerusalem the right place or Mt. Gerazim." It is not a matter of the physical; it is a matter of the heart. How insightful our Lord's response: "They that worship God must worship Him in spirit and in truth."

Our Lord gave two qualifications for acceptable worship. First, it must be done in spirit. That which is not of the heart, born of God, stirred by the Spirit from the depth of the soul, and absolutely sincere, is not acceptable to God.

Second, worship must be in truth. You must have a correct view of a holy God, come to him through the blood of his Son, Jesus Christ, and on the conditions and promises of his Word. That, and only that, is the way to worship him in spirit and in truth. Curiously, our Lord made no mention of style, volume, organ, or guitar. That is never the issue. It is, has always been, and ever will be the attitude of the heart and the foundation of truth.

Jesus told about a Pharisee who prayed "within himself." His high-sounding prayer was rejected. It was, he said, the humble, simple prayer of a brokenhearted tax collector that got through to heaven. He knew nothing of high-sounding phrases at all. The only "song of his soul" was "God, be merciful to me a sinner" (Luke 18:13).

The sincere worship of a brand new convert singing with a clanky old guitar is far more acceptable to God than a lyric soprano with a doctorate in music who does not mean the words she sings. Neither are acceptable worship to God based on their performance, accompaniment, quality, or style. The issue remains the sincerity of a devout heart and the changeless truth upon which it approaches God.

What then is the big attraction about the new music? Several things, I think.

First, and perhaps most importantly, it is *to* God, not *about* God. Sing again the words of your favorite hymns: "Oh, How I Love Jesus," "His Name Is Wonderful," "He Is Lord," and "Down at the Cross Where My Savior Died." It is a rare thing to find such words as "Have Thine Own Way, Lord" among the favorite hymns and gospel songs of the traditional church. They are glorious songs, beloved songs, accurate songs, but they are primarily *about* the Lord—not *to* him.

The young generation of today has been shaken by an unstable world, and it hungers for the stability of reliable, deep, consistent relationships. Where is their authenticity to be found? Where can they find secure relationships? I believe the primary reason for the popularity of the new music among the young is that it is *to* God, not *about* him.

"I Love You, Lord," "You alone are my Strength and Shield, to You alone may my spirit yield." Analyze these songs. Listen to them. They are from the heart to the heart, sung directly to Jesus.

Second, they are predominantly Scripture. Rare it is to find traditional hymns exclusively quoting the Scripture, but the majority of the new songs are Scripture set to music.

Third, it is a style of music with which young people and young adults are familiar. If you go as a missionary to Spain, you had better learn to speak Spanish. If you are called to Germany, you must become fluent in the German language. If you would reach today's youth, you must learn to speak to them in their language, and their language is their music.

Time magazine said recently, "There are 36 million Generation X-ers in America and 34 million have never been to church and aren't going. Their whole world is music. If they are starving to death, before they will buy a sandwich, they will spend their last $10 on the latest CD."

Is there anything holy or unholy about loud or soft, slow or fast, plugged or unplugged, B-flat or F-sharp? I think not. If we are honest, we will acknowledge that the musical style we grew up with and that we are comfortable with is really the issue, not "who is worshiping and who is not." To both groups I would say, "Live and let live." This I firmly believe: We have no right to judge the worship of another person.

We must not say, "I alone am truly worshiping, and your style of music disallows true worship." Unfortunately, I have heard both groups say that about the other. Strangely, our Lord said nothing about music, but he had a lot to say about the sincerity of the heart and about truth.

Charles and John Wesley clearly went to the secular world to learn their music in order to put Christian words to familiar tunes and get the gospel into the ears and hearts of sinners. Many of these former "barroom" songs fill our hymnals today.

Have you ever considered why, through the Book of Psalms, the Lord chose to preserve the words of the oldest worship music but not the music itself? I think he knew that *each generation would write its own music.* And, by the way, all of today's old familiar music was once new unfamiliar music, wasn't it? If things didn't change, we would be singing congregational chants now, wouldn't we. Let's be tolerant of one another. There is a place and a need in the church for both styles of music. It is not uniformity of music, color, length of hair, or financial status for which our Lord pleaded when he entreated the Father that we might "be one."

Uniformity and unity are two different matters. Things in uniformity are all alike. Things in unity are different things functioning as one. Bricks in a pile are uniform, but there is no unity in the pile. A house has bricks, lumber, plumbing, and wiring. These materials are different, but constructed into one house they have unity. The Bible has no uniformity of authorship or style, but it has unity. A body has no uniformity of parts, but it has unity. Different styles of music in one congregation are healthy for the body. It is unity of purpose, spirit, and truth for which our Lord pleads, not uniformity of music or style of worship.

Chapter 60

Dramas and Skits

First Baptist Church of Houston is widely known for its annual Christmas pageant. For twenty-eight years, Gerald B. Ray, the grand master of Christian pageantry and the minister of music, directed the church in presenting the annual "Houston Christmas Pageant" to approximately 45,000 people. It is, of course, not necessary for every church to attempt something on so grand a scale. The church for the deaf, one of the church's strongest missions, presents its own annual Christmas pageant in a small building to a few hundred persons at a cost of less than $3,000. It was equally blessed of God. But few things will be better attended and provide more effective outreach than dramas and pageants in your church.

Metropolitan Baptist Church in Houston, for example, presents an annual Easter pageant. Hundreds of churches are discovering the benefit and impact of pageantry and drama. Who could overstate the impact of Jeannette Clift George, the Christian playwright, actress, and producer. She and her talented and committed company of Christian artists have thrilled thousands across the world. This method of presenting the gospel through one of the world's oldest art forms is a powerful ministry as well as an overlooked opportunity for the church.

Somewhere in your congregation there is an artist, a person who would love to lead this ministry. There are people in your church who are good at drama, videos, makeup, costuming, and a hundred other things, who have never "found their niche" in the kingdom. That long-sought place of service might be in just such a ministry.

Frances Schaeffer went beyond the importance of the arts as a reflection of the culture to emphasize the necessity of the arts as a tool to impact culture. Why is it that the church has generally given so much attention to music and so little to art and drama, not to mention the dance? Our Catholic friends have outdone us in this area. Even the most casual tour of Italy cannot fail to impact the believer with the awesome power of the arts in the things of God.

But where to start? Perhaps a skit or a play, a small pageant, an art display, or a seminar in your church. Sculpture and painting can have much the same impact as music in our churches and in our homes. But it is generally given little attention by evangelicals.

Contemporary services often feature skits and videos, and this is a good place to start. The younger crowd that will be drawn to your contemporary service is accustomed to a fast-paced, electronic environment. We often show a video clip from a movie with a scene and dialogue pertinent to the message. For a very nominal fee, you can get blanket coverage to do this.

Your Christian bookstore has material available with many creative skits. Some of our best skits really "get the point across" with humorous material. Five minutes is the limit for a skit, and two minutes for a video clip from a movie. If they are powerful and pertinent, they can even be used as an introduction to your message. Again, Rick Warren of Saddleback Community Church is the pioneer. Rick even goes beyond the video and the skit to the live presentation. In virtually every sermon, instead of telling the illustration, he prepares some person to come up and tell his story himself. If a person is not available to do this, Rick will get someone on video in advance.

Our Lord gave us all of these rich and powerful tools to arrest attention and communicate his love. We have been embarrassingly negligent in using them. Perhaps the time to start is now.

Chapter 61

The Atmosphere
of the Church

E ach church has its own personality. Generally, three factors go into creating it: the traditional liturgy of the church, the personality of the pastor, and the socioeconomic makeup of the congregation. For centuries churches have been "churchy." Robes and stained-glass windows are, in the minds of most Americans, synonymous with "going to church."

About twenty years ago that began to change. As stated in our chapters on traditional and contemporary worship, the musical landscape of the American church is changing. Generally speaking, younger people like the new contemporary music. The church must, in some forum, offer this option. To fail to do so is to fail today and ensure failure in the future. Interestingly, in some quarters, some teenagers and young adults are going in the opposite direction, and extremely formal services are gaining in popularity. Perhaps this is a desperate search for the security that tradition represents.

Again, the key is to find what's right for you. While First Baptist Houston offered both traditional and contemporary worship services, each had a bright and warm atmosphere. Structured formality and joyous freedom are *not* mutually exclusive. Some Americans go to churches with guitars and videos, while others worship with organs and robed choirs. Most people, however, go to churches "right down the middle."

At the risk of the mundane, let me tell you the philosophy that drives my approach to worship: *"You can't hatch eggs in a refrigerator."* The purpose of the proclamation of the gospel of Jesus Christ is to change lives. It is that for which he came and that which he does best. There is a great distance from what I am to what I long to be. The transformation of human character brought about through repentance of sin and personal commitment to Jesus Christ is so radical that it can only be described in terms of a person becoming something he has never been before—born again! When he enters a life, everything is drastically changed.

This divine operation of the Holy Spirit occurs more easily in an atmosphere that is conducive to freedom. We are naturally resistant to God. We want our way. We want to "do our own thing." But music, fellowship, and worship with other believers and fellow strugglers breaks down our inhibitions and resistance to the work of God's Spirit. To do something as radical and unstructured as allowing God to transform my life in an instant may certainly be done in a formal and structured environment. But it is more easily done in an unstructured, informal setting. Six factors go into creating such an environment.

1. Prayer. Prayer during the service is important, but the personal time that you as pastor spend alone in prayer before the service is even more important.
2. Personal holiness. The Spirit of God has little freedom to circulate through a congregation of sinful, coldhearted people.
3. Warm music that speaks to the heart.
4. A friendly and approachable pastor.
5. Prayer time. Nothing in the service warms the heart like the opportunity to kneel at one's seat, or at the altar, and pray and/or be prayed for by the pastor and congregation. Start a prayer time in your morning service. Dim the lights, and invite your people to bring their burdens to the altar. Ask your deacons to come forward and kneel with them and pray for them. As pastor, pray audibly for the

needs of the people. A five-minute prayer time in each service can revitalize the worship experience.

The atmosphere of your church is very important. If people don't get past that, they may never get to what you have to say about the Lord and what he can do in their lives. In all things, let love and warmth be your priority.

Chapter 62

Recognizing and Receiving Guests

As Great Commission churches, our magnificent obsession is to touch those outside our fellowship with the gospel. Worship of God and edification of one another are intended to build up the body that we might be his "sent ones." Jesus' last command to the church was "go into all the world and preach the gospel to every creature." Everything we do is to fulfill his command. Indeed, the message of the cross is an offense to them that perish, but this in no way implies the messenger is to be offensive. A "consumer-friendly church" and a "noncompromising" message are not mutually exclusive.

If we do not deal with the outsider in a manner "as wise as serpents and harmless as doves," we might never have opportunity to tell him the life-transforming story of the cross. Truth with integrity and love is always in order. The wise pastor will lead his church to remove every barrier to the unbeliever—from parking to greeting, from dress to decor. Everything must be done to say, "You are loved, you are wanted, you are welcome here."

Every physical and spiritual effort must be made to make your guests feel welcome. I recommend referring publicly and in print to all who visit your church as "guests." The term *visitor* suggests a certain kind of interference with the status quo. It says, "You are an outsider; come in and watch us do our thing." The term *guest* says, "You are a welcome part of the family. Come on in!"

Good hospitality includes repaying a visit. "Following up" the guest with phone calls, letters, and visits is not only the hospitable thing to do; it is the expectation of our Lord. No greater failure exists than leaving live prospects uncultivated. Effective follow-up of those who come to your church begins the minute they drive on the parking lot. Those first good impressions must be capitalized on in the services as well. At some point, by some means, it is imperative that you identify those who have come to visit your church in order to do effective follow-up.

Increasingly, guests choose to maintain their anonymity, and they will do everything to keep from giving you their names and phone numbers. This issue should never be forced. People must be treated with respect. You will graciously attempt to learn their names and contact them, but this must be balanced with respect for the anonymity they may prefer. All is not lost. A good experience without any pressure will enhance the likelihood of their visiting again and again. Personal evangelism is best done after personal friendships are cultivated and trust is built.

Prospects must sense that you do not see them as a prize to be won or a scalp to be added to your belt. Are you truly interested in them, or are you interested in *using* them to build your church? People are more sensitive at this point today than you might realize. The high pressure of many television evangelists as well as some pastors and churches has, frankly, made a lot of good people "gun-shy." From the 1950s through the 1980s people visited churches three to six weeks before they joined. Today, that time is three to six months. It is most important to understand their sensitivity to your motives. Unfortunately, there is too often good reason for them to be suspicious.

Be honest with yourself. Examine your motives. Are you first of all a compassionate bearer of good news or a self-serving hireling interested primarily in building a reputation? A warm, sincere pulpit greeting is always in order. Acknowledge the presence of guests and sincerely love and welcome them on behalf of your congregation.

How does the church go about identifying guests in order to facilitate follow-up? The most important thing may well be what you do *not* do. People do not like to be singled out. For years, preachers asked guests to stand and be recognized. Believe me, that is not the way to do it today. Sensitive to that mistake, we modified our approach and began asking our members to stand in honor of the guests. That proved to be only somewhat more effective. Although the members of our church sincerely greeted those guests seated around them, our guests still felt some sense of having been "pointed out."

We have found a better way to do this. Attached to our Sunday morning worship guide is a perforated guest registration form. At some point during the service when guests are welcomed, they are asked to fill out the form, detach it, and place it in the offering plates as they are passed. It is, incidentally, wise to occasionally say, "We are not asking our guests to give," although some will choose to do so. Nor will everyone choose to fill out the guest registration form, but the opportunity must be given in an atmosphere that says, "You are welcome to do so if you choose." It is, of course, necessary to do this in the service before the offering time to facilitate completing the information forms before placing them in the offering plates. Another way is to place guest registration forms in the pew racks and invite your guests to fill them out in the same manner.

During the benediction, the pastor should leave the worship center before the worshipers. Everyone cannot be greeted individually, but the attempt should be made. Look into the eyes of the one to whom you are speaking, not over his shoulder. Some will choose to engage you in prolonged conversation as others simply walk by. All is not lost. Those whom you did not have opportunity to greet will notice that you gave undivided attention to each person. That person will sense, "If I ever need the pastor, he will do the same for me." When multiple worship services exits, it is important to rotate to different doors—Sunday by Sunday.

Guest receptions might be profitable as well. When this is done, an invitation is given to the guests to join you for a cup of coffee at a designated area. A corner of the lobby or vestibule of your church will do quite well. A table with formal tablecloth, coffee urn, perhaps orange juice and cups will have been prepared by a small group of hosts and hostesses who will assist in serving, form the greeting line, and assist the pastor. The pastor's spouse should accompany him. The advantage is that you can spend more time with people. Those who choose to come to the guest reception are good prospects. The disadvantage is that you will seldom get to greet your own members personally, nor, of course, will all the guests come to the reception. We have done it both ways at First Baptist Houston, and you will find the best method for yours.

Most preprinted registration forms contain boxes that say, "Interested in joining our church? Check yes or no." Customize your forms to include "undecided." Normally the registration form is filled out early in the service. The individual is asked to indicate his interest in the church without the benefit of having experienced the full service. The person who says no at 11:00 A.M. might say yes at 12:00 noon. Give people a chance to say yes, no, or undecided. A no normally means no, but an undecided is often a yes waiting to happen.

The guest registration forms will be received in the offering plates and taken to the church office. If forms are placed in pew racks, guests should be given the option of returning them there or placing them in the offering plates. These forms should be taken to a central location as soon as possible for processing. Copies of cards indicating "undecided" or "yes" should be placed in the hands of the pastor immediately. A Sunday afternoon telephone call to those who were in your service that morning is most impressive to a prospective member. Personal visits, phone calls, and other contacts by pastor and people to all guests should be made the following week.

If you do not have Sunday evening services, Sunday night is the best time to visit. If you do have Sunday night services, Monday night is best. Don't let the prospect cool off. Don't let the ripe fruit lie on the ground. Woe to him who neglects the prospects.

Chapter 63

The Use of Public Testimonies

The first inclination of Andrew upon coming to believe in Jesus was to tell his brother Simon Peter, "We have found the Messiah" (John 1:41). New converts should be encouraged to "go home and tell." The value of personal and public testimony cannot be overstated. The new convert, however, should be both seasoned and instructed before public testimony is given from the pulpit. Often, when conversion of popular and influential people occurs, our first inclination is to "put them up" for a testimony. Far too often, pastor and new convert have been embarrassed, not to mention the embarrassment brought on the name of Christ.

Any of us are subject to "going back," but the new convert is especially vulnerable. A time of personal discipleship must be spent with a solid sense of stability established before the new convert is encouraged to give his testimony publicly. Announcing that on a given date an influential person will give his testimony can be of great value. When the time comes, the wise pastor will encourage the person to write out his testimony, reading it aloud to himself or others several times. The pastor should then assist the believer in refining his or her testimony until it is "just right."

Those who give public testimony from the pulpit should be helped at three points:

1. *Timing.* Brevity is always in order. The individual must be led to understand the difference between a testimony and a life story.

Most testimonies run far too long and tell me more than I want to know. Few of us were born in log cabins. Seven or eight minutes is the "outside" limit for a testimony; five minutes is ideal.

2. *Every effort should be made to glorify Christ and not the individual.* Accounts of sin must not be overly descriptive. Good taste is always appropriate. Remember the children. Frankly, few people know how to give a good public testimony. The motivation might be pure and the concept might be beneficial, but the bottom line is that very few people know how to do it.

3. *Every testimony should contain three elements:* (1) what I was and how unfulfilled I was, (2) who made the difference and how it came about, and (3) what I am today and how I feel about it.

The apostle Paul traveled the Roman Empire confronting both religious and political establishments. Although he was the great intellect of the New Testament, his message was seldom theological. Rather, it was personal. His argument was himself, his personal testimony—his greatest tool. To the believer who knew Christ, he taught theology. To the unbeliever, he gave his testimony. Study the accounts. Three ingredients were always present—who I was, what happened, and what I am today.

Through the years, I have confronted thousands of persons with the claims of Christ. These included atheists and unbelievers, cultists and sinners, philosophers and intellects, rich and poor. Some were receptive; some were not. Often they debated the Scripture, the reality of Jesus, even the existence of God. But one common thread ran through every response. No one ever tried to rebuke my own personal testimony. "Let me tell you what happened to me" is the ultimate softener of the human heart. That you have sincere joy and care enough to share it is disarming to the unbeliever.

Listen again to John 1:40–42: "One of the two which heard John speak, and followed him, was Andrew, Simon Peter's brother. He first findeth his own brother Simon, and saith unto him, We have found the Messias, which is, being interpreted, the Christ. And he brought him to Jesus. And when Jesus beheld him, he said, Thou art Simon the son of Jona; thou shalt be called Cephas, which is by interpretation, A stone."

Notice the progression. He found his brother, told him who he had found, and then brought him to Jesus. In the traffic pattern of our lives, we regularly "find our brother." That which best prepares a person's heart and brings him to Jesus is following Andrew's example. The intermediate step between finding a person and winning him is our personal testimony: "We have found the Messiah."

In your personal witnessing as well as your public ministry, don't forget the power of the personal testimony, both yours and those whom you have led to Christ.

Chapter 64

Ushers and Greeters

The first impression of your church is the one that will linger in the minds and hearts of your guests. An impression of a cold, uncaring congregation will not allow you that second and third chance with those whom you want to reach.

I could not count the times I have walked into a men's clothing store, sized up the suits, and already answered no in my mind by the time the salesman asked, "May I help you?" Everything possible must be done to make those potential members who visit your church feel warm and welcome.

Your parking will make the first impression. Policemen or volunteer "car parkers" should direct the people as they approach your church and its parking lots. A sign that says, "Visitors or Guests, Please Turn on Your Headlights," is the first order of business. Those cars are then directed to the priority parking that you have marked and reserved in a portion of the parking lot nearest to the entrance.

Covered drop-offs for rainy days should be ample and obvious. Give consideration, as well, to special parking for expectant mothers, parents of infants, and small children near the nurseries. Ample parking for the physically disabled, as well as senior adults, should also be clearly marked and easily accessible to church entrances. Shuttle buses to the extremities of your parking lot should be provided and captained by a friendly volunteer. Sunday morning worship guides can be distributed on the shuttle bus, and questions about locations and activities can be answered.

In addition to car parkers, shuttle drivers, and captains, the progressive church will have outside greeters and inside greeters, an information desk, ushers, and volunteers who will, when needed, escort guests from the information desk to classrooms. Outside greeters will be of two types—(1) those who open the door of the car, introduce themselves, offer to carry the baby, and escort the family to the front door and (2) those who open exterior doors of the building and again welcome the guests. Those greeters should refer the people to the information desk just inside the lobby.

Information desks should be located at each main entrance to your facilities. The information desks should be staffed with knowledgeable, friendly volunteers, ready to go the second mile to answer the questions of the guests and make them feel warm and welcome. In cases of large facilities, information desk assistants may personally escort families or individuals to the appropriate room.

The next personal touch will be by an inside greeter. This person opens the door to the sanctuary, welcomes the people to the worship service, and hands them a bulletin or worship guide.

Once guests are seated, the service will begin. The atmosphere before the service is as important as that of the worship hour itself. Church members should be encouraged to introduce themselves and welcome and assist new people who are being seated near them. If a parent brings a baby in arms, it would be nice to say, "If you would like to take her to our nursery, I would be happy to go with you." It is important to be sensitive to the parent's response. Should a parent not choose to do so, he must not be made to feel uncomfortable or uncooperative by not placing the child in the nursery or preschool facility.

It is important that ushers be sensitive to the needs of the congregation during the service. If a child is crying, it may be appropriate to offer help. Again, this must be graciously done with no inference that the child is disrupting the service. If this impression is given, the young couple will probably never return. Ushers should be sensitive to other disturbances in the service. Occasionally, unintentional or even premeditated disturbances will occur. Two to four ushers in the area should go immediately to the person and deal with the situation without having to be directed to do so from the pulpit.

It is the responsibility of ushers to distribute the offering plates or other materials that might be called for during the course of a service. They should also be responsible for taking offering plates to an appointed place of security.

Greeters and ushers may or may not wear nametags. I strongly recommend that you have both male and female greeters and ushers. Young adults add much to the perception that yours is an alive and invigorating congregation. Great sensitivity, however, must be exercised toward older ushers and greeters who have served faithfully for decades. It is possible to rotate or blend in new and younger ushers and greeters without giving the feeling that you are putting older ones "out to pasture."

The Holy Spirit has blessed the church with members of varying giftedness. One of those special gifts is the "gift of helps." Within your fellowship are many wonderful persons who cannot sing a solo, give great sums of money, or teach a class. These are the "helpers," those without which no church can function. Identify, enlist, train, and honor them. They are an indispensable part of a ministry that functions at peak efficiency.

Chapter 65

The Question of Sunday Nights

Things are changing in America. Don't assume that all of those changes that affect the church are entirely bad. Styles of music, staff structure, and laity involvement are important issues worthy of constant review.

One of the more critical issues in the spotlight today is the value of the Sunday night service. The majority of churches in America—and this includes all denominations—do not have Sunday night church, and more are dropping them every week. Is this good, or is it not? Let's talk about that.

Dr. Herschel Hobbs, former pastor of First Baptist Church, Oklahoma City, and meticulous documentor of American Protestant history, writes that Sunday night church services were initially begun to appeal to people who were "hung over" from Saturday night and couldn't get out of bed until Sunday afternoon. Regardless of the reason for their existence, Sunday night services have been a part of the American landscape, particularly in southern and rural areas, since the turn of the century.

Many factors in American culture have caused the church to revisit the issue of the value and wisdom of Sunday evening services. Probably the most significant is the emergence of the working mother. In a large number of American families, both mother and father work five days a week outside the home. Evening family time is virtually nonexistent. Saturdays are spent going to Little League ball games, doing yard work, and running a variety of errands that have been pushed back to the weekend. Sunday morning is for church, leaving only Sunday evenings for a relaxed family time.

Sunday night has become "stay-at-home night" in America. Bars are empty, movies are empty, shopping malls are empty, but video stores are packed. Americans are home watching videos and television. The only vestige of family night that remains in most American homes is Sunday night.

Let me ask you some questions. Are Sunday services simply a tradition that we passionately preserve? Are Sundays necessarily biblical? Does hurriedly running around to more and more church services truly enhance the spiritual quality of our lives, or does it simply relieve the guilt of not continuing what we have been doing for decades? Does it make "the Lord's Day" a *harried* or *hallowed* time? And perhaps the most important question: "Are Sunday night services counterproductive to the growth of quality families that we are attempting to facilitate through other means and ministries?"

These and other factors led First Baptist Houston to make the decision to drop Sunday night services in 1997. We replaced it with a "night of outreach," and in-home visitation, attempting, in part, to capitalize on the fact that this was the best time to find people at home. After a time, some of our people began appealing to us to reinstate the Sunday night service. The primary appeal was, "Pastor, we teach and work in the classes and missions on Sunday morning, and Sunday night is our time to come to church and be ministered to without the pressure of a hurried schedule or another task waiting to be performed."

After a period of time we made the decision to reinstate the Sunday night service. At this writing its future is unknown. Like many of you, this church continues to probe and search for the best approach to Sunday night.

The purpose of this chapter is not to persuade you to a conclusive decision, but to share some ingredients for your thoughtful consideration. Above all, don't continue Sunday nights because we've "always done it that way." But don't drop them because everyone else is doing so. Seek the heart of God. Talk with your people, and make the decision that is right for you. If that decision is to have Sunday night services, consider the following elements:

1. Do not make the Sunday night service a duplicate of the Sunday morning service. If I have pizza at lunch, I don't want it again for dinner. The evening service should be different from the morning service. This can usually be accomplished by making one traditional and the other contemporary.

2. Start the evening service rather early—5:00, 5:30, or 6:00 P.M. Early evening worship gives people time to get home and still enjoy the evening with their family. Those good Sunday night movies don't usually start until 8:00 P.M. And don't forget the popcorn!

3. Occasionally, bring in guest speakers. It can be most difficult to preach multiple services in the morning and then preach again in the evening, especially since you must preach different messages.

4. Don't go too long. There is nothing wrong with a good crisp forty-five-minute or fifty-minute service.

5. Don't pressure the people. Let those who choose quality Sunday evening family time know they are honoring God. The same goes for those who choose to attend church. Don't put a guilt trip on your people about not attending on Sunday nights. The priesthood of the believer recognizes the privilege and responsibility of each person to find the will of God for himself.

Chapter 66

Supply Preachers

We're not talking here about the seminar speaker who comes for a weekend conference or the evangelist who comes for a week's crusade. We're dealing with the one-time "supply preacher" who is an occasional guest in your Sunday morning pulpit. Most of the time, this person is invited only to preach in the pastor's absence. But I encourage you to think about bringing such persons in occasionally even when you are at home and thus presiding over the worship service.

There is, of course, the matter of hearing a fresh voice and different perspective, particularly in a pastorate of long duration. But even in shorter pastorates, it's always nice to hear a fresh voice. It doesn't have to be Easter or the Fourth of July. Occasionally, it can be nice to invite a good speaker to your pulpit for no other reason than to bless your people. Not only will it allow you to pace yourself in those times you need it, but it will be stimulating to your congregation as well.

Booking a quality speaker means extending the invitation well in advance. The person you want your people to hear is likely in demand. He also has a schedule to control. Your best chance at getting him to come is probably to extend the invitation at least a year in advance. The lines of communication must be open and clear between you and your pulpit guest. Discuss honorariums, travel arrangements, housing, subject matter, etc. It is customary to pay all the expenses of your pulpit guest, including travel, motel, and meals.

Honorariums may be agreed upon in advance and presented in person at the conclusion of the service in which he speaks. Don't tell him, "Sorry, we couldn't get the check ready. We'll mail it to you." You've had a year to get ready—and everyone likes to be paid on time. "On time" for your pulpit guest is at the conclusion of the service.

Tickets for food are normally signed by the guest and charged to the hotel room, with the bill paid by the church. Many hotels will bill the church after the fact. Most will prefer a credit card from the church in advance. Honorariums can range anywhere from one hundred dollars to one thousand dollars. Smaller churches normally pay smaller honorariums, while larger churches pay larger sums. Regardless of the size of the church, however, it is unthinkable to fly a guest speaker across the country, take two or three days of his time, and give him only two or three hundred dollars.

Remember, it probably takes a Saturday to get there, particularly if it is a Sunday engagement, and a Monday to get home. That thirty-minute message for your church might have cost that person three days out of his week. Consider this, as well as distance and value of the ministry, in determining the size of the honorarium.

Often you will be inviting a friend. But don't invite him because you're comfortable with him or want him to invite you to preach in his church in return. If he is just another average, good preacher who will not really bring something new and fresh to your church, you might be better off to just go fishing with your friend rather than have him fly across three states to preach to your people. As a pulpit guest, his presence should be a special occasion, and his sermon should be a special message.

If you're interested in someone you do not know personally, get references, check him out, ask the hard questions.

One issue that always arises is the sale of books, tapes, and CDs by the visiting author or musical group. It is most appropriate to expand your guest's ministry and that of the kingdom by offering such material for sale after the service. It is never appropriate, however, for the guest to do that himself. Enlist some of your members to set up a table and handle the sales. Let the pastor make the announcement, just before the benediction, and let the guest stand by the table and sign his books if he desires. But for the visiting speaker to be seen as the money handler, the hawker, or the promoter is to destroy all the good that was accomplished in the service through his message.

Expenses for travel should be mailed in advance or reimbursed at the time the honorarium is presented. The guest should be encouraged to stay and mingle with the people, greeting them, answering their questions, and praying for them when appropriate. If circumstances are such that he must choose between this and signing books, what to do is obvious. It is always best to contact the individual personally in advance and to follow up with a written, formal invitation. It is always appropriate as well to send a letter of thanks.

Part 7

Programs and Ministries

Chapter 67

Organizing the Sunday Morning Bible Study

T he corporate worship of God's people is an indispensable part of the Christian experience. But there are other needs that can be met not simply in one's daily quiet time but in a small-group setting. Here Bible study and interaction occur and personal relationships develop. Many churches have changed the name of these groups from Sunday school to Sunday morning Bible study. I think this is wise. There is, particularly in the secular world, an image of Sunday school as "something that children go to" while Sunday morning Bible study allows an appeal to all ages and all kinds of people.

Questions abound as to the "best way" to do Sunday morning Bible study.

Shall we have small classes or large classes? I feel strongly that small classes are best. Admittedly, with fewer teachers and larger classes, the quality of teaching may go up, but a serious effort to train and develop good teachers can staff a large Sunday morning Bible study with many small classes.

Small classes are preferable not only for the purpose of building interpersonal relationships but also because of the opportunity to ask questions. Large classes tend to become minichurch services taught by a minipastor. Virtually no opportunity is offered for the interchange of ideas. Many people will leave with unanswered questions. In a smaller setting, members not only are allowed but encouraged to raise their hands, ask questions, present a different view, and discuss ideas. And we do learn best by asking. You will never preach a sermon that someone doesn't have a question about something you said. In the smaller class, there is opportunity to learn the answer.

Further, good small classes become good big classes, and good big classes can be divided to create two good small classes, which can grow again. New units grow faster than old units. There is no better way to expand the Bible-teaching ministry of your church than by the old axiom "divide and multiply."

Should classes be age-graded? Decidedly yes! Children should be in Bible study classes with other children their age, as should teenagers and adults. Singles should be given the opportunity to go to Bible study with other singles, young marrieds with young marrieds, etc. This grouping by age and marital status offers a homogeneous mix that is an essential ingredient in building a developing group.

Should the sexes be mixed in Sunday school? Should you have only boys' classes and girls' classes, or only classes for men and classes for women? The best answer is to offer an option. Certainly among children and teenagers, there is much to be said for classes for boys and classes for girls, but among adults it is important to offer a choice of classes. In our church, we offer couples classes for married adults as well as men's classes and women's classes and often two of each within the same departmental age span.

Men often lag behind women in their spiritual development and Bible knowledge. Even though we learn best by asking, most men in such classes will normally not ask questions in front of their wives. So there is a case to be made for both mixed and separated classes even among adults. I recommend offering a choice in each adult age division.

Most student age divisions coincide with school grades from kindergarten through college. Beyond that, the age spread must be wider, perhaps every three to five years. When you get to the upper end, forget trying to get people to tell you their age. Just have a class for the 60-and-up, such as the Golden Eagles or the Prime Timers.

Growing churches often face the question of multiple services. I suggest four possible models, primarily determined by space limitations within your building.

1. A central, unified Bible study hour with two worship services, one before and one after Bible study.
2. A central worship service with two Bible study hours, one before and one after the worship service.
3. Two worship services and two Bible studies that flip-flop.
4. A staggered schedule: Schedule A (Bible study, 8:30 A.M.; worship, 9:45 A.M.); Schedule B (Bible study, 9:45 A.M.; worship 11:00 A.M.). This is the schedule I prefer.

There are several advantages to the staggered schedule. First, it is easy to understand. You simply go to Bible study and church on one schedule or the other. You are either a "Schedule A" person or a "Schedule B" person. Second, everyone goes to Bible study and then church. This is the most naturally sequential, as no one goes to church and then Bible study. Third, this schedule will best facilitate traffic movement in your parking lots.

Sunday morning Bible study is a beautiful and wonderful thing. Make it high priority in your church. It is the place where people are loved and cultivated. It can be most difficult to get your arms around hundreds of people. But in the Sunday Bible study program, relationships flourish, needs are met, and the church is strengthened. Dr. Harry Piland, former leader of the Sunday School Division of the Sunday School Board of the Southern Baptist Convention states: "Sunday morning Bible study is a place to be known by name, missed when absent, and ministered to when in need."

And remember these words: Sunday morning Bible study is not an organization of the church; it is the church organized to minister. Just as an army has divisions, battalions, squadrons, and companies, a church should be organized into groups. The army of the Lord, fed the Word by her undershepherd, corporately experiencing great praise and worship, needs to meet in small groups to facilitate the Great Commission. Sunday morning Bible study is the place to do this.

Chapter 68

The Ministry of the Sunday Morning Bible Study

T he purpose of organized Sunday morning Bible study is five-fold.

Religious Education

In the Sunday school we teach God's Word. The Sunday school teacher should not simply appear and disappear after Sunday morning. The teacher should be involved in the lives of the students. To teach the Word of God does not simply mean to explain it; it means to apply it to one's life. And in good Bible teaching, the teacher will relate to his students, live among them, know their needs, and be conscious of meeting those needs when he prepares his lesson. The teacher who is not aware of the needs of his class will be answering questions no one is asking.

Bible study teachers should be trained by the pastor or minister of education. They should meet the standards of holiness, calling, serious preparation, stewardship, and faithfulness. In any church there will be gifted teachers who need little training. Many of your people will have been effectively teaching for years. But it is important to be constantly developing and training a fresh corps of new leaders if your Sunday Bible study is to divide, multiply, and grow.

Religious education is done in many ways. It is not only through lecture or dialogue that people learn. Videos, for example, as well as object lessons can be most helpful. On a recent Sunday morning my wife was teaching a lesson on our response to the needs of others. Before the class arrived, she placed a paper sack under each chair. Some were filled with only two or three grapes or one small fig, while others had three or four bananas or two or three apples. At the appointed time, she asked each person to reach under his chair and open his sack and tell how he felt when he realized he had only a little, while others had much, and vice versa.

Evangelist Hyman Appleman told the story of an Indian chief who was a Bible teacher in a church in Oklahoma. Because of his knowledge of the oil business and his familiarity with the various dialects of the Indians in Oklahoma, a large oil company from another state tried repeatedly to hire him. He refused their offer, and they raised it again and again. Finally he told them, "I am not coming at any price. Your salary is not an issue." Pressed further, he replied, "Your salary is big enough, but your job isn't." "Why?" they insisted. The answer of that humble Indian chief was simply, "My Sunday school class."

Out of that class came over thirty men who went into full-time Christian ministry through the years. The ministry of the Bible is to teach. The value of committed teachers is at once immeasurable and eternal.

Evangelism

The best way to do outreach evangelism is through the existing unit of the Sunday morning Bible study structure. There's no need to reinvent the wheel. The most likely person to visit a twenty-eight-year-old single woman is her teacher or another class member. Geographical proximity does not carry the weight of spiritual affinity. If I teach fifty-year-old men, I will likely drive across town to visit a fifty-year-old prospect for my class before I will go down the street to visit a teenager.

Assign prospects through the Sunday school. They may be visited through other outreach ministries of the church, but you can't show too much attention to a prospect. Whatever else you do, make assigning prospects to the appropriate Sunday class for cultivation and visitation your number-one priority.

Stewardship

There is no area of Christian responsibility that evokes the number of questions and subsequent need for dialogue as the matter of finances. It is in the setting of the Sunday Bible study unit that you best teach stewardship. Here the matter can be personalized and explained. Here questions can be asked. We distribute offering envelopes each Sunday morning to everyone in Bible study above pre-school age. You can't begin teaching stewardship too early. Seventy-five percent of our income comes through those envelopes; 25 percent comes through the plates in the worship service.

In a stewardship campaign, goals can be accepted by individual classes and departments. A personal testimony of God's faithfulness to the tither might best be received when given by a fellow class member. Teaching and developing financial stewardship is an important function of the Bible study unit.

Ministry

In a setting in which people are studying the Bible and praying together, personal ministry naturally occurs. Within each departmental age division of the Sunday school you need inreach leaders and outreach leaders. The responsibility of the outreach leader is to direct personal visitation to prospects. The purpose of the inreach leader is to direct the class in meeting the needs of its own whether they be domestic problems, health needs, financial needs, discouragement, or absenteeism.

When I was a pastor, I had a telephone in my car. When there was a death, I was contacted. Very often, I reversed direction and went immediately to the home. But in all these years, I had never made a death call but what members of the deceased's Sunday school class were already there. The highest quality of service afforded by our church was not given by professional staff but by our caring and gifted congregation. This caring ministry was done through the Sunday morning Bible study unit.

Fellowship

The family that prays together stays together, and the class that plays together also stays together. Every month or two each Sunday school class should have a fellowship, a lunch, a social—perhaps a cookout, a beach party, or other event. Meet the social needs of your people within the tight structure of their own Bible study unit, and you will build the rock of a solid church from the stones of great classes.

Great classes build great churches. The wise pastor will give high priority to the Sunday school.

Chapter 69

Ministry to Adults

Т

he educational, spiritual, and social needs of your adults are as different as the needs of children and the needs of teenagers. As the church begins to grow, it is necessary that separate ministry and Bible study units be designed not only for married adults and single adults but also for the three broad age divisions within all adults: senior adults, median adults, and young adults.

Senior Adults

The ministry to senior adults, for example, is the largest untapped gold mine of spiritual opportunity and resource you have. Consider this: For the first time in American history, there are more senior adults than teenagers. Senior adults are reachable. They are mature, serious, and thinking about eternity.

Teenagers feel they are immortal and will live forever. But the senior adult, as recently as his last medical checkup, came face-to-face with the reality of his own immortality. The older, more serious person is much closer to hell or heaven—or at least he thinks he is—than anyone else in your city. Therefore, when approached with the gospel, he has a built-in receptivity to spiritual things. You might find him to be much more receptive to the gospel of Christ than a thirty- or forty-year-old.

Senior adults have historically been considered hard to reach. Indeed, if a person does not respond to the gospel when he is young, he may become spiritually hardened. Some statistics indicate that as few as one in ten thousand people will come to Christ beyond age sixty. But things are changing. People are living longer. Not only are there more senior adults, but they are more secular than their ancestors were. Millions of them in our pagan culture have never been seriously confronted with the claims of Christ at all. Untold numbers have never truly heard the gospel of Jesus and are most reachable.

Senior adults are not normally best reached by their children or young or median adults. They are best reached by their grandchildren and other senior adults. Cultivate friendships. Take a busload to a recreation park or a ball game. Have a picnic. Invite them to socials. Build relationships. Show them you care. They will respond to the Lord. What a shame that most churches pay far more attention to teenagers than senior adults. They are indeed a field "white unto harvest."

Senior adults have time. They make great volunteers for your church and are just waiting to be asked. They will count the offering, stuff envelopes, greet incomers, organize prayer meetings, wait tables, carry out special projects. They love to keep busy, and they have lots of time to fill. Senior adults have money. Realizing their own immortality, developing an increasing sense that "you can't take it with you," they will respond to charitable and Christian causes. They are often the first to give to advance the gospel, the most sacrificial in giving to the building fund, and the most consistent in mission contributions. Wow, what a group they are!

Median Adults

These marvelous saints of God between the ages of forty and sixty are usually the backbone of your church. They are quite different from married young adults, who are still uncertain who they are, in debt up to here, and looking for a good time. Their needs are also as different as those of senior adults and teenagers. The median adults in your church and their lifestyles may vary greatly from small church to large church, blue collar to white collar, large city church to small rural church. Analyze your median adults. Learn their uniqueness. Understand their needs. Staff and program to meet these needs.

Married Young Adults

Married young adults *begin* at any age and are classified as high as thirty-nine or as young as thirty-four. I feel age thirty-nine is the normal break, and we normally age grade by the age of the wife. Through the years we have experimented with many models. But to our surprise, we have determined that the best teachers for married young adults are often other married young adults. There will always be those among your young adults who were raised in the church and who, though still in their thirties, are mature beyond their years. These might well be your best teachers for married young adults.

In our own church, we have a nearly-married department for engaged couples and a newly-married class. The nearly-married department confronts the issues that couples will be facing in marriage, and teaches appropriate Bible study material to meet them. In this department, friendships are already being forged that will "tie them on" to your Sunday school and church for years to come.

It is critical that married young adults connect with a group of other married young adult couples with whom they are compatible, with whom they share activities, and with whom they can build lasting relationships. The nearly-married couple is encouraged to attend their department from engagement until marriage, whether their engagement lasts two months or two years.

The newly-marrieds are allowed to stay in their department only one year. The curriculum repeats after twelve months, and it is a step up from that of the nearly-married. It is, of course, Bible-based and heavy on application. This group is one of the most delightful parts of any congregation. The goal of ministry to those who have grown to biological adulthood is to bring them to spiritual adulthood, helping them to leave the milk of the Word and to move on to the meat.

A sensitive pastor will design some unique approaches to these three widely varying age divisions within the adult division of the Sunday school.

Chapter 70

Ministry to Singles

Over the past thirty years, one of the most profound changes the church has faced is the growth of the "singles" subgroup. This group is diverse and multifaceted. Some have been married, others never have; some are motivated career people, others are living day to day; some are young, others are reaching retirement age; some have discretionary income, others live paycheck to paycheck. Some singles are parents, and most are in transition in their lives. This multifaceted group with its unique needs must be a key focus group for a growing church.

The culture as a whole makes the statement that each person is complete within himself. To need someone else is portrayed as a sign of weakness. Further, singles abound because of the uncertainty of marriage. For the last thirty years, divorce and broken families have created generations of hurt and wounded young people who are cautious about the marriage commitment. Not surprisingly, over one-half of the adult population is single. The average marrying age has risen from twenty to thirty. Cultural pressure for material gain for one's self is also creating a focus toward accumulating wealth at the expense of committing to another person in marriage.

With such diversity, transition, and mobility, leading a singles ministry can be like preaching to a parade. The mobility of society, the transition of early adulthood, and the reluctance to commit has created a unique subculture of adult singles deeply hungering for more. Many singles, perhaps at the height of self-centeredness, are just beginning to understand that independence and lack of accountability might not be worth the aloneness and isolation it brings.

Singles normally have high levels of frustration over short-lived, temporary relationships, and they long for stability and permanency. Ultimately, singles desire authentic relationships with God first, others second, and themselves third. The need to deal with their falleness because of sin, as well as a deep desire to deal with their aloneness and/or estrangement from others, creates a longing in singles' hearts to which the church holds the answer.

Our approach to ministry to this growing segment of society is critical to winning our world for Christ. The broad-brush stroke of ministry must break down into smaller, more intimate components that will ultimately develop singles into strong, maturing disciples of Jesus Christ. Event-oriented singles ministry has no long-term effect unless coupled with an equal commitment to discipleship.

Mark 2:13–17; 3:13–19; Matthew 10; Luke 10:1–23; and John 12:44–50 establish patterns of the four interactive practices of effective individual discipleship for singles.

The first is a habit of studying God's Word. Sunday morning Bible study and small midweek studies are both effective.

The second habit is the practice of ministry application. The maturing Christian single must engage in appropriate application ministry. The single person is a prime candidate to put his training into practical ministry. But ministry needs to fit the person's giftedness and personal interests. The purpose of ministry is not merely pleasing God. Rather, it is an effort to join God in his mission.

The third habit of effective discipleship is the component of Christian community. "Iron sharpeneth iron; so a man sharpeneth the countenance of his friend" (Prov. 27:17). We must allow God to use relationships to sharpen our character. The key to Christian community is developing feelings of safety and enjoyment, and safety is paramount. Growth can come only when we feel secure enough to really be ourselves without fear of judgment or attack, and when we are safe enough to receive loving correction. The singles group must be a safe place to fail without losing friendships or affirmation.

The Christian community must also be a place of enjoyment. Enjoyment breeds feelings of safety, and safety fosters the reality of enjoyment. What better place to have fun than a safe, loving, challenging, Christian singles group?

Several years ago, a group of our young singles were in our home playing pool. As they were leaving, I said, "I'm so sorry you don't have a family to go home to." "Brother John," they replied, "we are one another's family." I'm so glad they were secure in that.

Fourth, maturing Christian singles need accountability. This vulnerable time in life needs the one-on-one relationships found in a small, closed group. Many times an older spiritual mentor is helpful and important. This accountability component is the key to healthy Bible study, ministry application, and Christian community. In the personal accountability group, the single can say, "I'm not alone in my struggle with sin," and find acceptance, confidentiality, and support.

Singles want to enter in the group with a sense of anonymity and the ability to "check things out" safely before joining or feeling "checked out" themselves.

Another key to ministering to singles is to know that "singles follow singles." Critical mass, or the feeling that there are "others like me," is key to creating an atmosphere where singles feel safe and are willing to stay around. Singles, of course, want to be involved with other singles. Houston's First Baptist Church facilitates "Metro Bible Study," an interdenominational Bible study ministry of 1,000 to 1,500 singles every Monday night. Both large and small congregations utilize Metro as a connection point with other singles.

One Hispanic church in Houston was struggling with a small singles group of ten to fifteen individuals. Feeling isolated, they began going to Metro. Soon they started bringing their friends and the group grew to twenty-five or thirty. Eventually they had enough singles to run additional programs at their own church. But still this growing group comes to Metro the first Monday of every month. Why? Singles follow singles, and they need ministry bigger than their small group.

Perhaps more than any other group, singles have time and desire to serve the Lord. One of the great joys of my ministry in Houston was to watch our young singles grow in their passion for inner-city ministries. In the summer of 1998, 135 of our singles took a week of their vacation time to conduct Vacation Bible Schools, youth clubs, build churches, do street witnessing, and other inner-city mission ministries. In 1999 the number grew to more than two hundred! Many of these singles are now giving serious consideration to a life-long career of serving others in the name of Christ.

Additional ideas for "big picture" possibilities abound. Be creative. We did praise and worship nights called "Unplugged" (followed by Starbucks Coffee), weekend retreats, and ski trips, all with the idea of creating places where singles feel comfortable.

Be cautious of feeling the need to be the church that creates the big events. Why not join with others in programs that already exist.

Singles Sunday morning Bible study classes should be large. Remember the vital importance of critical mass. This makes for easy entry. Still, it is important that each group break down into multiple smaller groups, such as men's and women's accountability groups and coed Bible study groups.

Singles ministry should be the hot button for your church. Understanding singles and meeting their unique needs is of vital importance. Seek to meet those needs by offering large entry-point opportunities, and funnel them into vibrant smaller groups. These are the keys to developing singles into mature disciples of Jesus Christ.

Many of the finest deacons, teachers, and leaders in our churches are singles. Don't overlook this talented and delightful group.

Chapter 71

Ministry to Students

T he terms "youth director" and "youth ministry" are out. "Student minister" and "student ministry" are in. Teenagers prefer the term *student* to *youth* or *teen,* and their staff leaders prefer student minister to youth director. More important are the paradigm shifts that have occurred in effective "studen-reaching" programs. The twenty-first century student minister must be alert to these changes.

The heart of student ministry today is one-to-one relationships. Students are hungry for authenticity. They crave an "up-close" relationship with someone they can trust, who understands and cares about them. Many students feel they are aliens in their own home. Their natural craving for deep family relationships often goes unsatisfied by insensitive or overly busy parents. Far too often an intimate relationship with her boyfriend is only a girl's substitute for a relationship with an absentee father. There is danger here, of course. But the wise student minister will develop deep, godly relationships with his students.

Recent student ministries were characterized by a "compete-with-the-entertainment-world" approach. Bigger was better, and each weekly event had to be louder and greater than the one before. Auditoriums were often filled with big bands, bright lights, and burgeoning crowds. But the result was often little more than an emotional and spiritual roller coaster.

Articles in *Newsweek* which appeared the week after the shootings in Columbine High School in Colorado (April 21, 1999) stated that the students who make it in the real world have a significant adult besides their parents who invests time in them.

The second relationship a student needs is with other Christian students. Life in middle school and high school can be difficult and frustrating. Fellowship with other believers during student years makes it easier. Student ministry should emphasize unity, friendship, fellowship, brotherhood and sisterhood, family, and group. The affirmation and support of fellow *Christian* students is of great importance at a time when peer approval is everything. A young person's deepening relationship with God is greatly nourished by the approval and support of a peer, who himself hungers and thirsts after righteousness.

A growing relationship with Jesus Christ transcends the student years and carries young people through college, marriage, and parenthood. Your student ministry is a failure if your students do not know how to spend time with the Father, read his Word, and hear his voice.

Focused worship is another changing dynamic of student ministry. Students no longer want just music and singing. They hunger to experience true worship of God through the music they are singing. Music that only excites and thrills is out. Music that is a true avenue into the presence of God is in. Contemporary worship need not be divisive in our churches. We must come to the conclusion once and for all that we must meet students "where they are" musically.

Students in First Baptist Houston often stood in worship and praise for an hour and still felt slighted when the worship time was over. There is new hunger to worship among students. Never judge the authenticity of a student's worship because it is set to music he appreciates, understands, and loves.

Experiential, hands-on missions is another new and exciting paradigm in student ministry. There is a growing trend toward both local and global missions. In 1997 fifty-two students from our church went on mission trips. In 1998 the number grew to seventy-seven. And in 1999, more than one hundred and thirty students raised their own finances to go to the inner city of San Antonio and overseas to Ukraine to conduct Bible schools, do street evangelism, paint houses, and conduct numerous other ministries in the name of Christ.

Mission involvement contains the elements of prayer, boldness, spiritual warfare, evangelism, servanthood, unity, and love for others. In what other activity do we engage that can accomplish all of that? This new generation wants to be a part of something significant and something God-sized. Don't be surprised if more and more of your students feel a burning urgency to declare Christ to the nations.

Finally, there is an increasing love of personal evangelism within the hearts of students in recent years. The dividing line between believers and nonbelievers is sharpening in public schools. Christian students are decidedly more bold in sharing Christ. Wearing Christian T-shirts, carrying Bibles to school, playing Christian music—all these are indicators of the heightened spiritual intensity of a new generation that is serious about their faith in Christ.

Who will ever forget the testimony of Cassie Bernall, who lost her life in the Littleton massacre simply because she answered yes to the question, "Do you believe in God?" Christian students are bold. Christian students are winners. Show them how. Set the example. Believe in them and be patient.

This young generation is much more process-oriented than event-oriented. Some nonbelieving students might take months to make a decision for Christ rather than respond immediately to a one-time invitation. Exciting things are happening with students across the nation, and virtually every significant movement of God in history began among students. Encourage your student pastor, encourage your students, and encourage the parents of your students. You are doing more than building tomorrow's leaders today; you are tapping into the greatest potential resource in the kingdom of God.

Chapter 72

Ministry to Elementary Children

The children's ministry is organized to reach boys and girls grades one through five with God's message through Bible study, fellowship activities, and personal ministry in times of need. The foundation of this ministry is the Sunday school organization.

In age-graded Sunday school classes, children are led to discover Bible truths through activity-centered learning during small-group time, Bible teaching, creative writing, drama, salt maps, art projects, and many other creative forms. All Bible learning activities must, of course, relate to the specific biblical objectives in the Sunday school lesson.

During large-group time, children experience prayer, singing, Bible reading, teacher-led discussion, and application of the Bible lesson on their age level. Children are also led to develop Bible usage skills and memorize at least one Bible verse weekly. Bible games can also be used to reinforce and review learning.

Children's workers should be carefully chosen leaders who enjoy and understand children. Children need teachers who understand that *there is more to learning than listening and more to teaching than telling.* Children need role models who accept them as they are and who use words and concepts they can understand. Good children's teachers recognize that through Christian education we train children in the

Christian way of life. Children's teachers should emphasize Christian attitudes and values as well as Scripture explanation.

As children are given opportunities to practice these values through activities such as role-playing or finishing open-ended stories, they are able to translate these attitudes into behavior. The Bible is, of course, the textbook for Sunday school and is to be presented to children as God's Word to us. The Bible should be taught as the sole authority for how God wants us to live.

First Baptist Houston conducts a "First Grade Bible Presentation" event each year in a Sunday worship service. As first graders are becoming aware of words and are learning to translate print into meaning, they are impressed by books. When we give a child a Bible, we communicate to this impressionable new reader that the Bible is very important.

Christian fellowship is also important to children. Two enrichment activities that provide children with the opportunity to make new friends are Vacation Bible School and camp for third- through fifth-graders.

The third- through fifth-grade camp provides an extended time of Christian discipleship training in a leisurely setting. Children grow through Bible study, worship, and fellowship as they swim and participate in other recreational and arts and crafts activities together. For many children, camp is the first extended break from the security of their home. This provides children a time to learn to trust other Christian adults to meet their needs.

Each year First Baptist Church in Houston hosts over one thousand children in Vacation Bible School. Vacation Bible School not only introduces many new families to our church, but sixty to eighty children each year accept Christ as their personal Savior during the VBS decision service.

Each Sunday morning an ongoing children's new members class is provided for boys and girls who have recently made a profession of faith in Christ. This class helps children understand more fully the decision they have made and helps them get started in their Christian life. Children are also counseled individually about their salvation experience before their baptism. A third form of follow-up is provided by offering each child the six-week daily devotional book, *Now That I Am a Christian.* Parents are encouraged to work with their children to complete this six-week study.

Another vital part of our church's ministry to children is mission education. We invite children to learn to care about the needs of others around the world through mission study. Children are taught to become Great Commission Christians and are provided with opportunities to get involved personally in serving others. We also introduce children to missionary heroes and teach them our Christian heritage.

Royal Ambassadors (RAs) is our church's mission organization for boys, led by men who provide them with positive Christian role models, along with inspiring mission studies. Boys also enjoy sports, learn camping skills, and participate in events such as our annual Pinewood Derby Race.

Girls in Action (GAs) is our mission organization for girls, led by women of faith. Through GAs girls become actively involved by learning to care for the needs of others through sharing themselves and the crafts they make. Missions education and service are, of course, the heart of these two programs. More than half of the people in our Southern Baptist foreign missionary force are the product of Royal Ambassadors and Girls in Action.

Additionally, Children's Church is formatted like a worship service. During this time, children will experience all the elements of worship in "big church" except baptism, the Lord's Supper, and a formal invitation to make decisions and join the church. Children are taught to pray, sing, give offerings, and listen as the Bible is taught.

The Bible teaches that it is ultimately the responsibility of each parent to train his or her children to worship. If parents feel their children are ready for corporate worship in "big church," our church encourages them to continue to train their children in worship skills as they sit together. Children can gain much from watching their parents worship and discovering that worship is important to their family. But parents are also encouraged to have planned and spontaneous times of worship at home so children may learn that worship is a part of the normal daily life of a Christian.

The ultimate goal of the children's ministry is to establish a solid foundation for each child's faith that will result in commitment to Jesus Christ as Lord and Savior, followed by a life of fellowship and service. Everything children's workers do, from skating parties to Sunday morning Bible study, should help a child come to know God's plan.

During the years when children are in the children's division, most become aware that they often choose to disobey God. Children need to know and feel that in spite of their sin, God loves them and he gave his Son, Jesus, for their sins on the cross. Adults must prayerfully listen as a child expresses his faith so they will not prematurely push a child who is simply asking for more information or hinder a child who is ready to place his faith in Christ. Provide a quality ministry to children, and their parents will bring them to your church.

Chapter 73

Ministry to Preschoolers

T he preschool ministry of the church has a major responsibility
to two groups. The first and foremost ministry is to children.
The Bible says, "And Jesus increased in wisdom and stature,
and in favor with God and man" (Luke 2:52). Children too must be
ministered to as they grow and develop mentally, physically, spiritually, and socially. Each age and developmental milestone must be considered as children are taught in the church setting.

During these years of astounding growth, solid foundations must
be laid in the life of the child. Research has shown that during the first
six years, the child learns over half of all he will learn in his lifetime.
God has given children a very special period in which to learn.

The second ministry of the preschool is to the parents of
preschoolers. Most couples come to the experience of parenting with
little or no experience with children. Often parents know little about
child development and realistic expectations for their children. The
range of parental behavior can swing widely from those who are unrealistic and unreasonable to those who will not challenge the child in
any way. The wise counsel of Sunday school teachers and preschool
workers assists the parent in working with, playing with, and teaching
their children.

The work a church preschool ministry does with the child will
establish a spiritual foundation upon which each life can be built year
after year. Even the youngest infants should hear Bible truths presented in word and song. Short, easy-to-understand Bible verses and
thoughts are to be used with the children. Usually babies have

receptive language before they have verbal language. It is never too soon to sing and quote simple Bible truths to them.

As the child grows older, the challenge of the preschool staff is to take the Bible into the child's world of play. By using various activities to teach, the preschool teacher can make the Bible a reality in their lives. As a child colors, we thank God for his eyes. As a child sets a table in the home living area, we say thank you to God for our food. As a child hears the story of God creating the world, he plays with plastic animals like those God created. Blocks, books, the nature center, home living center, puzzles, music—all these present opportunities for the child to hear and internalize the truths of the Bible.

Since the language and vocabulary of preschoolers is limited, it is important that the child can relate the words he hears to reality. It is more important that a child *understand* what is being said than that he *memorize* it. It is useless to talk about kindness to a child who has no idea what the word *kind* means. If we are to teach kindness, we must do it in the context of doing a kind act. The child can make a basket of fruit and take it to a church helper or draw a picture to give to a friend.

In addition, young children view the world literally. We must, therefore, be careful with the words we use with this age child. We need to use literal words like *Bible, church,* and *Jesus* rather than *God's Word, God's house,* and *Lamb of God.* Choose to say things in a manner that the child can easily understand and make a part of his life.

Sunday school must also build a foundation of love for the child. As young children establish attitudes about things in their world, the church must provide them with a safe, loving, caring environment in which to be nurtured. The rooms for children should be equipped with toys and materials to meet the needs of that specific age group. These rooms should also be inspected for safety features, such as plug covers, objects which are sharp or easily swallowed, and other potential dangers.

Sadly, the physical risk to the child's safety is greatly heightened in our violent and decadent society. Incidents have even occurred where a divorced or separated parent has attempted to "kidnap" a child from a preschool or nursery while the estranged spouse was attending a worship service. Simple systems have been developed to protect against this happening. Even the most readily recognized member of First Baptist Houston may not pick up his child from "preschool" without following the procedures.

Each age group should be staffed with plenty of workers who have been trained to meet the needs of children. Adults working with children must be screened through a background check to assure the safety of every boy and girl.

Each age group has special developmental milestones to cross. It is important that the children know that their church family celebrates these milestones with them. Occasions such as beginning kindergarten or going to worship for the first time should be magnified. Both individual Sunday school groups and the entire preschool can have special events that celebrate the child. And, don't forget, holidays are a wonderful time for parties and activities in the preschool.

The preschool ministry of the church must partner with the parents of the children. As life begins, the parents should receive an in-home visit from the preschool ministry. The birth of a child is a time of joy, along with fear. This is an important time for the preschool ministry to encourage and aid the family with concerns they might have about bringing their child into the world as well as bringing him to church. Such things as safety, personal attention, and hygiene should be ensured.

The preschool area can provide ongoing parental education for families. It can help preschool teachers to recognize their important role in the lives of young families. The preschool ministry must help parents fulfill the role of one generation telling the next about the praiseworthy deeds of the Lord.

As preschoolers grow and mature, the solid foundation they have received as babies, ones, twos, threes, fours, and kindergartners will make a great difference. It is critical that this time not be lost but used in a productive and positive way to direct a child into paths of righteousness.

Enlisting committed preschool volunteers is among the most difficult tasks of the church—but nothing is more important. In addition to permanent workers, both volunteer and trained, preschool parents should be challenged to serve one Sunday in six. Give repeated commendation to those invaluable workers while placing great public emphasis on their work.

Preschool ministry is not religious baby-sitting. It is the very heart and soul of God's promise, "Train up a child in the way he should go: and when he is old, he will not depart from it" (Prov. 22:6).

Chapter 74

Planning and Training for the Sunday Morning Bible Study

D id any of these things ever happen to you?
- The power fails in the middle of "Jesus: the Light of the World."
- The RSVP fellowship has thirty-two drop-ins.
- The overhead projector blows a bulb.

Not only do bad things happen to good people; they even happen to good people who plan. Certainly most problems are unforeseeable and uncontrollable, but plan we should. To fail to plan is to plan to fail.

Don't jump to the conclusion that Jesus wasn't a planner just because he had five thousand hungry men and no menu. Luke 10:1–16 gives us insight into Jesus' planning skills. His plan included: how to send (70) (10:1); how to go (teams of 2) (10:1); where to go (10:1); what not to take (10:4); what to say (10:5); how to be supported (10:7); what to eat (10:8); what to do (10:9); what to do in case of rejection (10:10–11); and whom to claim as authority (10:16). Jesus was a planner.

Planning and relying on the Holy Spirit are not mutually exclusive. About fifteen minutes into the session where "we'll just let the Spirit guide us," things begin to fall apart and we wonder why. Has it occurred to us that God wants us to seek his guidance a little earlier than 9:30 A.M. on Sunday morning? Prophecy is just one indication that God is the consummate planner!

In staff meetings while I was pastor at First Baptist Houston, we weny through every detail of every future event each week about three months in advance. When the big day came, there was little chance for confusion. The five *W's* for event planning and promotion include who, what, when, where, and why. Following this simple rule in your publicity will answer most questions before they are raised.

This is very important in the development of weekly workers' meetings. These are best held on Wednesday nights and are essential in building a great Sunday school. Ideally, all age-graded departmental directors meet at 6:00 P.M. with the minister of education and or Sunday school director, followed by a 6:30 or 6:40 meeting of each director with his teachers. The joint directors' meeting should be held in a large assembly area, and departmental/teachers' meetings should be held in their individual Sunday school departments. Make good plans and start today. Someone said, "Procrastination is suicide on the installment plan."

One of the more critical areas for planning is the enlistment and training of new teachers for the Sunday school or Bible study hour. Not only will teacher resignations need to be filled with qualified leadership, but dividing and multiplying ensures growth. Breathing new life and new energy into the Sunday school is only one of the benefits of dividing and multiplying when new teachers are "waiting in the wings."

Where do these new leaders come from? That process begins the day people join your church. Identifying the interest, potential, and talents of new members is priority. As pastor or minister of education, identify those persons in your church with teaching skills and a passion for excellence. They are the ideal candidates to assume responsibility for the ongoing training program that will stock your Sunday morning Bible study program with an endless supply of good teachers.

Someone in the religious education division of your denomination will offer help for good ongoing programs of teacher training and development. Most of those courses are of thirteen- to twenty-six-week duration and are best conducted in the spring and fall. After they join the church, information should be gathered from new members about gifts, talents, experience, and interests relating to teaching and various other opportunities of service. Identify these persons and enlist them in your program of teacher training.

Excellent materials are available to develop the potential teaching skills of the novice and to refine those of the experienced. Training can also include semiannual group training, conferences, workshops, video series, Bible doctrine classes, study course series, etc.

Sunday morning Bible study is based on the service of precious volunteers who believe in the ministry of teaching and their willingness to prepare and commit to it. The wise pastor will affirm the importance of what they're doing. Invest your life in these leaders. This will keep the heart of your ministry strong!

Chapter 75

Special Bible Studies

S unday morning Bible study is the heartbeat of your church, but it should be pumping its life-giving blood through many other opportunities for Bible study beyond Sunday morning. The healthy church will provide other types of study at other times of the week. One of the most effective is the "support group" Bible study. This is the type of gathering where six or eight people—perhaps even as many as twenty-five or thirty—meet regularly around a common issue with a solid biblical base under the leadership of a fellow struggler.

About 1989 I was astounded to read in *Newsweek* that on any given Sunday, only eighteen million Americans were involved in Bible study, while thirteen million were attending weekly support groups. We are offering the world what we are interested in, while they are telling us what they really want.

Please hear me clearly: Support groups in your church are not a *compromise* but an *opportunity.* I would never suggest that the Bible be watered down or left out to attract the secular person who is looking for a support group. To the contrary, there is something very special about knowing the local church cares enough about a particular need or addiction to offer help. But these groups should focus on Bible study. Needs must be met through teaching, application, and discussion of Scripture.

Support groups also have the common bond of people who are willing to openly acknowledge their need and who are hungry to draw support from fellow strugglers. First Baptist Houston has Bible study support groups for alcoholics, drug addicts, recovering homosexuals, families with homosexual members, grief after death, divorce recovery, and postabortion anxiety—to name a few. Find a need, meet it, and people will come. Jesus always went to hurting people and they always responded to him.

Another category of special Bible studies are those led by your people in homes and marketplaces across your city. From 1971 until the present, First Baptist Houston maintained a weekly Bible study in the downtown/business community of Houston. This lunch from 12:00 noon to 12:50 P.M. included a twenty-five-minute Bible study, and it was a tremendous entry point into the church.

I personally taught that study for seventeen years. At the midpoint of that time we relocated our church to the area of town where most of the attendees live. Within the first six months, over 150 people who were attending this study joined our fellowship. Across our city today, approximately twenty-five groups of men meet at various restaurants for breakfast once a week for a time of sharing, Bible study, and prayer.

Weekday and evening Bible studies within the walls of the church also meet many needs. First Baptist's women's ministry offers studies in "John," "Isaiah," "Prayer," "Missions," "Worship," "Breaking Addiction," "Revelation," "the Church," "the Character of Christ," and "the Financially Confident Woman" as well as "Becoming a Friend of God." What an opportunity for the women of the city. The high point of the week is a Tuesday evening women's Bible study taught by the renowned Beth Moore. This year's theme is "Breaking Free: Making Liberty in Christ a Reality in Life." These Bible studies have a combined weekly attendance of over four thousand people.

Further, the church provides a weekly offering of seminars to both men and women. These meet Wednesday nights and Sunday nights. They offer such topics as: "A Biblical Portrait of Marriage," "Raising Kids Who Turn Out Right," "Experiencing God," "Grandparenting by Grace," "Finishing Strong," "When Life Caves In," and "Mastering Your Money," to name a few. They are taught in thirteen-week cycles by laymen and laywomen of the church who speak from their varied backgrounds and areas of interest.

Additionally, monthly Bible studies for men in the oil industry, monthly men's barbecue with guest speakers and Bible study, and men's ministry offerings are provided, including such topics as "Learning to Be a Man in Christ."

First Baptist Houston offers many opportunities for Bible study beyond 9:30 A.M. on Sunday morning. Plan ahead. Use your people, stay well organized, meet needs, and be creative. The church should offer many opportunities for spiritual growth as entry points into its membership.

Chapter 76

The Bus Ministry

T he double-edged sword of this unique program known as the bus ministry must be readily acknowledged. Let's talk first about the problems. To a large degree, the bus ministry—the rage of the 1960s and 1970s—is virtually extinct today. Certainly church buses and vans have their place, and I encourage those who have found door-to-door Sunday morning bus ministries to be advantageous. But the truth is that most churches that started them stopped them. Still, it may be that this is God's will for you in your particular church field. You must seek his heart and find his will in this matter.

The reason for the end of the bus ministry in most churches is simply that most pastors have found it to be easier to go to where the children live and conduct services there rather than transport them to their facilities. For starters, one of the big problems is the liability issue. It is also very difficult to enlist and maintain committed bus captains and church bus workers.

Combining bus ministry children with your "regulars" can present a problem. The spiritual development and biblical understanding of the ten-year-old who was born and raised in your church is much different than that of the child who is inclined to ride your bus, who has likely never been in Sunday school at all. A better quality of teaching can be done with your ten-year-olds who have always been in church if they are taught in one group. And a better quality of teaching can be done with a group of ten-year-olds who have never been to church if they are taught in another group. This can often be done more effectively in a building near where the children live rather than by providing transportation.

Hear me clearly when I say that it is not a racial, ethnic, or socio-logical issue. It is an issue of determining the best method of reaching and teaching boys and girls.

The second problem with this ministry is that buses always run late. Fleets of old church buses are notorious for breaking down. Drivers must wait for the children who are invariably late arriving at the bus stop. And the teacher must invariably wait for the entire bus whose arrival is seldom on time. Over and over again I have seen a teacher halfway through the lesson when a bus load of children arrived. They had no idea what has been going on, let alone what it meant.

Years ago First Baptist Houston changed its bus ministry into a missions ministry and went to the housing projects and areas where the children live to teach Sunday school and conduct services. At this writing the church has begun sixty-three local missions since 1980. Many of them have become strong enough to become churches. Including those that have become self-sustaining and those supported by the church, approximately the same number of persons attend the churches and missions on Sunday as attend Bible study and worship in the central facilities.

Let me tell you about two of them. In 1985 Stan and Karen Felder, directors of the children's missions ministry, began the Springbrook Apartment Ministry in Houston. For nine years Stan pastored that congregation, which grew to nearly ninety in an older apartment complex. From that ministry came fourteen children who became Christians, gave their lives to full-time Christian work, grad-uated from Texas Baptist universities, and entered the ministry. One of them, whose name I cannot share, has been in China the last two years as an underground missionary.

Another story: In 1989 one of the African-American missions, Faith Baptist Mission, began a prison ministry. Eventually inmate Anthony Simmons became a Christian. God called him to preach, and he was discipled by mission members while still a prisoner. Today

Anthony Simmons is pastor of that very mission church that won him to Christ.

I believe in the bus ministry. If God leads you to it, "go for it." But First Baptist Houston has found a better way. But if you determine the Lord would have you to enter the bus ministry, I suggest the following guidelines:

1. Appoint a bus ministry committee.
2. Take your time and select your workers carefully.
3. Train bus captains well.
4. Make a door-to-door survey and determine the need and interest level.
5. Start slowly. Buy a good bus. You can buy a bus for $500 that will run the ten or fifteen miles you need on Sunday, but you will probably spend $1,500 over the course of a year on repairs. Buy a good bus, and paint it anything but yellow.
6. Make adequate budgetary provisions. Storage, insurance, gas, and repairs will be more than you anticipate.
7. Provide a high-quality ministry to these precious boys and girls in their own environment. Bible study, worship, and ministry will be different from that which you provide in your own Sunday school, but it must not be inferior.
8. Be conscious of the home, social, and physical needs of the children. Boys and girls who need shoes, who are from homes that need food, must be ministered to through meeting physical needs as well as through Bible study.

Again, search the heart of God for his unique will for you and your church. There are many good ways to reach people, and one of these two may be just right for you.

Chapter 77

The Activities Ministry

C hristians ought to have fun. More importantly, they ought to be fun. The negative, sourpuss Pharisees drove everybody away. The happy Christian who is having a great time following Jesus draws people to himself and to his Lord. What better opportunity to meet the unbeliever halfway, as well as know and enjoy your church family, than playing softball together. An activities ministry or a recreation ministry will greatly expand your outreach to the community as well as enhance fellowship within your church.

Everything from crafts and hobbies to roller skating and flag football can be enjoyed at relatively little cost. First Baptist Houston has the luxury of a six-million-dollar activities building with everything from saunas to racquetball and bowling to ceramics. But your church is not limited if you do not have such a building. Basketball gymnasiums, public parks, private homes, bus trips, fellowship halls—many opportunities are available to enrich the life of your church.

Again, many churches have large facilities and full-time staff in this ministry. But whether your activities ministry is large or small, its twofold purpose is to reach people for Christ and build fellowship within the church.

Before the building was built, committees spent two years studying the finest church activities centers, military bases, Jewish community centers, and many others. They took the best ideas, put them together, and today this facility is a model for others. If you invest money in a building, take your time, look around, and build it wisely and well. One afternoon, driving around the facilities of Bellevue

Baptist Church, Memphis, Tennessee, with Adrian Rogers, I asked, "Do you receive any new members because of your activities facility, or is it primarily for your own people?"

"John," he replied, "it is the number one entry point into this church." Today I'm still staggered at that statement. Dr. Rogers, a powerful preacher, may have spoken modestly. One would think the persuasive pulpiteer would be the single most important factor in those who attend this church and subsequently join. But that's what he said, and that's the way it can be.

Keep before your people, particularly those in charge of your activities ministry, the two goals of reaching the lost and building fellowship among the members.

Because acreage is limited on the church campus, the congregation conducts many outdoor activities at other sites in addition to a massive offering of activities in its own facility.

Whether on your campus or off, keep activities focused on evangelism and fellowship. First Houston requires that every team have at least two nonmembers who are required to attend twice a month. At halftime or before or after an event, there is prayer and a brief devotional or testimony. Christian sportsmanship is demonstrated and verbal witness given as unbelievers come to be interested in the things of God while recreating with our people.

Within the church's facility, weight loss classes, jazzercise, saunas, and many other opportunities are offered. The secular world is always responsive to something of interest in a Christian environment. Study the churches with great recreational ministries. Adapt them to your own needs, expand your horizons, and get excited about developing a good activities program. You can reach people for Christ and have fun while doing it.

Chapter 78

Planning the Evangelistic Crusade

"A nd he gave some, apostles; and some, prophets; and some, evangelists; and some, pastors and teachers; for the perfecting of the saints, for the work of the ministry, for the edifying of the body of Christ" (Eph. 4:11–12).

"And he gave some, evangelists." I like that. It means he gave some special giftedness. But he also gave us some who *are* evangelists. The first step in planning an evangelistic crusade is to seek the heart of God about who the evangelist will be. Evangelists are God's gifts to the church, and we should use them.

In addition to full-time or vocational evangelists, however, there are many gifted pastors who have the gift of evangelism. The gifted evangelist is characterized by his passion for souls, his powerful delivery of the message, and his unique giftedness in extending the invitation. The ability to present the gospel forcefully and persuade people to respond is a Holy Spirit-given, Holy Spirit-endowed capacity that not everyone has. It is the ability to articulate clearly the claims of Christ and persuade men and women to respond to his love.

The evangelist you want is not a manipulator. He is not consumed with himself, his personal convenience, his love offering, or a large numerical response to enhance his reputation. He is an experienced man who loves people and who loves lost souls out of the pulpit as much as in, and who tries consistently to win them to Christ in the normal traffic pattern of his life.

The delivery of the evangelist is nearly as important as his message. The ring of authenticity must be there. Credibility and genuineness must be obvious. The fire of his passion for the lost must come from his heart, not simply his mouth and hands.

Years ago, a pastor asked a famous actor why great crowds came to see him act when he only acted out fiction. "I deliver the very oracles of God," the pastor said, "and yet they do not come to hear me preach in droves. What is the difference?"

The actor replied, "Pastor, you speak fact as though it were fiction, and I speak fiction as though it were fact." The facts of the gospel are to be proclaimed forcefully.

Evangelistic sermons should be warmly illustrated, and they should not exceed twenty-five to thirty minutes. The invitation should never be manipulated or overly extended. The evangelist should give God time to work, but at no time do God's work for him. Let the Lord convince the heart to respond. Most evangelistic services begin at 7:30 P.M. and should conclude by 9:00 P.M. Go to 9:45 or 10:00, and your crowd will go down night after night. A good evangelist will not berate the people who are not there. He will lovingly encourage those who are there. The people should be encouraged, not scolded into bringing their friends.

The first night or two of a crusade, the messages should be designed to stimulate the congregation to prayer, holiness, and witnessing, and some of this should be included each night. But the heart of the message for *most* nights must be to the lost. In any crusade, such subjects as the new birth, the love of God, the Second Coming of Christ, the simple plan of salvation, the need for repentance, and heaven and hell should be included. And first and foremost, present the cross.

In giving the invitation, be authoritative, be specific, be urgent, and be honest. The battle is not won by the emotional manipulation of the people, but by the passionate prayer of the pastor, evangelist, and congregation well before the crusade services begin.

The atmosphere of an evangelistic crusade must always be bright and upbeat. Sing choruses. Sing the great old gospel songs. "The Old Rugged Cross," "Saved, Saved, Saved," "Are You Washed in the

Blood," and "Jesus Saves" are always appropriate. Sing the new songs as well. More young people will come if you do. At some point in the services, everyone should stand and welcome one another with a handshake and greeting. Don't ask only the guests to stand. They already feel "on the spot." Let them stand with everyone else.

The appeal for the offering should be clear and brief. Love offering envelopes and/or expense offering envelopes should be distributed. Be clear about whether the offering is for expenses or a love offering for the evangelist. In the best-case scenario, crusade expenses are collected in advance, or they are in the church budget. Envelopes should not be distributed in the plates, but in the back of the pews or passed down the rows by the ushers at the time of the offering appeal. People cannot remove their envelopes, fill them out, and deposit them again in the plate in one procedure.

Use testimonies, but rehearse them to ensure brevity. Have a crusade choir and/or praise team and use a good soloist. Special guests can make a great contribution to attracting the crowd and preparing the heart. But there is danger here, because most special guests, having been flown in at somewhat great expense, will feel under pressure to "give the people their nickel's worth" and often take much too long. The testimony must be short, not exceeding ten to twelve minutes, no matter how famous the special guest might be.

Special nights are an important part of evangelistic crusades. In a church, a children's night with a hot dog supper before the service is an excellent idea. The evangelist should address the kids for a few minutes in order for them to feel comfortable with him. The same is true with a youth night and a pizza party. In such cases, it is best that the teenagers sit together. It is best that the children do not. "Pack a Pew Night," "Old Fashioned Night," "Bring a Friend Night," "Prospect Supper Night"—all of these are wonderful ways to help promote attendance and enthusiasm for your revival crusade.

Regular prayer meetings in the homes and/or at the church should be held at least two weeks in advance of the crusade. The pastor and the entire evangelistic team should meet for prayer at some convenient time each day of the crusade.

Open-air crusades in tents or stadiums as well as indoor crusades in off-site auditoriums and other venues are effective in cooperative crusades with several churches as well as crusades sponsored by just one church. In these settings, the children's meetings and/or teenage meetings can even be held every night of the crusade at another part of the facility with a separate speaker. Remember, the young people will generally be attracted by a different kind of speaker and music than will the adults.

In the days of Billy Sunday, crusades often went six weeks or more. When I "hit the sawdust trail" in the early 1950s, most crusades were two weeks. Then they became one week, but it has been a long time since I've heard of a seven- or eight-night meeting. Most church crusades are four nights, and most cooperative crusades are six.

You can, of course, have a meeting with other churches of your denomination.

I encourage you, however, to consider an interdenominational crusade. Methodists and Presbyterians, Nazarenes and Assemblies, Baptists and Lutherans can easily put aside their minor differences and cooperate in winning the lost to Christ. It is not difficult to find an experienced evangelist who understands the tact required to preach the gospel without causing division in such a setting, yet do so without compromise.

In cooperative crusades, urge the pastors to sit on the platform and let as many participate as possible. Opening prayer, announcements (which should be brief), offering appeal, offertory prayer, and benediction allow five opportunities each night for a different pastor to participate.

Follow-up should be done immediately. The best follow-up is done by the decision counselor who dealt with the person the night before. Contact either in person or by telephone should be made no later than the next day. All who have been missed should be visited in person in their homes on Saturday. This will normally ensure a great influx of public decisions being made on Sunday for those who "came forward" through the weeknights. A crusade that is not centered in the local church and that does not funnel back into the local church is a crusade that is not of God.

The old-time evangelistic crusade is a piece of Americana that is dying, but it ought not be. The medium of television has dictated the emphasis of one-to-one communication. But it's still a wonderful thrill to sit in a football stadium and watch scores of persons come forward to make decisions for Christ. I have never seen a Billy Graham crusade from the platform, from the audience, or on television that I did not weep throughout the invitation. Crusades inside and outside the church are wonderful. Let's not lose them.

Chapter 79

The Art of Effective Change

A stagnant organization is a dying organization. Change means growth and growth means change. Status quo is comfortable; change is uncomfortable. Change hurts. Our criteria for change is never the latest "church growth" fad or the newest innovation of that church down the street. Change is always the result of the prompting of the Holy Spirit and the leadership of the Father. Change for the sake of change is never appropriate. "This isn't working; let's try something different" is a blueprint for failure.

How does the wise pastor facilitate change? As you consider the needs of your church and opportunities of your community and seek the heart of God in prayer, the Lord will normally give you the vision and direction he would have you lead the church before he gives it to the congregation. This is not to say that only you hear the voice of God in your spirit, and only you know his will. It is not to say that good ideas seldom come up "through the ranks." It is to say that the job of leaders is to lead, and that means getting out in front.

Leadership is lonely. It is dangerous and risky. But it is for the purpose of leading your congregation that the Lord has called you to this ministry. Leadership will often require you to go before your congregation and share a vision of change.

The key elements of change are information and patience. When the Lord gives you the vision for a new ministry, new music, new direction for your church, or anything else, first gather your leaders and begin to discuss the matter. Remember to "bring along" those legitimizers whose support you will need because of their influence with broad numbers of your members. Slowly begin to explain the situation, listing possible solutions, and share with your people that you sense the Lord has led you to one of them as the answer. Every vision needs refining. The people will offer good suggestions, many of which have never occurred to you.

Don't call for a decision on the spot. Lay it before your leaders, discuss it, ask them to pray about it and meet with you at a later date. Continue the process through increasing numbers of your people. The next step is to speak to the appropriate committee, then your leadership group, and then the church. At each level, lay it before the people as something in which you sense the Lord is leading you. If a person says to me, "God told me," I am going to walk away. If he says, "God told me to tell you," I am going to run. If he says, "I sense the Lord is leading me," I will listen.

Good decisions are prayed over and carefully thought through. The decisions I have later had to acknowledge were wrong were decisions I made too quickly. Back-pedaling now is better than back-pedaling from the decision later. Patience is of the essence. Make a list of the pros and cons as well as potential obstacles. Discuss and pray about alternative ideas to deal with the obstacles. If the plan is of God, nothing will be insurmountable.

Prepare the hearts of your people for change. Before introducing a bold new program to win the world, spend some Sundays preaching about Jesus' compassion for the lost. Before you introduce that million-dollar building program for a new youth recreation building, talk about the needs of a dying generation of teenagers and the responsibility of the church to reach them. Remind the people that the apostle Paul said, "I am made all things to all men, that I might by all means save some" (1 Cor. 9:22). Emphasize Paul's use of the phrase "all means."

Remind your people that *the message never changes, but the methods must be ever changing.* Sharing the good news of Christ's love is ageless, but the means do change. The telegraph has been replaced by the radio, the radio by the television, the television by the Internet, and the end is not yet. Remind your people that God has placed within the hands of the church means for sharing the gospel of which our forefathers never dreamed. Take your time, give adequate information, instill the vision, and try to get everyone "on board."

Provide a forum in which to allow questions. "What will happen if we do this? What will we lose if we don't? What are the risks? What is the cost? Will there be a committee? Will this be done at the sacrifice of other programs in the church?" God's people are good people. They are wise, and they can handle the truth. In their hearts, they want to win people to faith in Christ. But change can be unsettling, even frightening, and the older we get the more that is true.

As mentioned, sometimes those ideas for change will come up through the ranks. In his book, *Unleashing the Church*, Frank Tillapaugh encourages us to release our members to begin ministries that are on their hearts. If a member comes to you and says, "Pastor, I think we should have a Bible study for those poor children in that housing addition down on Eighth Street, say, 'Good, you can do it! How can we help you?'" If a potential ministry is credible and the person is dependable, it is quite likely he is the instrument through which God has spoken to the church.

Use the church paper to announce a meeting next Sunday afternoon: "All those interested in starting a ministry to the poor children in the housing project on Eighth Street are invited to meet in Room 120." Assign a staff member or church leader to facilitate; let the person share his dream, and see who shows up. Help him find the funds and the methods to carry out the vision. Many of the most productive ministries in First Baptist Houston were begun in precisely this manner.

When you begin a new ministry, don't be afraid to experiment. Everything doesn't have to be forever. Perhaps the housing project ministry is not something the Lord wants you to do next year but wants you to do this year. Let the person feel the freedom to back out after a while. Do all you can to support his vision and commend him when it has run its course. Perhaps God will lead him to another.

While this is true, however, it is still important to make every effort to "see it through." Give new ministries time. The very best will often struggle at first. How unlike our world today is the world of the last century and the one before that. But the human heart is still desperately wicked and in need of the loving touch of the Savior. Be willing to change. Do whatever it takes to touch human need wherever you find it.

It might require some major adjustments to bring the light of God's love to the dark corners of a decadent society. But the church that will adapt without losing the purity of its message or the passion of its ministry will be an effective tool for reaching people for Christ.

Chapter 80

Witness Training and Outreach

T he Lausanne Covenant states, "Evangelism itself is the proclamation of the historical, Biblical Christ as Savior and Lord, with a view to persuading people to come to Him personally and so be reconciled to God." Jesus called this going into all the world to preach the good news to every creature. An unfortunate trend has developed, however, which calls evangelism everything from social ministry to fellowship to friendship. If we are to change our world, our people must have not only a clear view of evangelism, but have equipping that is personal, comprehensive, precise, urgent, and bold.

Unquestionably, our society is becoming less Christian. Traditional Christian assumptions are not readily accepted without living proof. Revivals and other group approaches will become less effective unless they center on reaching personal networks of influence. As much as I love crusades, the personal one-to-one witness remains the single most important method of evangelism.

The Living Bible version of Colossians 4:5–6 says it well: "Make the most of your chances to tell others the Good News. Be wise in all your contacts with them. Let your conversation be gracious as well as sensible, for then you will have the right answer for everyone" (TLB). A church equipping its members to reach out to their networks of influence is still the most effective means for reaching its "Jerusalem."

Unfortunately, many church growth experts have been so galvinized around "friendship evangelism" that they have rejected any sort of evangelistic visitation as "confrontational" or "intrusional." I think I remember the apostle Paul to have been rather confrontational.

Every local church must provide training to equip its members in evangelism. The approach to equipping its members must be comprehensive, including structured programs, methods, and outreach visitation. To exclude training methodology means that in most cases evangelism is more discussed than done.

Debating whether lifestyle evangelism or Monday night prospect visitation is best is like debating which of your children you love the most. Both are essential to fulfilling the Great Commission. The wise pastor will remember that neither will occur, however, unless there is an atmosphere of evangelistic intensity in the life of the church. Enthusiastic singing, warm fellowship, good preaching, and personal testimonies—all contribute to an ongoing consciousness of the people that "knowing Christ" has a contagiousness about it that must burst out of the seams of the church.

Over the years, at First Baptist Houston, it has been difficult to determine whether more people came to Christ through Monday night prospect visitation or through "lifestyle witnessing" by church members. But the degree to which both happen is inseparably linked to the motivation they receive every Sunday. Let's talk first about the structured visitation program.

Structured formal witness training opportunity should be regularly provided for your people. Sunday night classes are usually the best. The "Roman Road," "Christian Witness Training," "Evangelism Explosion" and "Faith" are among the many successful programs available. It is easy to teach your people how to lead someone to Christ. It can be most difficult to inspire them to actually do it. Classroom training should be followed by hands-on opportunity for in-home prospect visitation accompanied by a seasoned visitor. The best time is Sunday night or Monday night.

Teach your people to be "wise as serpents and harmless as doves." Don't carry a big Bible to the door. Pray before you go. Ring the doorbell. Never ask, "Mrs. Smith?" Her attitude might be, "Maybe I am Mrs. Smith and maybe I'm not. That depends on who you are." Don't ask the person's name; state the person's name. If it happens to be wrong, he or she will tell you. The most difficult part of the call is getting into the house. Here is how you do it.

Ring the doorbell, step back as the door is opened, and all in one smiling sentence say, "Hello Mrs. Smith, we are Bill and Mary Jones from First Baptist Church. May we come in?" Once you are seated, be sensitive to the mood in the house. Talk about them, learn their background, and determine their spiritual condition. Then present the gospel in the method by which you were trained and, if possible, lead them to Christ. A little bit of training and practical instruction goes a long way. At first, your people will be fearful of evangelistic visitation. But the good news is that once they have led their first person to Christ, they will be anxious to do it again and again.

Lifestyle witnessing can be equally thrilling. Certainly, gospel tracts can be given to total strangers on the first floor of the elevator with a "yes" response by the tenth floor. But the best lifestyle evangelism is cultivating friendships in the marketplace, the school, and the neighborhood and sharing Jesus in normal everyday conversation.

Years ago I discovered what I believe to be the missing ingredient in one-to-one gospel presentations—the all-important personal testimony. Listen again to the record of Andrew, the master soul winner:

> One of the two which heard John speak, and followed him, was Andrew, Simon Peter's brother.
>
> He first findeth his own brother Simon, and saith unto him, We have found the Messias, which is, being interpreted, the Christ. And he brought him to Jesus. And when Jesus beheld him, he said, Thou art Simon the son of Jona: thou shalt be called Cephas, which is by interpretation, a stone (John 1:40–42).

Note the order of Andrew's masterful method:

1. He found his brother.
2. He told him he had found Jesus.
3. He brought him to Jesus.

Don't leave out that important second step. The force of the personal testimony, "Let me tell you about Jesus whom I have found," is at once penetrating and disarming to the unbeliever. Through the years I have found it unnecessary to look for ways to bring Jesus into everyday conversation. Keep your heart and your ears open, and virtually every interchange with a fellow human being will contain some phrase which you can "pick up on" to turn the conversation to the things of God.

And, of course, remember that Jesus, the consummate trainer of evangelists, was first himself the evangelist. Set the example in your structured prospect visitation as well as in your lifestyle witness. Both your words and your example will be the pattern for your people.

Chapter 81

Vacation Bible School

E very church should have a summer Vacation Bible School. In the old days, these lasted for two weeks. Today, most such schools last only one week. In First Baptist Houston, we had Bible school immediately after school was out. The theory is that in doing so, we could "get the kids" before their parents left on vacation. I have often wondered, however, if the end of summer might be better. Perhaps in the dog days of summer when kids are getting bored and are not quite ready to go back to school, their interest in "something to do" might be heightened.

The best advertising for VBS will not be done through newspaper or radio but by the invitation of excited children to their friends. Times are normally 9:00 A.M. to noon, Monday through Friday, with attendance peaking on Thursday and dropping off on Friday. I have wondered, therefore, if Monday through Thursday would be better. But it could well be that attendance would then simply peak on Wednesday. Be aware that if you plan a "decision service" on the day when attendance is the highest, it will likely be the next to last day.

The Bible school must be directed by a trained, committed person. If the church does not have appropriate staff leadership, enlist a talented church member who has it on his or her heart. Good Vacation Bible School materials abound. Check with your local Christian bookstore or denominational headquarters.

During Bible school, the children meet in various classrooms for unique activities: hand painting, model making; the opportunities are endless. One year in our Bible school, my wife taught a class of fifth-graders. One of their projects was to write a script for a television newscast, in which each was a reporter or news anchor or witness, reporting the resurrection of Christ, his ascension, and the day of Pentecost. Their video was a classic.

Time-outs for playground activities, snowcones, etc. are always appropriate. One central rally should be held toward the end of each morning where all the children assemble together.

I recommend only one decision service. The message should be delivered by the pastor; it should be brief, simple, well illustrated, and totally without pressure. After a week in the Bible school environment, most children simply need to have the gospel clearly presented, with an opportunity to respond.

In the church, that annual "decision service" was only for third-, fourth-, and fifth-graders. Our sixth-graders were part of our middle school or junior high division, and high school students join adults as Bible school workers. A Friday night graduation service in which a program is presented, projects are displayed, and diplomas are awarded, is a good attraction for parents of the children as well as a good entry point into your church. Even with kindergartners, everyone likes to "see their kids graduate."

Expedite the process of follow-up for those who make decisions, but don't rush them into baptism and church membership. The following Monday, begin visiting the homes of boys and girls who have made decisions. If the parents are receptive, schedule a series of classes for the children to learn more about Christ, baptism, and church membership. First Baptist Houston is very thorough in following up children who made decisions in the church, doing its best to determine that they have truly come to know Christ in a personal way. Each child receives a personal interview, and the quality of their decisions and churchmanship has been rather high through the years as a result.

I encourage you as pastor to give high priority of your own personal time to "being seen" at Bible school. Go to the classes, learn the names of the children, romp with them, and eat snowcones with them. It is a wonderful bonding time for pastor and children. Bible school is an important activity for building great families and great churches. Plan your vacation time around Bible school. Postpone that golf game until the afternoon. Enjoy the Vacation Bible School experience with the children. You'll be glad you did.

Chapter 82

Summer Camps

How can I adequately state the vital importance of the ministry of "retreating" in the life of the church? Weekend retreats, overnight trips, lock-ins—all are of tremendous value in the spiritual development of God's people. There is, however, something very special about a week at camp. I admit to being just a bit prejudiced. I was "born again" at just such a camp.

During the summer of 1952, I traveled with a jazz band known as Paul Nielson and his Dixieland All Stars. Our last engagement was at Selma, Alabama, at the officer's club of Craig Air Base. Concluding a long summer of night clubbing, I returned home to Perry, Oklahoma, for a few days of rest before returning for my sophomore year at Oklahoma State University.

On my second day home, I chanced to meet the pastor of my parents' church. He invited me to attend Falls Creek Assembly in the Arbuckle Mountains near Davis, Oklahoma, which was in full swing. Falls Creek is the world's largest Christian youth camp. Each year over forty thousand teenagers from across the state gather for a wonderful experience. Almost as a joke, I accepted his invitation. Little did I know that in less than a week God would dramatically change my life.

Throughout the week my response to what I was experiencing turned from ridicule to moderate interest to great fascination. By Friday night the Holy Spirit had prepared my heart. "So many hundreds of you are making decisions each night," said Charlie Taylor, the preacher. "I really doubt the sincerity of many of you." "Tonight," he continued, "I don't care if one person comes. I want one who means business." In my heart I said, "I'll be that one."

Indeed, I was the first person to walk down the aisle on that hot Oklahoma summer evening. Beneath an old oak tree I fell to my knees as someone prayed with me and led me to faith in Christ in a life-transforming experience. Strange as it might seem, it was in that moment that Jesus not only came into my heart but called me into full-time Christian ministry. Three weeks later I would stand before the Immanuel Baptist Church in Pryor, Oklahoma, give my testimony, play the trumpet, and lead the music in my first evangelistic service.

Following twelve years as an evangelist, I would spend thirty-five years as a pastor. At this writing, that has been exactly forty-seven years and three days ago. Happily I report to you that I never looked back. I wouldn't trade it. The trail has been long and joyful with the blessings far outweighing the heartaches. How can one describe the joy of forty-seven years of knowing and serving Jesus Christ in full-time ministry? And it all happened because thousands of wonderful Oklahoma Baptists provided a youth camp for teenagers to get away from the crowd and give serious consideration to the claims of Christ on their lives. Let's talk about that.

We live in a fast-paced world. Thousands of impressions fill our minds through our senses every single day. There is so much to distract us, so much to deter and confuse us. The heavenly transmitter is speaking as clearly and loudly as ever, but our earthly receivers are so crowded and clouded that they rarely hear the voice of God.

Our Lord often rose before dawn to seek the Father's face in a quiet place alone. Three years ago, I prepared a literal prayer closet where the Lord and I meet virtually every morning at five o'clock. In that quiet presence the Father speaks to my heart. Ideas come. Direction is given. Convictions are strengthened and new commitments are made.

Elijah found the Lord, not in the fire or the storm or the earthquake, but in the still, small voice of God (see 1 Kings 19:12). That came to him as it comes to us—in the quiet solitude of our lives.

One of the great things that happens at a large youth camp is the inspiration of the sheer numbers who are there. Countless numbers of young people come from small churches and feel they are virtually the only young Christians in the world. What a powerful impact is made when they realize Christianity is no off-beat cult but the most powerful force on earth.

Another beauty of summer camps is their built-in attraction, which appeals to all young people. Many of the teenagers who go to Falls Creek or any other summer camp probably don't go primarily for spiritual reasons. They go because it is fun. The gals go because of the guys, and the guys go because of the gals. There is swimming and hiking, softball and music. What teenager, Christian or not, will not get excited about an invitation to spend a week having fun with hundreds or thousands of other teenagers?

Ah, but once they are there, things begin to happen. It always takes two or three days to deprogram them from the clamor of the world, particularly those who walk around listening to the latest rock CD on their headphones. Young people shouldn't be allowed to take radios, jam boxes, etc., to camp. It is a time to get away from secular distractions. After a few days, minds clear and the Word starts to get through.

For several years in Houston we had three summer camps: one for children grades three through five; one for middle schoolers, grades six through eight; and one for high schoolers, grades nine through twelve. Normally, a child who was just going into the next grade was allowed to attend the appropriate camp—that is, eighth-grade graduates are eligible to attend the ninth through twelfth grade summer camp. Christians and non-Christians of all kinds should not only be allowed but encouraged to attend. Every effort should be made to keep the tuition well within reach of everyone. There are always wonderful people in your congregation who will happily provide half or full scholarships for those youth who are unable to pay.

During the camp, mornings should be reserved for Bible study and worship, allowing ample breaks for refreshment and relaxation between each. Afternoons are for recreation and leisure. Evenings are for worship. Young preachers are the best camp pastors, and it is not difficult to find qualified, mature young men who can relate to your teenagers and spend time playing with them through the day. Let the kids have fun. Let them be themselves. Rules must be enforced, but the secret is to *not have too many rules.*

I recommend not giving an invitation for salvation, rededication, or full-time Christian ministry until the last two nights of the camp. Give God time to work. Let the Holy Spirit build.

Have ample sponsors. Have various kinds of competition between the different grades and cabins or dorms. Enlist sponsors who really love the kids. A joint sponsor-parent-camper meeting must be held in advance of the camp so parents and young people understand the rules. Every sponsor must be able to give spiritual counsel to their kids as well as be able to personally lead them to Christ.

Following the evening decision services, each sponsor should take those making decisions from his group to a quiet place for relaxed and protracted personal counsel and prayer. Camp sponsors should meet each evening for forty-five minutes to an hour before dinner to coordinate activities and events, discuss problems, and pray for the kids.

Back to Falls Creek for a moment. Since finding Christ there as my personal Savior many years ago, I have had the pleasure of being invited back five times to "preach a week" at Falls Creek. The last night, there are always several hundred young people who make decisions for Christ. Throughout my travels across America and the world, I do not recall having preached anywhere, in any city or any country, without having someone to approach me and say, "I made a decision the week you were at Falls Creek."

It might well be that more lives have been changed in camps than in all our crusades combined. What a great ministry it is. By all means, *take those kids to camp!*

Chapter 83

Planting New Churches

O n a warm, sunny afternoon in 1988, God tugged at my heart. His instrument was the chairman of the "declining churches" committee of our local Baptist association. For over an hour, we viewed slides of more than 125 churches in Houston that were near extinction. With windows boarded up, grass grown high, and other obvious signs of decline, it was apparent that something had to be done. Someone must do something to help these precious little congregations.

God spoke to my heart, "I want you to be that someone." I called a meeting of the pastors and asked, "What can we do?" Their answer was predictable: "We need prayer, people, and money."

The overwhelming majority of these "at-risk" churches were in transitional communities. As often happens, Anglos were moving to the suburbs and the remaining faithful few had no idea how to go about reaching the tens of thousands of ethnics who lived around them.

God had earlier spoken to my heart while preaching a crusade in Mexico about the 30 percent of the population back in Houston who were lost Hispanics. God was getting my attention. Little did I dream he would lead me to a "kingdom mind-set" and that I would spend the remaining years of my pastorate leading our people to "give themselves away." We have done that through the years, and I can assure you of two things: (1) the attitude of our people was, "the kingdom of God is more important than any one church" and (2) by far the greatest joy of my ministry was to lead our people to become a "kingdom-minded" church.

Since that time the church has begun sixty-three missions in Houston. Approximately half have become strong enough to "spin off" and become self-sustaining congregations. Today, the Sunday morning attendance in those "spin-off" mission churches, when added to the number of current mission churches, equals the size of the home church. Four to five thousand attend Sunday morning Bible study and worship in the main church, while about eight thousand honor God on Sunday through the mother church *and* the missions she has birthed.

But I am getting ahead of my story. Two other factors converged to bring about the conviction that I must lead our people to "give themselves away." The first happened far away from our city. At a conference in a major eastern city, I heard the question posed to the pastors of the largest churches in my denomination: "Considering parking distances, escalating building costs, multiplicity of facilities, crowded buildings, and other factors, how many persons can one pastor say 'grace' over? Does there come a time when we have to ask, 'How big is big enough?'" The consensus of the pastors was "about five thousand."

The second thing that happened about that time was a meeting with Bill Lipps. Bill was the pastor of a declining church at our doorstep. Barely a mile away, the wonderful facilities of his Westview Baptist Church were 90 percent unused. "Brother John," Bill asked, "what can First Baptist Church do to help?" Within a month, I took the public position that First Baptist Church would henceforth be a "kingdom church."

Through the years, over five hundred members have gone back into those churches, many of them the congregations from whence they came. A special offering is received fifty-two weeks of the year to support this ministry. Sunday school departments additionally give time, money, and labor to assist in everything from repairing roofs and building baby beds to distributing food and visiting prospects.

The people loved the "missionary spirit" of their church. I am thinking at this moment of two successful attorneys, a doctor and a wealthy businesswoman, who served the needs of the poor in these missions every Sunday of the year. From these missions have come hundreds of converts, at least twenty-five full-time Christian workers, and a benevolence ministry that exceeds $200,000 a year in food, furniture, clothes, and direct financial support.

Attempting to rescue small churches, however, is only a part of the "kingdom mind-set" of First Houston. Special ministries to jails and prisons, transients, alcoholics, homosexuals, and countless others are a part of the mission ministry of Houston's First Baptist Church. During the 1990s the church led about as many people to Christ outside the building as inside. Would these persons ever have come to us? Probably not. Would someone else have reached them? Perhaps. But this I know: they were born into the kingdom, at least in part, because the Holy Spirit birthed a passion for the larger kingdom of God in the heart of one pastor and his people.

If we are to take the Great Commission seriously, we must start thousands of new missions churches all over America. There are several reasons why we need to do this: (1) Most churches in America have less than one hundred people as regular attenders. (2) Nearly 80 percent of nonchurched Americans are low income or ethnic. (3) Most Americans choose to attend small churches. With the continuing decline of the American family, the number of persons seeking the family atmosphere of the small church will only increase. Planting new churches will not only build the kingdom, but it will also strengthen the "sense of family" for which the heart so desperately longs.

Dear pastor, hear my heart. Our church is a megachurch, but megachurches will never win the world by *addition*. The need is *multiplication*. The size and influence of your church is not paramount; the expansion of the kingdom is. New works grow fastest. The quickest and best way to fulfill the Great Commission is to divide and multiply.

There are 670,000 cities and villages in India. If Jesus had preached to one village per day in India, after these two thousand years he would just be finishing his preaching tour of India. But suppose he multiplied his ministry by preaching one sermon to one city, won one convert, and then trained him for six months. Then he and the convert repeated the process in two cities, dividing every six months. How long would it have taken them to preach in every Indian city? Not 210 years or even 100, *but only seventeen years!* During these seventeen years, they would have trained 670,000 evangelists and planted multitudes of new churches.

The apostle Paul told young Timothy, "And the things that thou hast heard of me among many witnesses, the same commit thou to faithful men, who shall be able to teach others also" (2 Tim. 2:2).

Church planting produces rapid growth, with the greatest percentage of growth in a new church coming within the first three years. On the day of Pentecost there were 120 disciples. But that day 3,000 converts were added to the church. A few days later the Book of Acts reports, "And the Word of God increased; and the number of the disciples multiplied greatly" (Acts 6:7). Historians suggest that within three months, their number grew to approximately 55,000.

I want to ask you to search your heart and answer this question, "Do I truly have a kingdom mind-set?" Is the growth of his work more important to me than the growth of my own? Please don't pass over this lightly. It is so easy to say, "Everything I do is for the glory of God." But is your own glory in there somewhere, just a little bit? How important to you is your reputation? Those records of growth might attract the pastor search committee of that megachurch you've had your eye on. That baptismal record might get you a write-up in your denominational paper, which in turn can mean prestigious speaking engagements.

But all these things accrue only to our personal benefit and the stroking of our egos. Take another look at the cross and ask yourself, "Does my approach to ministry emulate Calvary? Am I giving myself away? Am I leading my people to give themselves away?" The answer, which comes from deep inside your heart, will be inseparably linked to your decision to lead your church into a mission-planting "kingdom mind-set."

Chapter 84

Special Days

I love holidays—especially the holy days. What can compare with Easter, Thanksgiving, and Christmas? Secular holidays are also important, particularly Memorial Day, Independence Day, Labor Day. Let's talk about these special times.

Encourage your families to enjoy these holidays, and enjoy them yourself. Don't put a guilt trip on your people because they are out of town on a holiday. The annual drive to Grandma's house strengthens the family unit, which in turn strengthens the church. Encourage your people to go. Tell them to have a great time and assure them that you will be praying for their safety as they travel.

Capitalize on difficult holidays. A Labor Day can be a great time for a concert and church picnic. A Fourth of July weekend can be a special time. Place flags around your church. Ask the choir to sing "Battle Hymn of the Republic." Have a color guard. Salute the colors. Sing the national anthem. Have a testimony from a war hero or bring in a great preacher known for stirring patriotic sermons and advertise that you are doing so. Your attendance will go up, not down, if you make lemonade out of the lemon of holidays.

Memorial Day weekends are wonderful times to recognize families who have lost loved ones that year as well as those who have lost loved ones at any time in the military. List their names, recognize them, pray for them. Preach on heaven. Preach on being grateful for the sacrifice of others. Be creative and turn holidays into special days.

Be flexible. Be willing to adjust schedules and times. The Sunday after Christmas, we have no Sunday school and only one morning service. The consolidation of two low attendances into one strong attendance is "making lemonade." Christmas morning is a special time. Children squeal with glee as they open their presents. Families gather around the table for a special breakfast. Encourage your people to observe their family traditions and be willing to adjust your schedule occasionally to "fit in." There should be nothing sacred about a schedule.

Make good plans and advertise them well in advance. Easter Sunday brings the largest church attendance of the year. On this day it might be wise to add an additional morning service. Sunrise services appear to have lost their popularity, but they can be exciting and new to a younger congregation. Everything old is indeed new again, and many of your folks have never even heard of the old. Others will nostalgically appreciate your "bringing back the old days."

Place lilies or other flowers around the church platform. Use banners. Enlarge the orchestra. Make it special. There is no Sunday morning in the year like Easter. And don't make an issue out of whether it was initially a pagan holiday, and how too much emphasis is placed on new clothes and bunny rabbits. Point to new life through faith in the resurrected Christ of which these things are only a reminder. Don't attack the negative, especially not on Easter. Amplify the positive. Jesus Christ is alive and well.

Now hear this! Preach a very *short* sermon on Easter Sunday morning. The crowd will be large and filled with guests. This might be the only chance you will have at them until next Easter. Seize the moment. Be positive, and above all, get out on time. Better still, get out early and then do good follow-up visitation.

Easter week services may precede the great day. Noonday services are particularly attractive. In First Baptist Church of Houston, we commemorated the death of Christ through a beautiful Lord's Supper service on Thursday night. The holiday week begins on Friday. Although your people will be there in great numbers on Sunday, they are usually nowhere to be found on Friday. Move your "Good Friday" service to Good Friday eve. Your attendance will be low on Friday but high on Thursday.

Thanksgiving is family time. What a beautiful season of the year it is. Leaves turn, sweaters come out, football games abound, and people take trips to Grandma's with turkey dinners and all the trimmings. Who doesn't love Thanksgiving? Years ago I was preaching a crusade in Canada, where Thanksgiving came a week before Thanksgiving in America. What joy! Two Thanksgivings in one year!

Thanksgiving services at the church on Thursday will be poorly attended. Thanksgiving eve will be the same. Tuesday night is the night to have your Thanksgiving service. Again, the Lord's Supper, special decorations, great music, and personal testimonies of gratitude, with a brief message by the pastor are in order.

Thanksgiving services should be concluded with a special benevolent offering for the poor. Church offices should be closed on Thursday and Friday. Give your staff the day off, allowing leisure time to enjoy this great holiday with their families.

Christmas Eve services are special. Many churches offer more than one, some as many as four or five, even beginning in early afternoon. Multiple services may well be conducted by different pastors and staff. There is, however, something special about 11:00 P.M. Christmas Eve services. Dim lights, processions with candles, the singing of hymns by children and adult choirs—these are a treasure. Again, the message should be brief. One year I simply read the Christmas story without comment. It was most effective.

Make much of these special days. They are part of the great traditions that go into building great churches.

Chapter 85

Special Events

U nder this broad umbrella, the creative pastor will find the latitude to meet the special needs of his people and his community. Of course, there are church picnics and fellowships,
after-church socials, Bible schools, choir concerts, etc. But I refer particularly to those one- and two-day opportunities that present themselves from time to time, primarily because of the availability of special
speakers or musicians. Often a seminar speaker, author, or outstanding personality will be in your area. You might learn either directly
from them or by the grapevine that they are going to be nearby.

Make a list of all the speakers you would like to have and contact
them for available dates and/or find out when they are "coming
through." Many singing groups and seminars, for example, have a
fairly large travel expense budget which can be cut in half if they are
coming from one thousand miles away to be in your church one day
and a church in a neighboring city the next.

I am often asked, "Did you allow such secular meetings as a
Chamber of Commerce banquet or Rotary Club to use your facilities?" The answer is yes. Is it not wiser to welcome a hundred unbelievers who need a place to have their annual meeting about gardening
or the environment than to have the annual meeting of the mission
society in your facility? If we indeed exist for those beyond our membership, anything we do which brings the unbeliever into the brick
and mortar of our facilities is worthwhile. They have probably
requested the use of your church because you have ample room and
are well located. Having a good experience, learning your location,

and enjoying your hospitality might establish the best relationship with an unbeliever your church will ever have. These kinds of people are likely to return on Easter or Christmas. Then you can meet them, cultivate a friendship, and perhaps lead them to faith in Christ and church membership.

I urge you to dispense with any policy that does not allow secular groups to meet in your facilities. These are the very kind of people you *want* in your facilities. Too often people feel we view them only as prospects to be targeted for our own ultimate gain—that is, their money. Illustrating that we exist not for what we can get but for what we can give is a wise approach to the secular society we are trying to reach.

Throughout the course of a year many "crossover" events will present themselves to you. These are the type of activities that will minister to your people and be of interest to the general public as well—such events, for example, as an evening with Paul Harvey, Chuck Colson, or James Dobson. You will want to clear your calendar for speakers such as these and have them in your church any time you can get them.

Programs and seminars that offer help to the family, the hurting, the depressed, or the addict are always helpful to your people and attractive to the secular person. Who doesn't want help with a child addicted to drugs or assistance with a troubled marriage?

Concerts are of particular interest to both believer and unbeliever. Often costs appear to be prohibitive, but this can usually be overcome by selling tickets. Local Christian radio stations will often provide free advertising and even joint sponsorship of the concert, for no more in return than a ten-minute spot at intermission to talk about their ministry. What sanctuary would not be filled to overflowing to hear the Brooklyn Tabernacle Choir, Steve Green, or other popular groups and artists?

Honorariums, expenses, and other arrangements should be clearly spelled out in advance. These are usually negotiable and are always best done by contract. Both a love offering and an honorarium should never be paid; one or the other must suffice. When you have committed to pay for the expenses and honorarium of an artist or group, you will need the offering to help cover your own expenses such as advertising, security, etc. Of course, you cannot sell tickets and receive an offering. If tickets are sold, therefore, they should be sold at a price that will cover anticipated expenses, including honorarium for the artist with enough left over to cover your own expenses.

And, of course, the artist, group, or their representative should not be allowed to make the financial appeal for themselves if an offering is received. This must be done *only* by the pastor. Outside speakers and musicians usually have books, CDs, and cassettes for sale. Selling socks, T-shirts, and ties is strictly financially motivated and should not be allowed. Carrying home a book or CD is spiritually uplifting. Wearing "Sammy the Singer's" T-shirt is not.

Special events play a great part in reaching the unbeliever and ministering to your own flock. They also add a spark to the feeling of your people and your city that yours is the church "where it's at." By the way, put those big events on holiday weekends, which normally have low attendance. You can make lemonade out of that lemon.

Chapter 86

Seizing the Opportunity

T he creative pastor will always be on the alert for that opportunity that might never come again. It might not be obvious at first, but it is often there. A sign on the marquee with a comment about a current event might bring a picture to the front page of the local newspaper. A visiting dignitary—an outstanding Christian who is in your area for another engagement—might be available for a Sunday morning testimony in your church.

Every week opportunities to enhance and promote the work of the Lord come within your grasp. Treat every situation as an opportunity to spread the word. A speaking engagement in a distant city from which a certain company is transferring hundreds of employees to your city could be most advantageous. Serving on a community project committee with non-Christians can create friendships and open doors for the gospel.

Encourage converts who have not been baptized by the end of the year to do so on the first Sunday in January. This is a great way for them to begin the new year as well as a good means of beginning to make disciples of converts.

Giving an invitation at a Vacation Bible School commencement might not be customary, but it can be a golden opportunity to win parents to Christ who might attend your church at no other time. Visit prospects the day after they attend your church. Visit good Sunday morning prospects that very afternoon. Keep your eyes open, be alert, strike while the iron is hot, and seize the opportunity.

Always preach on important current issues. The Saturday night that Princess Diana was killed, I stayed up all night and wrote a sermon for Sunday morning. Its title: "What Shall It Profit a Man if He Gain the Whole World and Lose His Own Soul?"

Two nights after our hostages were released from captivity in Iran, our auditorium was filled for a patriotic welcome-home service and prayer meeting. Flags representing each hostage lined the altar as guests and dignitaries responded quickly to our invitation to speak.

Our Lord, who commanded us to be "as wise as serpents and as harmless as doves," constantly gives us opportunity to enhance the work of the kingdom. With your heart attuned to his Spirit, your eyes and ears open to circumstances, watch and faint not. You might be entertaining angels of opportunity unaware.

Part 8

The Church Staff

Chapter 87

Administering the Staff

F ew things are more important in building a good staff than building good personal relationships. Strangers can indeed wed into a spiritual unity of mind and purpose, but very often long-time friends in other settings make some of the best staff members in the new setting of your current ministry. But whether life-long or new, developing friendships between pastor and staff is high priority.

The best pastor and staff relationship is not that of employer and employee, but that of friend and friend. This, of course, begins by calling staff with which you are personally compatible. "Can two walk together, except they be agreed?" (Amos 3:2). Friendship develops out of time and trust. To keep confidences, be honest with each other, admit an error, confess a fault, to forgive and overlook are essential ingredients in building the trust level within a church staff.

Jesus complimented his disciples, rewarded their trust, and elevated their relationships when he said, "Henceforth I call you not servants . . . but . . . friends" (John 15:15). Make the effort to build personal relationships with your staff and their families. They will be some of the most loyal supporters and productive helpers in your ministry.

In spite of the best relationships, there will be times when corrections must be given and decisions must be overruled. When you do, never talk about a staff member behind his back to another person. And always be the initiator. Jesus said that if a person has anything against you, we should "leave there thy gift before the altar, and . . . first be reconciled to thy brother" (Matt. 5:24). Notice our Lord says you are to initiate the reconciliation. He did not say, "If you have something against him," but even if you don't and he has something against you, you are still to take the first step.

There's no such thing as a staff without problems. But disagreements need not lead to broken relationships. A church knows when a staff is not together, and the church will suffer because of it. Unity in the body is essential and must be maintained at any cost. Give high priority to staff professional and personal relations.

The busy pastor will always attempt to be accessible to his people. They are never an interruption to our ministry; they *are* our ministry. However, there will be those times when a response to a member's request for your time must be delayed or delegated to another staff member. But the staff should know that your door is always open to them. It is not possible to individually pastor every person in a church with two or three thousand members or more. The wise pastor, therefore, will pastor the staff, who in turn pastor their individual segment of the congregation. Be available to the staff and always be supportive.

In the context of the Holy Spirit, fluidity of personal relationships thrive. Nowhere is this more true than in the relationship between a pastor and his staff. And, by the way, please note that the pastor is not *on* the church staff; the pastor *has* a staff with which to work. Their first responsibility under God is to him and his responsibility is to them.

Because the Holy Spirit creates an atmosphere in which every relationship operates more easily, regular prayer is a high priority in the life of the pastor and his staff. While nothing takes the place of private morning prayer, our need to pray together, to pray for one another, and to be prayed for is great. The apostle Paul acknowledged this when he said, "Brethren, pray for us" (1 Thess. 5:25).

In First Baptist Houston, I often prayed with individual staff members when they approached me about a specific problem or need in their ministry. Beyond this, every staff meeting was opened with a season of prayer, usually from five to fifteen minutes. Additionally, we set aside Tuesday noons as an hour of fasting and prayer for our senior staff. This not only enhanced our relationship but also revitalized our church. If true revival comes, it will come on the wings of prayer, and it will not be unrelated to a people who are encouraged to pray because of the example set by their pastor and staff.

I am often amazed to hear that some churches never have a regular staff meeting. That's like a contractor trying to build a house without a plan. If the carpenter doesn't know what the plumber is doing and the roofer doesn't know what the electrician is doing, the result will be disastrous. For many years, we used the following schedule for Tuesday staff meetings:

1. 8:30 A.M.—individual staff division leaders or program staff met with their personnel, assistants, secretaries, etc. This constituted about fourteen staff division leaders meeting with six or eight individuals each.

2. 10:30 A.M.—program staff (fourteen division heads) met for one hour. This included ten to fifteen minutes of prayer and forty-five to fifty minutes of discussion. The pastor was in attendance, but the associate pastor presided. A printed agenda was distributed, reports were given, and decisions were made quickly. It was critical that the right hand knew what the left hand was doing.

3. 11:30 A.M.—all employees, including cooks, custodians, secretaries, joined the entire staff in prayer until 12:00. There was five or ten minutes of singing and worship and about twenty minutes of intercessory prayer for those requests made by the staff as well as those submitted by the congregation the previous Sunday.

4. 12:00—one hour of prayer and fasting in the pastor's office by the program staff.

All of this was preceded by a weekly Monday lunch in the pastor's office or at various restaurants as the senior staff met with the pastor and prepared the Tuesday agenda. It was at this meeting that many of the major decisions were made for the Tuesday 10:30 meeting, enabling us to simply facilitate the decisions that had already been made on Monday.

Moses died leaning on his staff. Don't die leaning on yours. It is your responsibility to help keep them alive and well. Love them, support them, pray for them and with them. And, of course, commend them publicly and personally. The great majority of good things that have happened to me in my ministry have been because of loving, supportive, and gifted members of my staff.

Chapter 88

Calling a Staff Member

T he easiest thing in the world to do is to bring a staff member on board. The hardest thing in the world to do is to release one. This is not to say that every staff member is not a wonderful Christian and a dedicated worker. It is to say that sometimes the right person is serving at the wrong church. Therefore, it is essential that you take your time and be sure that you have the right person to begin with.

Employees such as secretaries, assistants, cooks, and custodians are normally employed by the staff member with which they work and are not the responsibility of the personnel committee. *Employees are hired; staff members are called.*

The calling of a staff member to lead a major division or ministry in your church is best done in concert with the personnel committee. In certain cases there might be a related committee that will also work with the pastor in determining whom to call.

For example, First Baptist Houston called a minister of activities to direct the work of the activities building. In this case, the personnel committee, as well as representatives from the Christian Life Center committee, worked with the pastor and associate pastor in interviewing potential staff. In some cases where committee responsibilities overlap, it might be best to bring both committees together. In other cases, representatives from each committee will suffice.

A healthy church and mature committee members will recognize that the ultimate weight of the decision to call a high level staff member must rest on the pastor. There is a sense, therefore, in which the committee is really assisting the pastor by counseling him with well-thought-out wisdom and input. But he must make the final decision.

Don't let this concept frighten you. If God has brought mature believers to the committee, they will want it no other way. In every decision I have made about calling a major staff member, the appropriate committee has always been extremely helpful. Their wisdom, counsel, and assistance in the interviewing process and ensuing discussion always brought to light things I had not considered.

The search process normally begins with word spreading quickly across the church and denomination that a certain position on your staff is open. Recommendations will soon be written and called in. Use the church newsletter to solicit names from the congregation. Call four or five good friends in other churches and ask them to suggest names. Soon a list of fifteen to twenty names will emerge. You as pastor and perhaps associate pastor will need to think and pray over these and eliminate several.

The next step is to call the committee together with resumes and pictures of the three or four persons you consider to be the best candidates. After a meeting or two, the pastor, personnel committee, and any related committee will determine a priority order of those three or four. Start with number one. It is never best to interview three or four people and then decide. Try to determine the best candidate, the one to whom you feel the Lord is leading you, and deal with that person exclusively to a final yes or no.

The next step is for the pastor to contact the prospective staff person and determine his level of interest. If possible, the phone call should be to that person's home, not to his church. It is best not to upset the other church with preliminary information about your interests when, in fact, it might go no further. Most of the time the person will say yes or no regarding his interest on the first call. If he has some interest, ask him to pray about it a week or ten days, then call him back. Make sure that both of you understand there is no obligation or commitment by either one of you until a final invitation is given and a decision is called for.

The next step is to visit this person in his city or to invite him to your city, perhaps away from the church field for a face-to-face meeting. As pastor, you will want to take the appropriate committee chairperson with you and perhaps an associate. If all parties are still interested, invite him to come to your city for an afternoon and evening and look over your church and church field and meet with the committee.

Don't make a decision on the spot. Ask the prospective staff person to return home and pray. Assure him that you and the personnel committee will pray and meet again. Meet a week later. Hear the heart of the committee, get their counsel, ask everyone to be honest. If all concerned feel this is the right person, ask him officially to come to your church. Depending on the level of the position, some prospects might simply be invited to the position by the pastor and personnel committee. Some might need to be called by the entire church. In First Baptist Houston while I was the pastor, only the pastor and two or three other positions are "called" and voted on by the *entire* congregation.

It is most important that confidentiality be observed. Don't let the name of the potential staff member "leak" to the congregation. If it does, you may be assured that it will also "leak" from your church to his. He will have pressure to stay where he is before his church should have even known he was considering leaving. The first information that the other church should have that the staff member is coming to your church is after the decision has been made and announced simultaneously at both churches and not "leaked" to either. In many churches, the staff member then goes publicly "in view of a call."

Let it be clearly understood that with few exceptions, such as an audible voice from heaven, once you have committed to go "in view of a call," you are committed to accept the call if it is given. And pastor and committee, don't even think about asking someone to come "in view of a call" if you don't intend to call him. It is unfair, discouraging, and divisive to churches to get that far and then have either staff member or church back out of the inferred commitment to come.

When the pastor, committee, and potential staff member have agreed on a date to come before the church, the staff member should go immediately to his pastor and share his decision in confidence. The pastor should then release the information to his congregation, either at the same time it is released in the church to which the staff member is going or after. The announcement that Joe Staff Member is coming to your church "in view of a call" on "X" date should be made with a picture of him and his family with complete biographical information in your church paper the week before the Sunday on which he comes.

By far the best approach is to vote to call the staff member on the spot as he steps out of the sanctuary at the conclusion of the service in which he has been presented to the congregation. It is also very important that the staff member be prepared to announce his acceptance on the spot. Waiting a week or two to vote or voting and waiting a week or two for an answer is not a good idea. It will set the ministry of the staff member ahead by six months if you allow an immediate bonding of the people as they rejoice and embrace him at the moment of his acceptance.

Such matters as staff structural responsibility, salary and benefits, moving expenses, dates, etc. should be spelled out in writing between the church and the new staff member. Discuss health insurance, retirement benefits, the furnishing of an automobile, gasoline expenses, vacation time. Leave nothing to chance. The church should pay all travel, motel, and food expenses for the staff member during the times he is coming to your church for interviews and "in view of a call."

An additional trip for the staff member's spouse, when the process has moved to the status of serious, is also expected. All expenses for the staff member and spouse for three or four trips to your city to look for a house during the interim should be paid by the calling church, as well as all moving expenses. Many churches also pay a relocation allowance to help with such things as utility hookups, storage, new carpets, etc., sometimes even including short-term, no-interest loans for a down payment on a new house. You will know no greater joy than the beauty of working with a godly and productive staff member. A staff relationship is very much like a marriage. Don't rush into it. Take your time and be sure.

Chapter 89

Reassigning and Releasing a Staff Member

When a staff member is deemed unproductive or uncooperative, every effort should be made at redemption. Have you clearly communicated? Does he know you are dissatisfied? Have you shown him how to improve? Have you pointed out why you are displeased? It is incumbent upon you as his pastor, friend, and employer that you go the second and third mile to help save this person. And remember to put yourself in his shoes. Kindness and charity are always in order.

One of the most effective ministries I have ever performed was reassigning staff members who were good and faithful persons but who were simply in the wrong position. Each of us has our own giftedness. If a person has a loyal heart and a great spirit and you cannot make him into what you feel you need, the next step is to examine the possibility of reassigning him to a different position. A different responsibility might better match his spiritual gifts.

Let me cite two good examples. Karen Lennard on our staff served as associate in the singles ministry for four years. Karen was not ineffective. She was talented at whatever she did. But somehow we began to feel there might be a better spot for Karen. Twenty years ago we shifted her to librarian. That responsibility began to expand with the addition of a tape ministry, audiovisual aids, and all types of media. Today we probably have the finest church library in America, and she is the unquestioned premier librarian and resource center director in all the land.

Another example is Rick Jones, who was serving as activities minister. After three years we moved Rick to pastoral care. Although he was good in activities, he was outstanding in pastoral care. His compassion in hospitals and homes in times of bereavement was a wonder to behold. Both of these people were *good* at what they *were* doing. Today they are *outstanding* in what they *are* doing. We shuffled some of our staff about more than once in my thirty years in Houston, and every move proved to be a good move. Talented staff members can serve in many positions. Always ask, "Is this person serving in the right position on our staff?"

There will, however, be those times when problems are unsolvable and differences are irreconcilable. When a staff member must be dismissed, it should be done with the consultation and support of the personnel committee. Every staff member will have built up a following. Their constituency might comprise 5, 10, or 20 percent of your church. Among them will be personal friends, and therein will lie problems.

Just as a good personnel committee can be insulation between you and making bad decisions, so they can be a buffer between you and the reaction that may result when tough decisions must be made. That the personnel committee made the determination to release a staff member is more palatable to the congregation, and certainly easier on you, than that you made the decision to release this person.

At such times, the importance of grace and mercy cannot be overstated. Above all, consider the feelings as well as the potential for future ministry elsewhere for that staff member and his family. They have a reputation to maintain, feelings to be considered, and bills to be paid. We have continued to pay staff members for many months on occasion to help them "land on their feet" in another church. Again, above all, put yourself in their shoes, be considerate, and be gracious.

Occasionally a situation will arise where a staff member may have no future and you cannot in good conscience recommend him to another church. From time to time, people in this situation will be considered by another church whose pastor will call you for a recommendation. There are many ways to handle this problem, but for me, the best way has been not to return the phone call. Soon the pastor gets the point, and I am free of having put out the bad word on a fellow Christian.

If a person is unworthy of future employment, that responsibility will be the Lord's. Vengeance is his, and he will make whatever repayment is necessary. Put yourself in this person's shoes, and go the second mile in this difficult situation.

Chapter 90

Delegating Responsibility

I magine trying to lead two million persons across a desert with no map and no food or water. Moses had an administrative nightmare not only in leading the Israelites and providing for their needs, but in judging them in matters of personal and national decisions. His was an impossible task. You know the story. Moses' father-in-law, Jethro, helped him get organized. The people were divided into groups, assistants were named, and the work was done more efficiently. Our Lord, of course, referred to himself when he said, "Upon this rock I will build my church" (Matt. 16:18). Yet he poured his life into developing twelve leaders who would be the human instruments through which he would carry on this awesome responsibility.

The pastor of a growing and vibrant church must learn that he cannot be a jack of all trades, make all the decisions, and do everything himself. He must have help. The telephone and the United States Postal Service are two of the most available and most inexpensive forms of help. The staff, secretaries, deacons, teachers, and the church membership comprise a large untapped reservoir of talents and abilities. Right now there is probably someone in your congregation just waiting to be asked.

The elderly can telephone the shut-ins for you. There is probably a retired minister in your congregation who can help visit the hospitals. There are women who can address envelopes. There are teenagers willing to distribute handbills for the next revival and men who can mow the lawn. There are people who know how to design ads, take surveys, handle legal work, and do a hundred other things that need to be done. But don't delegate responsibility at random. The new member's packet should contain, among other things, a talent survey card. Keep a master file of your people's talents, hobbies, and occupations. When you need something done, go to that file.

There is a mechanic who cannot teach a lesson, but he can repair the church bus. There is a carpenter who cannot give great sums of money, but he can build bookshelves for the children's department. There is a talented lady who can help improve the quality of the church meals. There is a groceryman who can assist in the ordering of foods in quantity for weekly church meals.

When you have a job to be done—whether it is painting a room, following up new members, or recruiting and training ushers—get a layman to do the job. Call him into your office and have a heart-to-heart talk. Tell him you need him. Tell him the work of the Lord needs him for a special project that only he can do. Tell him how much you are counting on him and how important he is to the work of the kingdom. Teach him how to do what you want done. Ask him to enlist others, oversee the job, carry it through, and give you a report when it is completed. Thank him publicly when the job is finished. Think! There is an easier way, and there is probably someone who can find it. You can't do it all, and there are a hundred good people wanting to be used.

Larger churches, of course, have the luxury of being multistaffed. While there are those who are called and paid to assist you in the work of the ministry, don't forget the wealth of services that are available within the laity of the congregation. One Sunday morning I preached on the importance of being available to God for his service. I will never forget the man who approached me. "Pastor, I would never come forward on an invitation to be one of the crowd to say I am willing to serve," he said, "but I will never turn you down if you ever pick up the phone and call and tell me there is something special you need me to do for the church." Even though you have a paid staff, give equal importance to the volunteer spirit of your people.

Within the staff structure at First Baptist Houston were many levels of administration. There were directors of education, music, counseling, cleaning, school, etc.—each with a level of leaders under them who administered others within their area. One thing in common made each of these leaders effective: they were all good delegators. Being a delegator, getting people to help and trusting them to do it, begins with a sense of personal security that rests on our security in Christ. It is an insecure leader who feels the need to do everything himself, check up on everybody, look over every shoulder, and trust no one but himself to get the job done.

The apostle Paul tells us our Lord is the head in heaven and we are the various members of his body on earth (see 1 Cor. 12:12–20). The beauty of this body is its diversity. As a functioning body has various organs and limbs, so the members of the body of Christ bring varying gifts and talents to the service of our Lord. So turn it loose. Let someone else do it, and trust him or her to get the job done. A few people will disappoint you, but most will bless you.

This is particularly true within the church staff. Early in my ministry I greatly belabored the matter of checking up on my staff. Finally, I decided if I was going to do my job and theirs, I might as well get paid my salary as well as theirs! Make every effort to hire competent, committed, hard-working, talented people and turn them loose. Even the member of the smallest staff whose commitment to our Lord is of a high degree is probably capable of doing more than you imagine.

Don't just give your people errands; give them projects. Give them the goal and let the Holy Spirit work through their own creativity to determine how to reach it. Looking back through the years, I truly believe that in the majority of such cases, the staff member or church member found a way to do it that was different from, and better than, the plan I had in mind.

As Moses found others to help him, as our Lord poured his life into his trusted disciples, so we, as pastors, can enhance the effectiveness of our ministry. We can do so by entrusting to others the sharing of the task that the Lord has entrusted to us.

Chapter 91

Observing Anniversaries

K nowing and recognizing birthdays and anniversaries of your congregation is a marvelous way to express your love and endear yourself to the hearts of your people. A card or telephone call will take only a moment of your time, but it will bring hours of joy to some wonderful people. Remember to use that cell phone during those wasted hours of travel spent in your automobile. In a growing church it will soon become impossible to call everyone. If such is the case, call your leaders and staff as well as those people observing special twenty-fifth and fiftieth anniversaries and eightieth, ninetieth, and one hundredth birthdays. On the occasion of a hundredth birthday, have the person stand in the service and let the congregation sing "Happy Birthday."

Recognizing the anniversaries of staff is equally important. There is no greater delight to a pastor's heart than a faithful and loyal staff. Having around you those who serve Christ by serving their pastor is one of God's choicest blessings. Most staff members could make more money in the secular world, not to mention the tragedy of inadequate retirement so often provided pastors and staff by their congregation. The least we can do is say thanks.

It is important that your church establish some kind of "anniversary policy" for its staff and pastor. This should be done in a handbook that explains other policies such as time away, retirement, medical benefits, dress codes, etc. This handbook should be given to each new staff member and employee. Most large churches will be happy to share a copy of their employee handbook to assist your church in writing its own.

Generally, bonus checks are given and recognitions made for each employee and staff member. Receptions are normally held for ministerial staff in five-year increments, beginning with the fifth year. Christmas bonuses are always in order as expressions of appreciation for a job well done.

Major denominations provide an avenue for ensuring other staff benefits. The Annuity Board of the Southern Baptist Convention, for example, provides retirement benefits for its pastors and staff members. Regular contributions are normally made by the church and the staff member. The Annuity Board's slogan is "Serving Those Who Serve the Lord." With or without such assistance by an agency, the church is always right to honor those who honor the Lord.

Part 9

The Church Finances

Chapter 92

Overseeing the Budget

Our Lord warned against the folly of failing to plan. The cost of everything from the next evangelistic meeting to next year's operating budget must be well thought out in advance. When you fail to plan, you plan to fail. The order is: enlist the budget committee, prepare the budget, subscribe the budget, and administer the budget.

The finance committee, appointed by the committee on committees, is to be comprised of persons who are tithers to the church, mature, supportive, knowledgeable, and who have great faith. They should represent a broad section of the congregation and be instantly recognizable as men and women of respect. No church member should ever be able to say, "He's on the finance committee? You're kidding!"

Budget preparation should begin three months before each new fiscal year. Hearings should be held with representatives of the staff, and various entities within the church should be allowed to present their program budget and defend it. The finance committee will, with the pastor, make the final determination on which line items are increased or decreased in the new budget to be recommended to the church.

Annual budget increases should reflect a measure of optimism and anticipated growth. Nonproductive ministries should be reduced or eliminated. New ministries and programs should be funded adequately to ensure that they are birthed with a good chance for survival and success.

When the budget has been recommended by the committee and approved by the full board, it should be voted on by the entire congregation. On a given Sunday morning, the budget should be adopted by the entire congregation with a commitment to its support. Discussion of individual items within the budget should, however, be done on Wednesday night before the Sunday morning worship service in which it is adopted.

Simultaneous with this process, a special budget promotion committee appointed by the pastor or committee on committees will conduct a thirty-day annual stewardship campaign to prepare the church for adopting and pledging the budget. The stewardship campaign should be simple—comprised of one or two sermons, several testimonies, and at least one Sunday school lesson on stewardship. Stewardship testimonies to fellow class members during Sunday morning Bible study are most effective. One or two worship services might include such testimonies, as well, all in the context of an effective stewardship publicity campaign.

The people should be fully informed that on the Sunday following budget approval by the church, the entire membership will be given the opportunity to pledge. Pledge cards may be distributed to the congregation or inserted in the bulletin. But they are more effective when distributed at the conclusion of the sermon. After a brief time of prayer, background music is provided as members have two or three minutes to fill out their pledge cards. They should then be passed in to the waiting ushers, who will prepare them for those who will count the total.

A follow-up letter with an enclosed pledge card should be mailed to all members who did *not* pledge on pledge Sunday. It should include the statement, "If you were not here last Sunday, or were in attendance but unable to pledge at that time . . ."

Additional pledge cards should remain in the pew racks for the next two Sundays. Call attention to them and ask that they be filled out and placed in the offering plates when passed.

Administering the budget should be done on a weekly basis by the pastor, administrator, or other appropriate staff member. Monthly finance committee meetings should also be conducted to oversee the budget. Let there be no secrets. Full disclosure is important to the financial health of the congregation. The budget committee will take under consideration necessary seasonal spending in dealing with overages in particular line items.

Care must be taken to seek the Lord for a good balance between faith and reason in planning and administering the church budget. Here we will do well to observe our Lord's admonition to be as "wise as serpents, and harmless as doves" (Matt. 10:16).

Chapter 93

Ensuring Financial Responsibility

L
et me put it bluntly: I have personal knowledge of at least two cases in which handling the church collections on a regular basis was too great a temptation for a church member. Not only shalt thou not tempt the Lord thy God; thou shalt not tempt thy brother, the offering counter. Cash should never be handled except in the presence of two persons. Nine hundred and ninety-nine out of a thousand Christian people are honest. But even the best among us are capable of yielding to temptation, particularly when there is overwhelming financial need in one's life.

The smallest church can afford a safe. At the conclusion of the offering, the ushers should take the offering plates to a designated secure place. At least two persons then secure the money in the safe to be counted on Monday. Ideally, a safe should be purchased that requires two persons to open. Each person should have different parts of the combination in his or her mind. Deposits should be removed by two persons and counted in the presence of at least two or three people, with money counts and deposit slips completed appropriately. You might save yourself and someone else a lot of heartache if this procedure is followed diligently.

Money should never be left overnight in the possession of any person—pastor, staff, or church member. Money should not be kept locked in a staff member's drawer to be placed in the vault the following day. It should never be kept in the possession of any individual at all. Our church financial policy states in part: "No staff member may keep cash in his desk overnight."

As I write these words, I am reminded vividly of a serious problem. An employee was terminated from First Baptist Houston because he was videotaped removing from a staff member's desk $1,600 that had been left there overnight in violation of church policy. The employee was arrested and the staff member was reprimanded. God's people trust us with their money. It is as important that it be well secured as that it be well spent. The wise minister will keep himself above possible reproach and never handle the church's money. First Thessalonians 5:22 says, "Abstain from all appearance of evil."

It is the responsibility of the finance committee, with pastor and administrator, to oversee the church budget. Depending on the season and the need, the church finance committee of First Baptist Houston met at least monthly and sometimes weekly, with full accounting given to the congregation in monthly business meetings. The other side of the coin is that the finance committee is to be trusted with the responsibility of expending funds previously approved in the adoption of the church budget. Once the budget has been adopted, the church should not *reapprove* individual expenditures within that budget. That is the responsibility of the pastor, staff, and finance committee.

What good is a system in which authority is given to a finance committee, only to have other committees and boards look over their shoulder and second-guess them? The finance committee should be trusted to handle the business matters of the church.

Each year a professional audit of the church's finances should be conducted by an outside accounting firm. Seldom, if ever, are improprieties found, and finding them is not necessarily the purpose of the audit. The purpose is to ensure the congregation that professionalism prevails at every level of the church's finances. A good firm will occasionally recommend procedural changes to enhance the effective functioning of the church's financial matters. Annual audits can cost as little as a few hundred dollars or, as in the case of First Baptist Houston, as much as $30,000.

Given an occasion to do so, the first thing the secular world will jump on your church about is your finances. Here you want to be squeaky clean. Seize the initiative and see that from collection, to deposit, to expenditure, to accounting, your church finances are above reproach.

Chapter 94

The Issue
of Borrowing Money

There is no way to overstate the problem and burden of debt in our time. Individually and corporately we should aspire to be debt-free. Some churches, however, are causing great confusion with their teaching on the issue of borrowing. The church must have a balanced perspective of the biblical view of borrowing and lending. It is erroneous to extrapolate from Scripture a teaching that borrowing is unbiblical and, as taught in some quarters, downright sinful.

At the root of the controversy over borrowing is Romans 13:8: "Owe no man any thing, but to love one another: for he that loveth another hath fulfilled the law."

Even the simplest exegesis of the context verse makes it obvious that the subject is not money but love. Because of Christ's love for us, we owe a debt of love to one another. The apostle Paul said simply, "Pay the debt. Don't fail to meet the obligation you owe." It is an amazing "stretch" to extrapolate this clear teaching into a prohibition against borrowing money.

The eminent Old Testament scholar, Dr. Phillip Williams, stated, "The earliest record of borrowing and lending was done as an honor to the poor, to allow them to save face by not having to take charity." It added to a person's dignity and sense of self-worth to say to them, "I believe in you; I believe in your future; I believe you can pay this money back."

In the days of the Old Testament, lending money was an honored profession among the Jews. There are great issues, however, regarding the matter of usury—charging exorbitant interest. Taking advantage of one's brother in this manner is an obvious breach of ethics.

Deuteronomy 28:44 is often cited as a proof-text against borrowing money: "He shall lend to thee, and thou shalt not lend to him: he shall be the head, and thou shalt be the tail."

Verse 12 of the same chapter, however, casts quite a different light on the subject. "The LORD shall open unto thee his good treasure, the heaven to give the rain unto thy land in his season, and to bless all the work of thine hand: and thou shalt lend unto many nations, and thou shalt not borrow."

Read the entire chapter. In context, it is clear that God is saying that if Israel honors and obeys him, he will prosper and bless them so greatly they will not need to borrow money. In fact, they will be in a position to lend money to others. Conversely, God says in the last half of the chapter that if they do not obey him, they will be in the position of having to borrow money.

Is it possible our Lord is promising Israel if they will obey him, they will be in a position of doing something sinful—that is, lending money? Clearly, if it is a sin to be a borrower, it is a sin to be a lender. And what of our Lord's statement in Matthew 5:42, "From him that would borrow of thee, turn not thou away"? Jesus taught four parables about lending and borrowing. In no case did he infer there was a moral issue connected to either. The issue was the attitude of the borrower and the manner of repayment.

As in all things, it behooves us as believers to set the precedent for right. Borrowing for you and your church might or might not, at any given time, be the right financial decision. Many factors will go into determining that. But solid biblical scholarship dictates that we clearly understand it is not a moral issue in and of itself. There may be *related* moral issues such as exorbitance, usury, failure to repay, etc., but the issue of the morality of incurring debt through borrowing is, biblically, no issue at all.

Chapter 95

Steps to the Building Program

The first issue to be resolved is this: Are we absolutely certain that now is the time to construct the new building? Has every other possibility been explored? Has dual usage of existing buildings been considered? Has serious consideration been given to beginning new missions? Have the people been given adequate information about projected cost, options, and the pros and cons of building and not building?

Take your time and bring your people with you. Start on your knees, and when the Lord has given you peace, first present the dream to your leadership. Take your time. Don't stampede your people. Most of them are not yet where you are.

Measure the pulse of your congregation about the proposed building program. Do they truly love the Lord and hunger to see the church grow? There is often apprehension among longtime members about all those "new ones" coming in. Is the church financially able to build? Has it been long enough since the last building campaign? What were the problems then, and have they been resolved? Is the church in unity? Do the people love the Lord and readily follow their pastor? Things must be *just right* to enter a building program. Building programs can be a tremendous blessing, or they can cause great stress within the fellowship.

Once these matters have been satisfactorily resolved, the first step is to appoint a qualified building committee. Again, this can be done by either the pastor or the committee on committees. The building committee for the new facility is quite different from the existing building and grounds committee that is charged with the responsibility of the maintenance of existing facilities.

The committee's first act should be to interview potential architects. This process should be opened up to those who are members, as well as nonmembers of your congregation. Be advised that church members under consideration for architect might end up with hurt feelings if they are not selected. Nonetheless, select the best architect for the job. The person should be a Christian with knowledge of how churches think and operate and one who ideally has plans for other such projects.

Discuss fees, concepts, dates, etc. The architectural fee is normally in the 7 percent range and includes both designing and overseeing the building throughout its construction, in concert with the building contractor. The selection of the architect, determined by the committee, must be approved by the board and the church before documents are signed. The people should be invited to make suggestions regarding elements of interest to them, including everything from hallways to classrooms to color of bricks, etc. Let the people take ownership. Let them have input. Jesus said, "Where your treasure is"—and this includes the treasure of time and ideas—"there will your heart be also" (Matt. 6:21). It will take approximately three months for the architect to put the ideas of your people on paper.

Next, a general sketch will be made of the floor plan with an exterior sketch and possibly a model of the building. Take your time. Once the model has been approved, display it in the lobby of the church for a month. Let the people see it and experience it. Ask for their opinions and input. After blueprints are drawn by the architect, ask him to estimate approximate costs. The church will then approve the project and the cost and vote to proceed.

Once final plans are approved, they are "put out to bid" to a select list of five or six potential bidders. A list of qualified contractors, who will be allowed to bid, should be prepared in consultation with the architect. It is also possible to put the plans out to bid on a "come one, come all" basis. I have found it to be much more effective, however, if the committee and architect prepare a list of qualified construction companies that will be invited to bid. You will also need to determine whether or not you will simply accept the lowest bid. Surprisingly, other factors come into play. Inform every potential contractor whether or not you are looking for a low-bid offer.

The architect will help you determine a closing date for bids to be received as well as a time line for completion of construction. The building schedule will be built into the contract with appropriate penalties included for time overruns. Weather delays must, of course, be a part of this consideration. Expect the time from the first meeting of the building committee to the groundbreaking for the new building to approach one year. Construction time will average nine months. In your cost projections, include building construction costs, architect fees, any special site work, ample contingency, landscaping, and equipment. And be prepared for this: The entire project *will* cost more than you anticipate.

Two months before the building is completed, plan a dedication ceremony and "move-in" date. Our Lord is building his church upon himself. What an exciting privilege it is to be a part of building the facilities in which his church will meet!

Chapter 96

Conducting the Capital Campaign

O nce you have determined to buy land, build new buildings, or remodel existing facilities, the next step is to determine the method of financing your project.

Normally called "the capital campaign" or the "fund-raising campaign," raising the money to build can be as exciting as the building project itself. Fund-raising programs are normally conducted to finance four types of projects. The excitement level of the people in descending order of projects will likely be:

1. Constructing new buildings.
2. Purchasing new land.
3. Remodeling existing buildings.
4. Reducing/retiring existing debt.

In rare circumstances, if the giving potential of the church is extremely high and the financial need is not overwhelming, it is possible to excite the people and stimulate them with the challenge of giving all the money in a cash offering on one Sunday. Very seldom, however, is this successful. The better way is to think in terms of three-year pledges. People are accustomed to signing three-year notes for appliances, automobiles, etc. Over a three-year period they can and will give much more than on any single day.

Some church members will say, "I don't believe in pledging." Help them to see that, in fact, they do. We pledge virtually every day to those things that are of value to us. Every time you write a check, you are making a pledge. Each time you use a credit card, you are making a pledge. If you have served in the military, stood at the marriage altar, or signed a mortgage, you have pledged. The issue is not, "Do I believe in pledging?" It is, "Will I pledge to that which is far more important than any of these lesser things—the expansion of the kingdom of God?"

Share with your congregation that a pledge is not a legal contract; it is a spiritual commitment that helps the church plan its work. When adequate pledges are in hand, borrow the money for interim, short-term financing and begin your project. Some banks might wish to hold the pledges, but they are never used as legal collateral for the loan. If all the money does not come in during the three-year pledge period, extend the loan or get a new loan for a short duration.

Waiting three years until all the money is in hand to begin building is counterproductive. Escalating building costs mean the project will cost much more three years in the future than it does today. People will also grow discouraged as they see nothing happening. Construction stimulates giving. Conduct the campaign, get the pledges, borrow the money, and begin.

The typical pastor will want help in conducting a major capital campaign. Let me urge you never to borrow from another church materials that have been purchased from a professional fund-raising organization. It is morally wrong and might be downright illegal as well. Several opportunities of assistance are afforded to you.

There are many large professional firms such as Cargill Associates, Resource Services Incorporated (commonly called RSI), and In Joy, as well as smaller firms such as Sabbath Stewardship Ministries and Paul Gage and Associates, to name a few. Certain denominational programs are also available that are conducted by full-time denominational employees.

The only book on the subject available in bookstores, however, is my book, *How to Be Your Own Fund-raiser*. Some pastors are comfortable with doing their own programs. Many pastors and churches, however, feel the need to have a consultant actually visiting the field and giving personal direction. For this reason, my company called

Shepherds Group was put together. It is comprised of pastor-consultants who have actually completed my program in their churches successfully. This new pastor-to-pastor approach has replaced the usual objectionable features with positive and creative features.

Public announcements of a person's pledge are never in order. By God's grace, every campaign goal has been more than successfully reached without them. This is true in part because the correct formula has been followed in determining and setting reasonable goals. Beware of setting unrealistic goals. One fund-raiser asked a church that could not reasonably pledge over $300,000 how much they would like to raise. "One million dollars," the pastor replied. Anxious to get the contract, the fund-raiser responded, "Good. The goal is a million dollars." How sad!

Whether you get help from my book or from a company, get help. A well-done capital campaign will bless your people and prepare them for the next. A botched-up job done in a high-pressure manner will assure failure and might cost you your job.

Information on "Shepherds Group" is available at www.SHEPHERDSGROUP.com

Chapter 97

The Benevolence Ministry

Jesus made it clear he has little patience with those who think only of themselves. So much of his ministry was directed to the hurting and the poor. It has been no surprise through the years to find the secular world often measures our sincerity as believers by our compassion for the poor.

Admittedly, there are always phonies among us.

The Pharisees asked of the woman who broke the alabaster box, "Why wasn't this perfume sold and the money given to the poor?" (Mark 14:3–9). They didn't care about the poor. They only cared about trapping Jesus. I have asked more than one reporter, "How much does your newspaper give to the poor?" But compassion on those who have nothing might be the most consistent badge of our sincerity as well as the most natural response of our hearts.

Determining the reality of a need can be difficult. For years a woman stood at an intersection near our church, begging every car for money as hundreds of exiting worshipers passed by. One day we asked the hotel just across the street to give her a room in conjunction with our adopting her other needs as a church. The hotel manager laughed. "Why, we offered that woman's husband $36,000 a year as a maintenance man, plus free room and board for her family." Her response? "Why would we want to do that? We're making $600 a day on the streets."

I seldom drive by a beggar on the street without rolling down my window and giving him something, but I never do so without thinking of that woman. Perhaps if we err, it should be on the side of doing too much rather than too little. But through the mission ministries of our church and a hundred other avenues, we are well aware of an endless stream of hurting people who do need our help. Generally, at First Baptist Houston we attempted to meet benevolent needs in three ways.

Within the more than three hundred Sunday school classes of the church, we encouraged an atmosphere conducive to helping one another. Thousands of dollars every year flowed around the church budget directly from one hand to another within the Sunday school classes. I knew of cases where people had lost their jobs, had their house burn down, or had great illness where classes gave them $1,500 to as much as $10,000—and that's all right. It's all God's money. These compassionate givers are generally those who have learned the joy of giving by being consistent tithers to the church budget.

A second source of benevolence was special offerings in the services of the church. Six times a year, at Christmas eve services, Thanksgiving eve services, and four Lord's Supper services, we received an offering for the poor. These were second offerings received at the door after the regular offering for the church's budget had been received. These gifts totaled several thousand dollars a year.

The third avenue of meeting needs was through our missions center. One of the many mission ministries of our church was called the Mission Training Center. This was the drop-off and distribution point for food, clothes, furniture, appliances, etc. It was also here that the financial assistance ministry was coordinated. Over $200,000 in food, cash, clothing, and other items were distributed here annually in the name of Jesus.

All distributions were made at the center. In some ministries, a nominal fee—perhaps ten cents for a pair of shoes or a dollar for a suit—was charged. There is something to be said for this. If a person pays at least something, this may enhance his sense of dignity and self-worth. God will lead you to the best way for you and your church. But develop a planned and coordinated benevolent ministry in your church. Some of the most gifted servants of God in your congregation are just waiting to be asked to direct the work of this ministry. They may not be able to give great sums of money themselves, but they can serve in this ministry if this is where their heart are.

Nothing will bless you more than helping people as Jesus did. He reminded us that even a cup of cold water given in his name would receive a disciple's reward. Never have we more opportunity to be his hands and feet than here. A smile, a touch, a tract, a kind act—these "cups of cold water" given in his name and with his love—are of high priority to our Lord and should be to us as well.

Chapter 98

A Financial Potpourri

Here are several small flowers to brighten the garden of your church's financial health:

1. *People give more money in colored envelopes than in plain white envelopes.* Perhaps subconsciously they feel you have cared enough to make the offering special by preparing special envelopes. Perhaps it is that lovely pastel colors such as yellow, pink, green, or blue are more pleasing to the eye. But for whatever reason, the fact is that on average people give more through softly colored envelopes. Pink seems to be the best color.

2. *Distribute the envelopes before the offering appeal.* They may be mailed to the home, placed in pew racks, distributed as inserts in the bulletin, at the door, or in the plates. However you distribute them, give your people the opportunity to receive their envelopes in advance, see them, touch them, hold them, and be comfortable with them before the appeal for the offering is made.

3. *When offering envelopes are mailed to the church membership in advance, don't assume that everyone will bring them back.* Some will, but many will not. Distribute envelopes again and again. If they have brought their envelopes from home, they will simply bypass the opportunity to receive another. Just as church members will give more through pink envelopes than white envelopes, they will also give more with envelopes than without.

4. *Allow your people to give as they wish.* Frankly, I preferred that every member of First Baptist Houston give one check per week to the

unified church budget. I recognized, however, that some of them preferred to give only to the fund for new hymnals, a new organ, or a favorite mission project. Giving is to be encouraged, not discouraged.

5. *Encourage noncash gifts in the form of stocks, bonds, automobiles, notes for property, real estate, beach homes, jewelry, etc.* All of these may be given to the church for tax-donation credit if one prefers them to cash. This, too, should be encouraged, not discouraged. While we preferred the cash, it is possible to encourage noncash contributions without discouraging cash.

When this type of contribution is made, the church should translate it into cash as soon as possible. We are not in the real estate business, nor are we in the business of speculating in the stock market. Sell stock gifts the next business day. Convert every noncash contribution into cash at the earliest possible moment after the gift is received.

The person making a noncash contribution has the responsibility of placing a value on the contribution and reporting it to the Internal Revenue Service. The church is not allowed to estimate the value of such gifts and give the individual a receipt for that estimate. It is only allowed to give a receipt that states the nature of the noncash gift. The amount claimed is between the donor and the Internal Revenue Service. In such cases, the member is wise to obtain a professional appraisal of the value of the gift for his records.

6. *When a special offering is to be received on a certain day for a specific need, write a personal letter to ten or twenty of your largest contributors.* Encourage them to give generously and remind them that the offering will not be successful unless a few of the church's special contributors come through in a generous way.

7. *Be an opportunist.* Keep your eyes open. Be alert to things that happen spontaneously in the course of a stewardship campaign or a worship service. Sharing the news about a $15,000 pledge by a nonmember that actually occurred in the course of one of our stewardship campaigns made quite an impact on the church.

8. *Report the results.* If the occasion is just right and you are relatively sure a goal is going to be reached—or at least an encouraging amount will be received—ask the finance committee to count the

offering during the service. Then make a victory announcement at the close of the service.

9. *Consider consolidating various special offerings of the same type into one major offering.* In my denomination, churches normally receive three special mission offerings per year in addition to our Sunday-by-Sunday offerings for the unified church budget and local missions. In our church, however, rather than three separate mission offerings, we had one big missions month offering. The corporate effect is that by strongly promoting missions annually, rather than laboriously returning to it three times a year, we gave much more to each of the three causes than before.

10. *Receiving offerings for the poor at the conclusion of services in which the congregation participates in the Lord's Supper has been a tradition among Christians from time immemorial.* Churches that partake of the Lord's Supper on a weekly basis will likely find this a bit much. But those churches that observe this ordinance three, four, five, or six times a year will find this offering to be a special experience.

11. *Mail the offering envelopes from the church on a monthly basis.* By the time summer and fall arrive, most members have misplaced the offering envelopes they received back in January. A monthly or quarterly mailing of packets of envelopes to the church membership is a regular but gentle reminder of the church's need and of their obligation.

12. *Give the congregation the opportunity for special, selective giving through the offering envelopes.* Two boxes on the envelope marked "budget" and "building fund" are not enough. Envelopes should contain a third box labeled "other/specify." This is another way to encourage giving. Why make it hard for people to give? Do everything possible to make it easy!

Part 10

Facilities and Operations

Chapter 99

The Importance
of Location and Relocating

P eople cannot attend a church they cannot find nor will they likely attend one that is hard to find. Three things are important about the public's ability to find you: Location, location, location.

We are of all people most blessed. First Baptist Church of Houston is located at the intersection of the major arteries of the city. The geographical heart of the county crosses on the church property. Each day more than 125,000 cars pass this site. Visibility and proximity to those who pass by your property are very important.

If relocation is impossible and you are not satisfied with your present location, do the best you can where you are. Make the buildings look nice, pave the parking areas, advertise the church, maximize entering and leaving, and be alert to the possibility of purchasing additional land. Adjoining land is always the best, but it is not out of the question to consider the purchase of land within a short distance of your church.

Often businesses with ample parking will either adjoin the church or be located nearby. Virtually all of them will consider entering into a relationship with you that allows you to park on their facility Sunday morning while you allow them weekday access to your parking.

But if your church continues to grow and you are simply out of space, there are four possibilities that are discussed at length elsewhere in this book: (1) multiple services, (2) buying additional property,

(3) relocating, or (4) sending your members out to start new missions. The fourth option is what First Baptist Houston decided to do when no more property was available and multiple services were already being successfully conducted. Sixty-three such missions have been established by the church since 1986.

I have a firm conviction that relocation should not be done because things are not going well in your church and you feel they will get better by moving. Indeed, you might have a short burst of interest from people in the new area, but the probability is that if you're not doing the job where you are, you'll not do much better in the place where you move.

How many restaurants have you been to that had the reputation of being the best in the city, were always packed, and were difficult to find? Lakewood Church of Houston, Texas, is a prime example of that scenario. If there's anything this church doesn't have, it's location. Yet they have done very well with what they have. People make the extra effort to get there because it is exciting. So there are those cases in which growth can happen in difficult places, but unfortunately they are rare.

If, after serious prayer and consideration with your leadership, you determine multiple services and the purchase of additional property are not feasible, you must at least *consider* relocating your facility. In making the decision to relocate, the church must give serious consideration to the following essentials:

1. Has every other possibility been explored and exhausted?
2. Have we prayed about the matter and determined it to be the will of God?
3. Do the people favor it? It is doubtful that 100 percent of your congregation will affirm the move, but the strong majority of the people must be behind it. I don't like minority rule, and neither do you. But a church that votes 55 percent to 45 percent to relocate needs to question seriously whether it is the thing to do at that time. It might be the right decision, but the wrong time. I have learned that timing is important to God. *When* he does something is as

important as *what* he does, and now might not be the time to relocate.

4. Are we prepared to buy an adequate amount of property? First Baptist Church of Houston relocated because the church was landlocked downtown. Unfortunately, the congregation bought only eighteen acres and is landlocked again. God has used this, however, to thrust the church into the mission-planting business. Consider buying twenty to fifty acres when you relocate.

5. Are you moving to an area with high growth potential? Is the area growing now, and/or will it grow in the future? Don't move to an area where the population has already grown past.

6. Does the new location offer high visibility to the public? Proximity to freeways and main arteries is important.

7. What kind of businesses and neighborhoods surround the new location?

8. Is it possible to purchase the corner? If so, do it.

9. Can we afford to pay for the new property?

10. What is the salability of our present property?

Giving thorough and objective consideration to these issues and taking plenty of time to relocate assures the church of making the right decision regarding its all-important location.

Chapter 100

The Importance of Parking

Your people will never grasp the importance of parking until they get hold of this statement: "The church is the only organization in the world that does not exist for the sake of its members." As God's people, we are willing to endure inconvenience in parking as well as other areas in the life of the church. The unbeliever who attends your church, however, is not. If I am devoted to Christ and his church and am physically able to do so, a ride on a shuttle bus or a two-block walk across a rainy parking lot matters little.

But understand the unbeliever is looking for a reason *not* to go to church. Inconvenience in parking might be just the excuse he needs. Studies of young adults indicate five things are important to them in choosing a church: relevant sermons, warm spirit, the opportunity to develop personal relationships, great nurseries, and good parking.

That which may be most difficult to change is the inclination of your people toward willingness to sacrifice their comfort in parking for the sake of reaching others. This includes giving money to construct covered drop-off entrances, parking in the extremities of the parking lot, and even riding a shuttle bus. Close-in parking should always be reserved for your guests. Parking lots should be well-marked and well-lighted, with greeters on location to escort guests to the nursery, classrooms, or sanctuary.

If you want your church to remain small, buy three or four acres. If you want it to grow, buy thirty or forty acres and cover most of the site with good, well-drained, well-lighted, nicely-landscaped parking.

"Nothing to us," you say, but it is everything to those you are trying to reach. All other things being equal, prospects will opt for the church with better parking virtually 100 percent of the time.

Some churches attempt to enhance existing parking by getting more cars in fewer spaces through striping particular areas for compact cars. Usually this doesn't do much good. If it is raining, if it is hot or cold, or if they are running late, people are going to park where they want to. Big cars will simply take two spaces. They will park in the handicapped zones; they will park in the flowers and drive over the bushes to park close to the building. My opinion on striping for compact cars? Don't go to the trouble.

As you make projections for future growth, consider this. Allowing for entrances, exits, and parking, you can put 110 to 120 cars per acre. Survey your people to determine how many come per automobile each Sunday, averaging it out over four Sundays. With the large singles population of our city, our average is about 2.2 to 2.3. If your anticipated percentage of singles is less, these numbers can go up to 2.5 or 2.6. Suppose the number is three. If you realistically believe within the next ten years you can grow to nine hundred people in attendance, you will need three hundred parking spaces or about three acres. Add the number of acres needed for other buildings, add an additional two or three, and you have the amount of land you need.

I strongly urge you to consider the purchase of every piece of adjoining real estate that comes up for sale. North Phoenix Baptist Church in Phoenix, Arizona, owns forty acres, most covered with parking. First Baptist Church in Orlando, Florida, has 120 acres. Bellevue Baptist Church in Memphis, Tennessee, has over three hundred. Often, costs will be prohibitive. We quit purchasing available adjoining land when it went to one million dollars an acre.

When this happens, only two possibilities exist: run shuttle buses to other lots or build parking garages. The wisdom of building parking garages is, in part, determined by entrance and exit points from your church property. If they are limited, they may only compound the problem. In such cases, rent or buy shuttle buses to run to other available parking areas as close as possible.

Shuttle buses should ideally be driven by one person and "captained" by another. Think how nice it would be on your shuttle bus next Sunday morning if a vibrant person with a warm personality greeted each person as he boarded, called him by name, gave him a "worship guide," and told him about the events of the day. Real estate, parking garages, and shuttle buses cost money. But the most costly thing of all is the decision not to invest in good parking.

Chapter 101

Building and Grounds

The word *church* in the Bible has two meanings. Neither of them mean the physical buildings in which you meet, but both the local church and the worldwide church need a place to assemble. That place should be well located, functional, comfortable, attractive, and well kept. You may have the most wonderful services within the walls of your sanctuary, but large numbers of people will never come in and experience them if they can't get past those ugly buildings on the outside.

Whether your building is metal or wood, brick or marble, large or small, you should do everything possible to maximize its appearance. In well over half the towns and villages I drive through, there are church signs on the edge of town with faded and crumbling paint. On vacation, I always look for a church to visit. I often seek out denominations other than my own to expand and enrich my own worship experience, but I never stop at a church with a crummy sign or run-down buildings.

The steps may be wooden, but they can be in good repair. The lawn may be small, but it can be well manicured. The sidewalk may be old, but the holes can be filled. Put this book down for a few minutes. Walk through your church. Look in the closets. Check out the bathrooms. Go into the nurseries and Sunday school classes. Is the paint peeling? Are the floors unpolished? Are the windows broken and the trash uncollected? If you think people are going to leave the surroundings of a beautiful, well-kept home six days a week and go to a crummy-looking church building on the seventh, think again.

It doesn't take a lot of money to buy five gallons of paint or a pickup load of new boards. It isn't difficult to plant flowers. It's not costly to wax the floors. Your church facility might not be valued on the real estate market at more than $50,000, but it can and should "look like a million."

Drive around your town and look at another church or two. What is your first impression? Do you like it? Does its condition say, "We care. We think the house of the Lord is important?" Years ago I heard a woman singing on the radio. Her voice was off-key and her guitar out of tune. As she began, she said, "You know, folks, this here ain't gonna be too good, but just anything is good enough for my Lord." I for one don't believe that. Nothing is good enough for our Lord unless it's the best. It should be done right if it is done at all. To fail to do our best is to dishonor Jesus Christ.

Build a line item for "upkeep and building repair" into your church budget, and keep things fixed up and "in the pink."

In our Houston church, we had a properties committee that worked with our systems manager, maintenance people, and grounds-keepers to oversee the maintenance and repair of the facilities. It was a serious matter with us and one to which we gave much attention. I considered our building and grounds or properties committee to be among the five most important committees of the church.

As your church grows, you will need more and more specialty help. Our church had a full-time painter; electrician; systems manager for telephones, computers, etc.; a kitchen crew; a maintenance crew; and a grounds crew. Your church might not yet be at the place where you need such a large staff, but employ people who really care about the beauty and efficiency of your facilities. To bring honor to God's house is to bring honor to him.

Chapter 102

Your Physical Environment

T he building, sound, lights, colors, and room arrangement in which you worship are very important. Most things are obvious. Adequate offices, well-located classrooms, and ample restroom facilities are an important part of good facilities. But to the preacher, what surrounds him in the worship service is most important. Let's consider four areas.

Size and Shape

Too many sanctuaries are overbuilt. A one-thousand-seat worship center with three morning services is better than a four-thousand-seat sanctuary with three thousand at one time. Construction costs, utility costs, maintenance, and, most importantly options for the worshipers—all these play an important part in determining the size of the worship center. Great worship centers that seat eight to ten thousand people dot the American landscape. But the wave of the future is smaller buildings and more usage.

The traditional church building is rectangular. Modern church architecture, however, follows the rule of thumb, "more people, closer in." Sloping the worship center forward, bringing the balcony closer, expanding the sides, particularly near the pulpit, and other creative options abound. But the prevailing thought is to have the maximum number of people as close to the front as possible.

The attraction of the new professional football and baseball stadiums across America is the proximity of the people to the action. I never understood the inadequacy of our own Houston Astrodome until I attended a game at The Ball Park in Arlington. What excitement! I have never experienced a sporting event like it. You will have to experience it to understand it. The stadium is so designed that you feel you are part of the game. I can't wait to get back there for another game.

In 1972 we set out to relocate our church and build a new worship center in a new location. Ideas were solicited from the people. Suggestions regarding everything from rest rooms to colors poured in from the congregation, and many were utilized. I made only one: "Build an auditorium conducive to giving an invitation." We now have a sanctuary about which everything physically and psychologically says, "Come on down."

Our architect went back through history and came up with a Roman amphitheater style that is marvelous. The lower floor is sloped downward toward the front, with side balconies as wide as the top balcony. Everything flows together in a common front. The feeling is created that whether upstairs or down you are a part of the same congregation.

Give maximum attention in your remodeling or building to the size and shape of your sanctuary.

Pulpit

Preaching from a manuscript, preaching without notes; standing still, moving around; stationery microphone, portable microphone—all these are factors in determining the size and style of the pulpit. Everything should be done to keep the pulpit from becoming a barrier to good communication from pulpit to pew. The popularity of conversational communication as opposed to oratory has enhanced the effectiveness of preaching with no pulpit at all. If a pulpit is to be used, it should not be one that the preacher "gets into" but "stands behind."

The first Sunday I preached in our Houston church in 1970, I was appalled at the size of the pulpit. It virtually wrapped around me and struck me at my chest. The next Sunday it was gone. Our church members wondered what happened to that old pulpit, and I never told them. I replaced it with a small pulpit, an ornate lectern, from a forgotten storage closet. It remains today.

More recently, a transparent Plexiglas pulpit was donated for the chapel. It, too, was most effective. The pastor must be comfortable in his preaching environment. The sensitive church should consider allowing the new pastor to select a pulpit "just right" for him, or at least modifying it to his personal preference.

Sound

The church is in the business of communication. The apostle Paul asked, "How shall they hear without a preacher?" (Rom. 10:14). I ask, "How shall they hear without a good sound system?" Through the years I have probably preached in a thousand different church buildings in America. I have heard only a handful of really fine sound systems. The pastor might be as good as Chuck Swindoll or James Kennedy, but of what value is that if he cannot be heard? *Invest in a good sound system. Borrow the money. Pay it out. Do what you must, but get the best.* The right place for the speakers is immediately above the pulpit. One speaker is never enough. A cluster of several is required. Sound technicians will determine the right amount and quality of mixers, tweeters, woofers, etc., but get help and do it right.

To find the best sound company in the city, determine who does the sound for the rock concerts in your area. Hire the company that does the sound when the bands come through, and you will have the best. Don't skimp at this point. To the degree you do so, you lessen the effectiveness of your message.

Lights

Well-placed, modern, uniform lighting is nearly as important as the sound system. Dimming capability in various places in the worship center is important. For three years I traveled with evangelist Hyman Appleman. Often the lighting technicians would dim the lights on the congregation, virtually spotlighting him as he preached. "Turn the lights back on," Dr. Appleman would say, "the people are the attraction." Brighten up your auditorium with good colors and bright lights. It is a great honor to him who is the Light of the world.

Most churches are smaller churches, and can make great improvements in lighting and sound with a modest investment. To hear the gospel and see its messenger are key ingredients in communicating God's love effectively. Give priority attention to the physical atmosphere in which the miracle of preaching happens.

Chapter 103

Security

G od's loving arms protect his people. Often he does so, however, through human instrumentalities. In the church, that
human instrumentality is us. As leaders of the congregation,
it is our responsibility to ensure the safety of the people and their possessions.

The initial implementation of safety procedures for your church
begins as the people enter your parking lot. Policemen and "volunteer"
car parkers add to safety, both perceived and real, as your facilities are
first approached. If as many as even two or three hundred cars are
being parked, the visibility of a police officer can be very important.
Tragically, recent events have again emphasized the vulnerability of
even the smallest churches in our land. In our own church, every parking lot except one required crossing a public street. Protection and
assistance must be visible and efficient. An additional uniformed officer inside the church gives an additional sense of security as well as real
safety.

Someone in the worship center should be designated to "keep an
eye on the service." Hopefully, you will spend your entire ministry
without incident. But precautionary measures, which prevent just
one, are well worth it. This person should have the ability to communicate electronically in an instant with an officer. In the event of a
problem, ushers should be trained to go instantly to the assistance of
the "inside watcher" who will be the first to respond. Occasionally
there will be people who so disrupt a service or are a threat to do so
that they must be barred from your facilities. Your policeman will be

trained to handle and enforce such situations. At this writing, First Baptist Houston has six such officers.

In larger cities and congregations, an added sense of security may be achieved by the presence of one or two designated persons who drive their cars through the parking lots at peak attendance hours. A simple, battery-operated, yellow flashing light on the roof of that car will suffice. The theft of hubcaps and automobiles will stop immediately as will a sense of insecurity by your people.

Safety for worshipers as they leave the property is also a high priority. There is a high concentration of automobiles in a small amount of time as the people exit. Again, one or more officers should be employed to expedite the movement of traffic, as every church parking lot exits to a public street. In some cases the city traffic department can be petitioned for traffic lights at your main exits. Officers may then hold those lights on green, waving through large numbers of automobiles as they leave the church parking lots.

Officers may also be of great assistance in the event of threats to the pastor. High-profile ministers who preach on controversial subjects have regularly been the object of such threats. It is not unreasonable to assume that this problem will increase because of the hostile nature of the environment in which the church exists. There are two subjects, which shall remain unnamed, that have generated at least six such threats in my ministry. Inform the officers in such cases. They are well qualified to take it from there.

The medical security of your congregation is equally important. Again, someone in your worship center should be prepared to identify any medical problem and contact security instantly. Our people are prepared with stretchers, oxygen, and other first-aid assistance. Seizures, heart attacks, accidents, and blackouts are not uncommon.

Through the years I was proud of the professional manner in which our volunteer leaders and staff handled these situations. A doctor, paramedic, or nurse "on call" should be at every service. It might be well to consider a church committee to coordinate securing the medical welfare of your congregation. An incident that saves only one life for each fifty-year history of your church is well worth the investment of time and preparation.

The securing of possessions is also important. Purses left in choir rooms, desks left unlocked, offerings left unsecured—these are trouble waiting to happen. Securing the offerings has been dealt with in another chapter and might on the surface appear to be overly protective. But it is imperative not only to protect the valuables of your people but to protect them against temptation as well. One incident, improperly handled, can cause your church great damage through the negative publicity it receives. A word to the wise is sufficient.

Chapter 104
Food Services

E arliest Christian history makes clear the importance of Christian fellowship to the people of God. Within the New Testament community, the practice of breaking of bread from house to house, so often mentioned in the Gospels, likely refers to the Lord's Supper instituted by our Lord. But fellowship and good food are also biblical. Today's version of church fellowship has its roots in the New Testament community. An unbroken thread runs from Jesus feeding the disciples a breakfast of bread and fish at the Sea of Galilee to today's "all-day singing and dinner on the grounds" at the country church.

Christian fellowship around eating together is here to stay—and well it should be. From Sunday school fellowships to church-wide ice cream socials, God's people like to "meet and eat." The growing church, however, will have needs far greater than those which can be met by the traditional "potluck supper."

Even the smallest congregation will have a volunteer hostess who has likely been in charge of cooking and coordinating church dinners since the days of Noah's ark. In those rare cases in which no such person exists, seek out the volunteer services of a good church hostess. This person will have a warm personality, good cooking skills, and be a gifted administrator. Enlisting and coordinating volunteer workers for those weekly church suppers will be as important as getting the seasoning "just right" in the meat loaf. One of the wisest investments a church can make is to include some level of monthly financial reimbursement for this type of part-time person.

As the church grows, consideration should be given to the employment and addition of a full-time food services director to the staff. The need for such a full-time position usually develops as the church increases to an attendance of approximately one thousand and as the "activities" calendar grows correspondingly. Appropriate kitchen staff will be added part-time and/or full-time under the direction of the food services director as church membership and activities expand.

Coordinating the calendar of activities of the church cannot be done without the involvement of the food services director. Many factors go into church programming. Such matters as time, place, date, public-address system, lights, chairs, tables, advertising, ordering, cooking, serving, and cleaning require the attention of one person with full responsibility for coordinating them all. An uncoordinated church calendar that gives too little attention to even the slightest of these factors can leave your church program in shambles.

As with other important positions, the food services director will be interviewed, employed by, and made accountable to the personnel committee and appropriate staff member. That person will generally be the church administrator and/or minister of education.

Occasionally, a different model may be considered. In our own church, we changed to "outsourcing" our food services. The reason, in our unique situation, was the addition of food service responsibilities for a five-hundred-student grade school, housed within our own church facilities. Additionally, day camps and an in-house restaurant plus a sizable activities calendar made this the right decision for us.

Regardless of the sophistication of your food preparation and distribution system, volunteers are always appropriate. Our Wednesday night church supper was high priority. Hundreds of persons came straight from work and went directly from the evening meal to various kinds of education, music, and mission meetings. At each of these Wednesday night dinners—the centerpiece of our food-service ministry—a different adult Sunday school class volunteered to serve. Not only was money saved but the opportunity to be of service was afforded and fellowship was enhanced.

In the integration of the food-services ministry of your church into the life of the congregation, it is essential that accurate records be maintained. Requests for food service for a Sunday school class dinner, for example, must include all pertinent information about type of food, numbers, paper plates or china, etc. These instructions should be written in triplicate.

One copy of those instructions is for the administrator's office; one is for the food services director; and one is for the properties director, who will be responsible for set-up and clean-up. Forms should be completed in writing a month in advance when possible. All things should be done decently and in order. Our Lord is not the author of confusion.

The food and fellowship aspect of your church is very important. Your people will be coming from various walks of life, representing many races, geographical locations, socioeconomic statuses, and ages. In Christ's church they find common meeting ground. Here everyone is equal. Here only Jesus Christ is exalted supremely above all. Relaxed times to get acquainted and come to know and care about one another are essential. In planning to build this dimension into the life of your congregation, don't overlook the importance of breaking bread together.

Chapter 105

Should the Church Own Vehicles?

T o buy or not to buy—that is the question. There is, however, no question about the importance of transportation in the life of a congregation, whether vehicles are owned or rented. That which promotes togetherness is good for the church family. Trips, cookouts, and ball games are almost as important as trips to conferences, conventions, and crusades. Retired adults especially like to take long trips together. A bus trip to a national park or other venue of a week to ten days' duration is of great value, particularly to those who would never go alone.

Large church buses are virtually a thing of the past, nor have repainted, second-hand school buses "survived" the cut. Most churches today use fifteen- to thirty-passenger vans and mini-buses. The necessity of shuttling people from distant parking areas has increased the Sunday-by-Sunday value of such vehicles far beyond that of the occasional trip.

There are pros and cons on both sides of the rent-or-own question. A committee should be appointed to make a serious study of the cost of each option before the decision is made to purchase or rent. Remember, there are more issues at stake than simply the financial cost. Issues of reliable and qualified drivers, liability, storage, etc. must be given consideration. When I first came to our Houston church, the deacons were opposed to owning church vehicles. With the exception of the school, that opinion remains today. Through the years, we spent hundreds of thousands of dollars renting vehicles. While the financial wisdom of this might or might not be clear, it is certainly convenient to do so. Pick up the phone, call the bus company and reserve a date, and you are through. They furnish everything when you rent. When you return from your trip, say good-bye, and it's over. And there's something very nice about that.

But is it economically feasible not to own? In determining that, don't overlook:

- cost of vehicle
- maintenance
- gasoline
- insurance
- storage
- driver (trained, licensed, insured drivers are required)
- safety

In some states, passengers may not legally be transported in the typical church van or bus. Special equipment must often be included, with safety reinforcements adding to the cost. Again, it is important to study carefully the issues of convenience, safety requirements, etc. as well as carefully detailed financial costs. After years of living exclusively with rented vehicles with professional drivers included, I was still fifty-fifty on the matter. You and your church will make the decision that is right for you.

Part 11

Other Important Matters

Chapter 106

Ordaining and Licensing Ministers

Every denomination acknowledges God's call and approval of its ministers in different ways. In many churches the first step is licensing the minister, to be followed subsequently by ordination. In Southern Baptist life, both these steps are done by the local church. In other disciplines it is performed at the denominational level. In a Southern Baptist church, a license means, "You tell us God has called you into full-time Christian ministry and we believe you." An ordination means, "We have had time to observe you and we also believe God has called you." The first says we believe you believe it; the latter says we believe it.

I recommend that a church have a licensing and ordaining council. After a person has made public his conviction of a call to the ministry, he will petition the church for a license. The council will interview the candidate and recommend him to the church for approval. A license from our particular church does not authorize a person to perform weddings. It is primarily a pat on the back, a "God bless you, we're behind you, now go prove yourself."

In many denominations, seminary graduation and proven service are necessary for ordination. Within Southern Baptist churches, proven service is normally required; seminary completion is not. Ordination at the hands of a Southern Baptist church means the ordained person may perform marriage ceremonies as well as the ordinances of the church—the Lord's Supper and baptism. While models vary from denomination to denomination, both license and ordination certificates may be revoked by the ordaining church for reasons it deems appropriate. Because a license does not qualify a person to perform marriages, it is not necessary that it be registered with state or local authorities. Ordination certificates, however, should be registered with the appropriate government agency to make marriage ceremonies legal in the eyes of the state.

A religious ceremony is not required to make marriage legal. All that is required in the eyes of the state is simply that the marriage license be signed by a minister or other official. To the legal system, the religious ceremony is an option and has no binding effect on the legal status of the marriage. During premarital counseling the minister should inform the couple that they must have the marriage certificate *in hand* before the wedding ceremony can be conducted. At the conclusion of the ceremony, it is to be signed by the minister.

The certificate will indicate whether witnesses are required. While groomsmen and bridesmaids generally perform this service, it may be done by anyone in attendance. Once signed, the marriage certificate is to be mailed to the county courthouse within ten days to be legal. The minister generally assigns the best man the responsibility for performing this function.

The gifts and calling of God are without repentance. God doesn't change his mind about planning to use us. He intended to do so before we were born. God told the prophet Jeremiah, "Before I formed you in the womb I knew you" (see Jer. 1:5). The ordination process of the church is an expression of its affirmation of the ultimate ordination of God upon the life of the minister. The ordination ceremony is a significant event and should be accompanied by grace and sincerity in the presence of loved ones and friends.

Let the ordained minister respect the high level of confidence placed in him by the ordaining church that affirms his call from God. If the time should ever come that the minister no longer holds to the doctrines and standards of the ordaining church, he should relinquish his license or ordination voluntarily.

Chapter 107

The Library
and Resource Center

B e advised that the above name is not in vogue today. The new
name is "media library" or "resource center," and it's about a
whole lot more than books. A well-stocked, well-run resource
center is a valuable tool for the personal enrichment of the congregation. The persons who impact tomorrow are those who write or record
their ideas today. I have a high regard for the value of church libraries
and Christian bookstores. Thank God, men and women of noble
character and keen insight are writing today.

We are the benefactors of the legacy of great books left by those
who have gone before. Imagine life without the writings of Charles
Sheldon, Oswald Chambers, Spurgeon, and others, not to mention
today's writers such as Chuck Swindoll and Max Lucado, to name a
few. I could not have pastored my church without the benefit of commentaries and word studies of those who have gone before.

In our Houston church, we had the benefit of a highly dedicated
and competent full-time resource center staff. But virtually every small
church has, among its membership, a gifted person who will gladly
volunteer or who can be paid a part-time salary. Don't see the church
librarian as an antiquated and stuffy old lady. This stereotype is a gross
error. He or she is a bright and productive person whose value to the
kingdom of God is incalculable.

Our church was blessed with a large, two-story media center of
approximately six thousand square feet. It contains fifteen thousand

volumes of books, not to mention tapes, films, and videos. Our resource center staff advised pastor, teacher, and laity where to look for resources, what to look for, and then help them do it. They were organized, trained, disciplined, knowledgeable, thorough, and most helpful. During the course of writing this book, I called Karen Lennard, our resource center director, at least a hundred times to look up something for me. Within ten minutes, she was back on the phone with the answer.

Our resource center had several reading areas with couches, upholstered chairs, and good lighting. One of my great joys was the two children's reading areas. There the children sat on stuffed sheep and big floor pillows and read children's books or watched children's videos in two different areas appropriate to their age group. There were also weekly children's reading times when parents could bring bring their children and be read to for storytime. Our resource center was widely used and most profitable.

The resource center administered the ministry of films, slides, videos, and audiotapes. A wide selection of each was available. It was also the responsibility of this ministry to record the weekly sermons of the pastor on audiotape and offer them for sale at a nominal price to the church membership and the public.

In another area of our building was a Christian bookstore. The sale of Christian books, however, can also be done by the media center if desired. Whether through print, audio, video, television, the Internet or any other means, it is important to disseminate God's Word. Give attention to developing an excellent media center in your church. Somewhere there's a room available for this ministry, and there's no better time to find it than right now.

Chapter 108

Starting Schools

First Baptist Church of Houston was instrumental in starting three schools in our city. Houston Christian High School was begun in cooperation with First Methodist, First Presbyterian, Grace Presbyterian, Braeswood Assembly, Spring Branch Community, First Nazarene, and Brentwood Baptist Church. Each church was pastored by a warm-hearted, conservative, Bible-believing pastor, and the fellowship was great. Miraculously, all eight of us agreed on an extremely tight, conservative doctrinal statement of faith at our very first meeting. Today brand-new facilities stand on forty-five acres located in the fast-growing west side of Houston on the Sam Houston Toll Road.

First Baptist Academy was a brand new four-million-dollar pre-kindergarten through eighth grade school located on First Baptist's home campus. Enrollment in its second year of operation was four hundred.

First Kids, First Baptist's child development center, had approximately 150 children and was located within our current facility, while First Baptist Academy was a new addition to it. The child development center is for children six weeks through four years of age.

Few experiences have been more rewarding in my own ministry than being a part of starting these three schools. This means that from six weeks through the senior year of high school, it is possible for a child to be taught the Word of God five days a week in a classroom setting through the ministry of this church. Let's talk about that.

American education is built on three primary foundations: public education, private and parochial education, and homeschooling. I want to be clear that personally, and as a church, we fully supported all three.

No one blessed me more than the young people, teachers, and administrators who were being salt and light in the public education system. We recognized them, we honored them, we encouraged them, and we prayed for them daily. Most people who worked in the public schools do so in spite of great obstacles.

Private Christian education will continue, however, to be more important with each passing year. Our country is losing its soul because God has been removed from the public classroom. Someone asked, "Where was God in the massacre at Littleton High School?" Unfortunately, God wasn't allowed in and hasn't been since the Supreme Court so decreed over thirty years ago.

Homeschooling is growing at an awesome rate. Recently James Dobson's broadcast, "Focus on the Family," presented a powerful discussion on the high quality of children being produced through homeschooling. But the subject at hand is the beginning of private Christian schools by your church.

The issue is often raised, "Are we encouraging working mothers to spend less time with their children by providing them day care in a Christian child development center?" The wise pastor will always recognize that while some things are ideal, we often have to minister to situations that are less than ideal. I encourage all mothers not to work outside the home unless it is absolutely necessary, particularly for the important first five years of their children's lives. But there are those circumstances where the mother absolutely must work, or chooses to work. It is to these parents that our church ministered in offering the child development center.

If God leads you in this direction, be aware that start-up costs are high. City and state ordinances governing fire codes and other safety issues for children are strict. These requirements are generally more rigid for day-care facilities in which children meet eight hours a day, five days a week, than for one hour on Sunday morning. Schools that exist within your facilities and share classroom space will create a problem of coordinating desks, cabinets, posters, scheduling, etc. Conflict between Sunday school teachers and school teachers using the same space is to be expected. This can best be diffused through meetings with the pastor or appropriate staff member and the two entities well before the opening day of school.

Our facilities were quite nice, and they met every Sunday morning's safety requirement. But when we made the decision to use those facilities for a daily child development center, $175,000 worth of changes had to be made to meet state requirements. Requirements for weekday care exceed those for Sunday-only occupancy. There are state requirements for licensing as well, such as the training and quality of your teachers and director. He or she, too, must be licensed by the state. This means paying a salary for a person who has paid the price to become qualified to do this kind of job. Good consultants are available who will advise you regarding the ramifications of starting this or any other kind of educational ministry.

As pastors, we should not see people simply as objects to build our church membership. But schools should never be started only to teach the child. They should also be started to offer an opportunity of ministry to both child and parent which may, in turn, present an avenue of entry into the church. Don't start a school and forget it. Walk through the halls. Meet the parents. Be involved with the children. Eat lunch with them. Go to their plays. Pick up the little ones and become the pastor to the school. You will not only enrich their lives and offer ministry to their families, but many will one day choose you as their pastor.

The same is true with beginning a Christian grade school or high school. At this writing, the question of whether a tax credit should be given to parents who have their children in private school is under discussion among lawmakers. On the plus side, I support it, and it does seem the logical decision. On the negative side, it could open the door for every kind of charlatan to "have a school." Pray that God's will shall be done in this matter.

If you decide to begin a school, understand that parents expect a safe environment in a Christian atmosphere as well as smaller classes and a higher standard of education than you can get in a public school. This presents a major problem. That higher standard of education comes only with better qualified teachers, and they earn higher salaries than less qualified teachers. The church will be faced with trying to hire teachers at a rate higher than public school teachers with less financial ability to do so, because church school programs do not receive government financial support.

Many excellent teachers are willing to teach in a private setting because they feel called of God to do so. But know that there will be these kinds of difficult issues. Confront them before you open the doors of your new school.

Teachers in Christian schools must be Christian. They should also love to teach, love the Lord, and truly love the child. Children should be encouraged, not ridiculed; commended, not humiliated. The Bible should be taught regularly in the classroom with at least weekly chapel services conducted. In Houston Christian High School, every teacher is committed additionally to personally discipling a number of students.

Private Christian education is taking its rightful place alongside public education and homeschooling. It is not an inexpensive proposition, but one that is extremely rewarding to the student and to the life of the church. I encourage you to consider making the investment of time and money required to begin a good school.

Chapter 109

The Question of Childhood Conversion

Eighty percent of America's churches are plateaued or declining. Of the other 20 percent, 19 percent are growing by swapping members and baptizing their own children. In this atmosphere the pressure to "produce" may tempt pastors to be overly aggressive in evangelizing their children. Few issues in your ministry will need to be handled with greater sensitivity than the question of "childhood conversion."

As with adults, the conversion of children must always be allowed to take place by the sovereign movement of the Holy Spirit and not through human manipulation. The age of the conversion of children is not fixed in Scripture. Some children may be ready to make a profession of faith at six or seven; others will not be ready until eleven or twelve. Many factors enter into the timing. It should be noted, however, that children are becoming exposed to blatant sin much earlier today than in the past. It is important, therefore, to allow for earlier conversion because children experience earlier guilt.

Throughout the history of my own denomination, huge numbers of adults who made decisions as children have been "rebaptized." Often it is said, "The children didn't know what they were doing." My observation, however, is that it was more often the adults who dealt with them who didn't know what *they* were doing. Parents should be cautioned to respond to the questions of their children without offering additional information that might create pressure on the child, resulting in premature professions of faith. Children want to please, and any authority figure must be cautious at this point. When a child makes a profession of faith, he should be counseled gently, in a quiet and unpressured manner.

It is important to separate conversion from baptism and introduction into church membership in the mind of a child. For this reason, we offered a six-week preparation for baptism and membership course for children as well as adults. The length of the time between profession of faith and baptism, therefore, was even longer. Children in churches that offer catechism should be made to understand clearly that completing the catechism, answering the questions, and being baptized is *not* tantamount to being born again.

If special "decision services" for children are offered during evangelistic crusades, camps, Bible schools, etc., they should always be only for older children. Preschoolers, first-graders, second-graders, and perhaps even third-graders should not be involved. That is not to say some second-graders and third-graders may not be ready to make a decision for Christ. It is to say that we must not do that which is conducive to hurrying the process. Conversions of children at earlier ages usually happen best at home. Several factors, however, support the validity of childhood conversion at virtually any age.

1. *The allure of sin.* Children are being exposed to sin at an earlier and earlier age. More than ten years ago the *Dallas Morning News* ran an Associated Press story about New York City schools training kindergarten teachers to detect signs of drug addiction. Sin appeals and sin addicts. The older one becomes, the harder it is to turn from sin to Christ.

2. *The ability of the children to understand.* To become a Christian one must do two things—repent of sin and receive Jesus Christ as personal Savior. Repentance and faith are at the core of the conversion transaction. You don't need to worry about an adult's love of sin. He has plenty of that by experience. You have to be concerned, however, about his faith. It is not easy for adults to believe.

With children, it is exactly the opposite. They have plenty of faith. It is easy for them to believe in Jesus. You do, however, have to worry about their knowledge of sin. Be certain they understand not only what sin is, but that they have a personal conviction of guilt about their *own* sin. Help them to understand that sin is not simply disobeying mommy and daddy; it is disobeying God.

3. *Children are not ashamed.* Jesus said, "Confess me before men and I will confess you before my Father which is in heaven. Deny me before men and I will deny you before my Father which is in Heaven" (see Matt. 10:32–33). When children "walk the aisle," looking around, chewing their gum, and smiling, it is not because they are not sincere. It is because they are not inhibited.

4. *Children have their entire life to give to Christ.* Charles Haddon Spurgeon stepped off the train upon his return from an evangelistic meeting in a small church. One of his men greeted him and said, "Pastor, how many were saved?" "Two and one-half," Dr. Spurgeon replied. "Two and one-half?" questioned the friend. "Yes. Two children and one adult. The two children have their entire life to live for Jesus. The adult has only half."

Jesus said, "Suffer the little children to come unto me, and forbid them not: for of such is the Kingdom of God." He added, "If anyone offend this little child that believes in me, it were better for him that a millstone were hanged around his neck and he be drowned in the depth of the sea" (see Mark 9:42). The word *offend* means "impede forward progress." Let God do the work. He knows the right time for each child. Don't do anything to manipulate the process, but don't stand in the way when it begins to happen.

Chapter 110

The Use of Radio

Our Lord, in his grace, has allowed us to live in the day of greatest opportunity the world has ever known to communicate the gospel. Opportunities abound. Fax machines, E-mail, the Internet, radio, and television are only the tip of the iceberg in emerging electronic technology. In the day of state-of-the-art, super-tech communication, don't overlook radio. That men such as John MacArthur, Joseph Stowell, and James Dobson have opted out of television speaks volumes about the importance of radio.

There are many reasons for this, not the least of which is the high cost of television. You can probably have a daily radio program for less money than the cost of a weekly television program. By all means, use television to advertise your church and televise your services if you are financially able to do so. But don't ignore radio.

Radio is inexpensive. Radio is everywhere. Radio is readily accessible. Television sets are rarely in automobiles and never in the front seat. Radios, conversely, are in every automobile. How can we say enough for the rich ministry of Christian radio? Knowing that I can turn the dial to any of several Christian radio stations in Houston is a great encouragement. How often have I been listening to the news—murders, fires, burglaries, rapes, lies, pressure of world events—and said, "Who needs it?" Then, with a touch of my finger, I have changed my environment to a beautiful song of praise to our Lord Jesus.

There are obviously three uses of radio that may be within the reach of your church budget. The first is spot announcements. Being on the radio, like being on television, spreads the gospel and advertises your church and its events. It also gives a good sense to your congregation that you are busy with what is important. Your people take pride in what you are doing when you spread the gospel through radio and television and do it well.

Spot announcements can be purchased very inexpensively when contracted in large quantities. Fifteen seconds is enough—thirty seconds at the most. Keep it happy, bright, and short. Don't preach. Just give listeners the facts about your church and/or the event you are publicizing. Purchase time in "drive time." More people are in their cars between 7:00 and 9:00 A.M. and 4:00 and 6:00 P.M. than any other time of day. The increased cost for ad time during these hours will be well worth it.

Another possibility is a daily radio program. Many local churches now have three- to five-minute programs every day of the week. To tell the truth, most say it just about as well as they would in fifteen or twenty minutes. If you commit yourself to a daily radio program, be prepared to pay the price in time and preparation. If you want me to talk on any subject for an hour, I'm ready to ramble. But if I have to say it in three or four minutes, it will take me a while to prepare.

The third use of radio is obviously the live or delayed broadcast of the weekly services of your church. For more than thirty years, we broadcast our Sunday morning services live on the largest Christian radio station in the city as well as an early tape-delayed broadcast on the NBC radio affiliate. If possible, broadcast your service live. There's something exciting and special about that.

Above all, move the service along and don't let the music portion of the broadcast drag, or you will lose your audience. Make announcements of interest only to your congregation before or after the broadcast. And be certain to get the entire message on the air. It is extremely frustrating to your radio audience for you to go off the air the last two or three minutes of the message.

I love radio. Worldwide ministries have been built on radio. Undoubtedly, that was at least in part in the mind of Jesus when he said, "And this gospel of the kingdom shall be preached in all the world . . . and then shall the end come" (Matt. 24:14).

Chapter 111

The Use of Television

L et me put it simply: If you can get on television, do it. The advantages are obvious. A few words to the wise, however, are in order. The television ministry of your church will be very costly and time-consuming. Often it can be done only at the sacrifice of other valid ministries. It should not become the tail that wags the dog. I know a few churches that "have a television ministry." I know a lot of television ministries that "have a church."

It might be necessary to employ a part or full-time, paid technician or director. But the best service is performed by committed, trained members of your congregation who volunteer their time and talents as a service to the Lord and his church.

Someone in your congregation has interest and experience. A small amount of time and money may be invested wisely in getting them the increased training they need to "do the job" for you. Backup personnel must always be available for cameramen, producers, etc. who may not be available on any given Sunday.

A prerecorded and edited production is normally in order if you intend to distribute your program to stations out of your area. But there is something special about a live Sunday morning telecast from your church to your city. Frankly, I feel too many pastors suffer from "delusions of grandeur" and are on nationwide television. They would be better off simply broadcasting their morning worship services to their own city. There may be a few television preachers worthy of national exposure. But are we doing more harm than good with hundreds of less-than-effective preachers filling the airwaves?

When we began televising our services in 1971 at First Baptist Houston, we were one of only two local television ministries in our city. Through the 1970s and mid 1980s, we determined by survey that fully 30 percent of our congregation had joined our church because they first began watching our telecasts. Due to costs, we were off the air for two years. But we entered the market again on an even larger and more prestigious station in the early 1990s. After two years of broadcasting on one of the largest stations in the South, nothing happened. I could not point to one person who joined our church during those twenty-four months because of television.

There were, I believe, two reasons. The first was an oversaturation of the television market with second-rate presentations, creating an increasing tendency to "turn it all off." But the second and perhaps most important reason may be laid at the feet of certain televangelists:

- constant haranguing for money,
- claiming of miracles,
- bizarre carnivalistic acts performed in the name of Jesus, and
- exposure of the moral character of some televangelists.

Five years ago we pulled the plug on television. We began to put that money into buildings and staff, radio and missions, benevolence, outreach, and religious education. For us, it was the right decision. God will lead you to yours. Give it serious prayer and thought. But let me say frankly that television is not for every church. Said another way, not every preacher should be on television. If you ask him with a humble and sincere heart, our Lord will show you the way in this important decision.

Chapter 112

The Use of the Internet

The Internet is all the rage today. It is not possible to live even a day without hearing a conversation about it. What is the Internet? It is simply a collection of computers of all sizes, wired together in one big computer network. In fact, it is the largest network of any kind in the world.

The Internet began as a government project for the U.S. Department of Defense, a computer network called ARPANET. The general public used the Internet very little until the development of the World Wide Web in the early 1990s. Since then, its growth has been phenomenal. In 1993 there were only about 130 Web sites; today there are millions. The number of computers on the Internet approximately tripled between January 1994 and January 1996. At last count, this number was doubling every year.

No one authority controls the World Wide Web. With today's authoring tools, anyone who has access to a computer can post a Web site and contribute to the content of the Internet medium. Remember, *you shape the Web.*

What does the Internet have to do with the church? Jesus told us to proclaim the Good News throughout the world to all people. Think of the potential for evangelism. The strongest Muslim country in the world, for example, cannot stop its people from receiving the gospel on the Internet. The same medium that allows pornography must allow the good news of Jesus Christ.

It is vitally important that your Web site not be static. Technology allows people to respond and interact with your site. Make it as interactive as possible. Constantly update it. Times must be correct and the information must be fresh and relevant. When it becomes stagnant, it will be passed over after the second hit.

Consider the following uses of the Internet.

E-church billboard or sign. You probably have a road sign announcing and directing people to your church. The Internet is simply an electronic road sign.

E-newsletter. Gather E-mail addresses from members and visitors and E-mail much of the same information that is on your "paper" newsletter. It costs next to nothing to do this.

E-forum or E-meeting. Committees or groups can use chat rooms or forums to gather together. An online forum can even be designed so members can meet and comment throughout the week at their leisure. At the least, set up a Web forum where members can E-mail ideas among one another. This is much less expensive than distributing information in its traditional printed form.

Showcase your church services and events for other churches to see. Is your church doing something unique in a service, group, event, or mission that others could profit from? The Internet is an easy way to advertise your church's uniqueness and help build up others within the body of Christ.

Today's Internet technology allows you to broadcast your church services live. With streaming media, like real audio and video, think of the Internet as a broadcast medium like radio and television. Your church service can be a "live" event. It's also possible to offer archived messages on the Web as you would cassettes or videotapes.

The Internet can also be a convenience to your members. Many of your people are on the net every day. An October 1998 Georgia Tech survey revealed that 35 to 40 percent of the respondents between the ages of eleven and fifty were on the Internet one to four times a day. Those numbers are undoubtedly higher today. (Source: GVU's WWW User Survey www.gvu.gatech.edu/user_surveys.)

As Internet penetration continues to grow, substantial budget savings can be realized. Look for a diminishing demand for printed material. Your Web site can post prayer needs, ministry opportunities, sermons, events, menus, schedules, activities, etc. Think of the

Internet as a "live" medium, as you would audiocassettes or video-tapes.

It is even possible to receive tithes and offerings over the Internet. Members can make contributions on a secure page with "cyber-cash," direct deposit, debit cards, or credit cards. A growing number of people pay their bills online today. Just look at the electronic offerings from banks. Occasional attenders may prefer this method of giving, especially if they are "Internet members."

Before you design your church Web site, ask yourself a few questions:

- What do you want to "do" with the Internet?
- Whom do you intend to target?
- What are your objectives and goals?
- How will you reach those objectives?
- What is your church's specific vision or mission statement?

I recommend you start with a good Internet connection. Find an Internet Service Provider (ISP). All providers are not alike. Do the research and know what you are looking for before you sign up for service. All connection speeds are not created equal. Connections can be made with a modem, ISDN, DSL, T1, or other technology. Connection speeds range from 28,800 to 1,500,000 and higher.

There are individual connections which allow only one computer to connect, and network connections, which allow your entire church staff to connect. If you have more than one person using the connection at a time, or if you plan to host your Web site in-house, you will need a faster network connection. If only two or three staff members will use the Internet, you can get by with individual modem connections, with each user dialing onto the Internet as needed. The individual modem connection, however, makes it mandatory that your Web site be hosted outside your church.

After your connection is in place, use the Internet search engines to gather ideas for your Web site. I like Yahoo for individual word searches, Alta-Vista for searching for items by sentence, and Hot-Bot for searching for people.

There are several elements that make up the creation of a Web site.

1. The site map or plan (if this were a movie, it would be called a storyboard).
2. Graphics and text (the graphic design will make the difference in load-time and determine whether your site looks amateur or professional).
3. Layout or paste up (you should direct the visitor's eye to what is important and how to navigate).
4. Hosting (develop a relationship with a company that offers good speed).

Give thoughtful consideration to the technical element in making these choices. Do you have a Web-savvy staff member? Do you have lay experts who can help? Should you form a committee? Should you outsource your Web development? Seek the answers to these questions for your church through prayer and consultation. Our Web site is still being developed and is certainly a challenge for us.

The good news, however, is this: You don't have to know the chemical makeup of the ink in order to use the pen. Don't let the technology scare you! The Internet is not the wave of the future; it is the wave of the present. Fail to use it at your loss.

Chapter 113

Preparing the Church for an Interim

In some churches a new pastor is appointed by a bishop or appropriate denominational governing body. In a Baptist or Nazarene church, for example, a "pulpit" or "pastor search" committee seeks out a new pastor. Once the committee is elected by the church, their responsibility is to seek the heart of God in finding the person they will recommend to the entire congregation for ultimate approval. Let's walk through that process.

To begin with, whether retiring or moving to a new ministry, the exiting pastor has a responsibility to help prepare both the church and the search committee for their task. A wise pastor will not be involved in selecting his successor. But he will give every help possible to the committee in its responsibility to do so. The search committee should be instructed, in part, in the following ways:

1. *Prayer must be the priority.* God will direct the hearts of sensitive, sincere men and women who hunger to know his will.

2. *Personal preferences and agendas should be laid aside.* To say, "I want a pastor who has been to seminary" will create a problem with a fellow committee member who says, "I want one who hasn't." For a committee member to have an agenda such as, "I want a man who likes this kind of music or that kind of style" is a mistake. The committee should confront immediately the member with an obvious agenda.

3. *No restrictions should be determined.* The committee that begins with the restriction, "We are not calling a man who has not been to seminary," has just excluded the possibility of Billy Graham being their next pastor. It is equally wrong to say he must be under fifty, or over thirty, or have "X" number of years in his present church. Let God be God. If you will release him to do so, you will get God's pastor for your church.

4. *Solicit names of potential candidates from your congregation, friends, and fellow churches.*

5. *Be wary of one name recommended from many sources.* The possibility is strong that the person might be calling his friends, asking them to "recommend me to this church." Occasionally, multiple recommendations come because God is indeed spontaneously putting one name on the hearts of many people. But far too often it is a personal campaign orchestrated by an unhappy or ambitious pastor who is trying to move.

6. *Don't get in a hurry. Take ample time for names to be submitted.*

7. *Eliminate, eliminate, eliminate.* Feel no obligation to run all over the country hearing thirty or forty prospects just because someone recommended them. Ideally, only four or five individuals will need to be heard in their own pulpits before a decision can be made. This can easily be done by the use of God's great gift to the pastor search committee: *the video.* Why spend tens of thousands of dollars flying the committee to thirty or forty cities when they can sit in a committee member's living room and view the videos of all the candidates?

8. *Don't ask the pastor to send you a video.* He will send you his "sugar stick." Find a way to get several videos without his knowledge. Audiotapes can be helpful when videos are not available. Reduce the most likely candidates to three. Spend two or three weeks in prayer and come to agreement over the one to see first. Whatever you do, *do not* talk to several potential candidates at once; start with the person whom God has put on your heart and pursue him all the way to a "yes" or "no" from both the committee and the candidate.

9. *Once you have "zeroed in," call the church to find out when the pastor will be preaching, but don't identify yourself.* Visit the church two

or three times. Don't walk in as a group. Go in as individuals at different times, sit in different places, and don't identify yourself. Don't tell the candidate you are considering him until you have determined you are serious enough to invite him to meet with you. Meet with him in his city, on his church field, before you invite him to yours. And don't make it public with either his church or yours that you are talking about his candidacy.

10. *When you have determined to invite this person to be your pastor, inform the church of the date on which he will come "in view of a call."* Follow his desires in coordinating the release of information in his church that he will be preaching in view of a call at yours.

11. *Remember, you do not want a person who is anxious to move.* The pastor who is not happy where he is, who is looking for greener pastures and is anxious to move, will not long be happy with you.

The story of the Exodus is replete with preaching material to encourage the church during its interim. Challenge the people with at least one sermon on the principles by which God leads his people through times of transition. Following is an outline of just such a sermon I preached from Exodus 12 and 13 prior to my retirement:

1. *Unite your hearts.* Exodus 12:38 records that a "mixed multitude" came out of Egypt. That mixture would be the source of great difficulty. The people were divided, confused, and complaining. Different levels of faith, varying agendas, and conflicting opinions prevailed. The church, like the pastor search committee, must hunger for God's will and his alone. Let united prayer be priority in the church.

2. *Purify your life.* Exodus 13:2 calls for sanctification. Verse 3 adds, "No leaven is to be eaten." Leaven is the biblical picture of sin. God cannot speak to impure hearts.

3. *Honor the past.* In Exodus 13:6–10, God established the institution of the Feast of Unleavened Bread. We are to tell our children the great works of God from the past. Commemorating what God has done in times past encourages faith in what he will do today and tomorrow.

4. *Stay in the battle.* Exodus 13:17–18 states that God led them to the promised land, "the long way around." They had to be

strengthened for the journey. They put on their battle gear and pressed forward. The interim is a time for the church to gird itself for battle and stay harnessed in the army of the Lord.

5. *Look for the fire.* God led the Israelites with a cloud by day and a pillar of fire by night. The direction of God's Holy Spirit for New Testament believers comes not by fire in the sky but by fire in the heart. He leads his faithful people into his perfect will.

Take responsibility for preparing your church for the interim that will follow your departure.

Chapter 114

Retiring: Getting It Right

*(Retirement Sermon Preached by
John Bisagno, June 20, 1999)*

F rom the beginning of time, God has commissioned men and
women for a predetermined, specific amount of time to accomplish a specific purpose. When that task was completed, they
passed the baton gracefully to their successors. They knew a joy
beyond anything they had ever experienced in their own ministry;
they reveled in the blessing their people would know as others built on
their foundation for decades, even centuries to come.

Although our Lord's earthly ministry lasted only three brief years,
it was so well done that he could say to those who would continue to
build for centuries to come, "Greater works than these shall he do"
(John 14:12).

Moses finished the task the Father had sent him to do and passed
the baton to Joshua. Joshua led the children of Israel into the promised land, where they would do even greater things in the future than
they had ever done in the past.

The same was true with the mighty prophet Elisha, whom God
empowered to do even greater things for Israel than did his predeces-
sor, Elijah. Paul passed the baton to Timothy, Silas, John Mark, and
Barnabas. He had trained these people so well the church is still
vibrant, triumphant, alive, and well after almost two thousand years.

As Moses looked into the promised land across the Jordan River into what would be a great new day for Israel, so stand I today at the edge of the river of a new millennium. I have a deep and settled knowledge that now is the time for our dear church to begin to walk across the threshold of her greatest days that lie just ahead with a great new young Joshua at the helm.

For almost three years, Uldine and I have had a deep and peaceful sense that 1999, the conclusion of thirty blessed years, would likely be the year for our retirement from the responsibility of the active leadership of our beloved First Baptist Church. The first of February 2000 A.D. will allow us to complete thirty wonderful years as your undershepherd, as pastor and people have together followed our heavenly Shepherd.

But in order that we might enjoy a relaxed final holiday season with our church family, and with our own children and grandchildren, and to allow time to begin the prayerful journey for the church to find its new Joshua, I will preach my final sermon as your pastor and turn the interim leadership of the church over to Dr. David Self on Sunday morning, November 21.

Those who know how much we have loved our little farm in Brenham often ask if we don't feel a bit sad now that it has been sold. In fact, to my utter amazement, we have had a tremendous sense of freedom and joy. And as the days grow closer, we are, in the same way, feeling just that same way more and more about our dear church. Tears and a sense of loss at leaving have turned to excitement and joy about our future and yours. Let's talk about that.

First, I am excited about our past. The late 1960s were hard times for First Baptist Church. Spirit and attendance were so low that serious consideration was given to the possibility of disbanding. These many years later, church statistician John Vaughn stated last week that you have become one of the top one-half of 1 percent of the largest churches in all the world. This is all by the power of God, the faith of this congregation, and to the glory of the Father.

Since 1970, you have given approximately a quarter of a billion dollars to the work of our Lord. Five hundred of our sons and daughters have gone into full-time Christian work, over one hundred to the foreign mission field. We have begun sixty-three missions, received more than forty thousand new members, matured disciples, developed incomparable leadership and unprecedented ministry, and built a staff generally recognized by their peers as the finest in the Southern Baptist Convention. In addition, there are the three schools, a full-time retreat center, support groups, a counseling ministry, a nation-wide health ministry, and much, much more. We have much on which to reflect, much for which to bow our heads and thank the Lord.

Second, I am excited about our future. Today we stand at the crossroads of our destiny. Everything that has been for the past 30 years and the 130 before that has been only a foundation for tomorrow. We stand at the crossroads not only of the city but of eternity. We have the best people, the best leadership, the best location, and the greatest love of any church in the world. You are a people of deep purpose, doctrinal maturity, mission commitment, unwavering confidence, and unshakable faith. You have a spirit of indomitable conquest. Today you stand just on the rim of the cup, right at the rising of the sun, at the bank of the Jordan, and the best is about to begin.

For Uldine and me, it will be the deepest joy of our lives to observe the process as you begin to seek the heart of God and find your Joshua. And we will be your number-one fans—praying for you, cheering for you, weeping for joy—as my successor, your new pastor, leads you into a day beyond anything you have ever known. This will happen with all stacks smoking and all flags flying as you watch the dawn of the new millennium across the banks of the Jordan.

Third, Uldine and I are excited about our own future. For thirty years, you have recognized my passion for the greater kingdom of God—my commitment to the whole body of Christ beyond the borders of our own membership. You have unselfishly allowed me to expand the ministry and influence of this great church without a word of criticism or restraint, as I sought to give a reasonable response to the endless flood of invitations to "come over and help us"—to speak at seminaries, retreats, conferences, conventions, churches and crusades, carrying the light of this church to many dark and discouraged corners of the world. You will never know what your influence has meant to the kingdom of God.

For fifty years, First Baptist Church of Dallas was the only megachurch in the Southern Baptist Convention. But through the years, virtually every megachurch pastor in our denomination has said that because we were the first to break out of the mold, the first to break the four-minute mile, they believed they could do it, and they did, and so did others. Today there are well over a hundred megachurches like this one in the Southern Baptist Convention.

I am excited about being your worldwide ambassador to the ongoing kingdom of God with broadening needs and expanding opportunities of influence. I believe because of what you have invested in me, I can in the years to come expand the ministry of this great church's immeasurable contribution to the kingdom. I also hope to have a little extra time for Uldine, the kids, the grandkids, and my favorite fishing hole.

Now, I want you to hear carefully something your pastor of nearly thirty years considers to be very important.

In the history of the church of Jesus, there has to my knowledge never been a smooth and easy transition into new leadership following a ministry of long duration. We are firsthand witnesses that those who follow pastors or staff members of twenty to thirty years duration almost always have a difficult time. But this need not be. It must not be. By God's grace and the maturity of this congregation, *it shall not be.*

You were the first new megachurch in half a century. You set the pace and you showed the way and now you have the chance to do it again. Today, the first wave of pastors of these so-called "superchurches" are all in their sixties, and will soon be considering retirement. Could it be that God will use this church to again set the example in how a great church not only follows the leadership of their pastor for thirty years, but how to make his exit as smooth as was his entrance?

In First Southern Baptist Church of Del City, Oklahoma, we were the first church in twenty-four years to baptize three hundred persons. There was a great deal of apprehension about whether a church built on evangelism could survive the departure of an evangelistic pastor. When you called me to Houston, I challenged our Del City church to "stay by the stuff," to be steadfast and loyal not just to a man but to the Lord Jesus himself. Believe it or not, the church called a new pastor within six weeks. During that interim of six weeks, they did more in the way of attendance, giving, and conversions than they had accomplished during any six-week period in the history of the church. But even then, its best days were still before it. Today, this church is also among the top ten churches in the Southern Baptist Convention.

Can First Baptist Church of Houston, the congregation that has so long been God's instrument in setting the pace, yet show the way this one more time in how to *"pass the baton without dropping the ball"?* I say to you that these closing days, these transitional days, these interim days can and must be our finest hour.

I have dreamed of a day in the future—a special time when I might return and lead the installation service for a wonderful new, young undershepherd—that I might have the joy of experiencing the passing of the baton in a manner that is exemplary to the world, honoring to the man, glorifying to God, and worthy of this congregation.

Therefore, I am this day asking you to make four vows to God:

1. *A vow of gratitude.* Normally, we would be abuzz with "how shall we celebrate the past, how shall we prepare for the future, who will be our new leader, when will we elect the search committee?" But I am going to ask you instead to spend the next two weeks thinking and talking only about the awesome greatness of God, and reflecting upon his immeasurable blessings upon us for the past thirty years and for the 130 great years before that. For the next two weeks, let us simply praise the Lord and thank him for the legacy of his faithfulness and the faithfulness of those who have gone before.

2. *A vow of prayer and fasting.* I am going to ask from this moment until your new Joshua stands in this pulpit that you fast every Tuesday noon meal of every week and spend that hour in prayer. Our staff has been doing that for a year, and we believe it is greatly impacting our own lives as well as our church.

3. *A vow of faith.* When our church set out to find a new pastor thirty-one years ago, they got it right. No one candidated to be on the

search committee and no one pushed for anyone in particular to be the new pastor. In faith, they knew God would bring about the right committee and hence the right person. I want to urge you to trust God completely and to do that again. Let there be no candidating, no circulating of names that you would like to see on the search committee, no petitions for this pastor or that pastor. Just leave it to God. Trust the Lord.

The less we trust our own desires and methods, the more we will trust God to do it his way, and the sooner we will find the man, and the greater will be the certainty that he *is* God's man. And when he comes, follow him as you have always so sweetly followed your pastor. Trust the Lord. Let God orchestrate it all, and you won't believe what he will do in the future.

4. *A vow of faithfulness.* This is not the time to even think about looking around for another church. That would not be of God. If ever your church needed you, it needs you now. There is something right about the church paying some attention to a consumer-oriented society that asks, "What can the church do for me?" But John F. Kennedy said it well when he said, "Ask not what your country can do for you; ask what you can do for your country." And what can I do now for my church? Be faithful!

Ours is no average church. It is a special church. It is a great church. Its impact on the world is legendary, and its people must be more loyal and more faithful in the months to come than they have ever been in the past. The greatest influence you will ever have, the greatest example you will ever set, the greatest gift you will ever give to the Lord and his church in her 160-year history—and, if our Lord tarries his coming, in our 160-year future—is what you as God's blessed family are and do and become during these next several months.

As you bridge the gap from the past from 1837 to 1999 and across the threshold of January 1, 2000 A.D. and beyond, this time is the time. The real time. The only time. The right time to arise, to unite, to rise up and *be* the church.

For this you were born in the heart of God from the foundation of the world. Wonderful First Baptist Church, beloved First Baptist

Church, church of my heart, church of my soul—arise now! Arise together as one, now and forever—for the sake of those who have gone before, for the little ones, for the children, for the young, for the aged, for the gospel, for the lost world, for the kingdom, and for Jesus. Beloved church of God, beloved First Baptist Church, let the church arise, the church triumphant, the church alive and well. *Let the church be the church!*